PROPERTY RIGHTS AND NEOLIBERALISM

Law, Property and Society

Series Editor:
Robin Paul Malloy

The Law, Property and Society series examines property in terms of its ability to foster democratic forms of governance, and to advance social justice. The series explores the legal infrastructure of property in broad terms, encompassing concerns for real, personal, intangible, intellectual and cultural property, as well as looking at property related financial markets. The series is edited by Robin Paul Malloy, and book proposals are welcome from all interested authors.

Robin Paul Malloy is E.I. White Chair and Distinguished Professor of Law at Syracuse University College of Law, USA. He is Director of the Center on Property, Citizenship, and Social Entrepreneurism. He is also Professor of Economics (by courtesy appointment) in the Maxwell School of Citizenship and Public Affairs, Syracuse University. Professor Malloy writes extensively on law and market theory and on real estate transactions and development. He has authored six books (one now in its third edition and another in its second edition), and edited five additional books. He has also written more than 25 scholarly articles, and contributed to 12 other books. His recent books include: LAW AND MARKET ECONOMY (2000, in English and translated into Spanish and Chinese); LAW IN A MARKET CONTEXT (2004); and REAL ESTATE TRANSACTIONS 3RD EDITION (with James C. Smith, 2007).

Property Rights and Neoliberalism

Cultural Demands and Legal Actions

Edited by

WAYNE V. McINTOSH
University of Maryland College Parks, USA

LAURA J. HATCHER
Southern Illinois University Carbondale, USA

ASHGATE

Published by
Ashgate Publishing Limited
Wey Court East
Union Road
Farnham
Surrey, GU9 7PT
England

Ashgate Publishing Company
Suite 420
101 Cherry Street
Burlington
VT 05401-4405
USA

www.ashgate.com

British Library Cataloguing in Publication Data
Property rights and neoliberalism : cultural demands and
legal actions. -- (Law, property and society)
1. Right of property. 2. Law reform. 3. Culture and law.
I. Series II. McIntosh, Wayne V., 1950- III. Hatcher, Laura
J.
346'.04-dc22

Library of Congress Cataloging-in-Publication Data
Property rights and neoliberalism : cultural demands and legal actions / by Wayne V. McIntosh and Laura J. Hatcher.
p. cm. -- (Law, property and society)
Includes index.
ISBN 978-0-7546-7892-2 (hardback) -- ISBN 978-0-7546-9760-2 (ebook) 1. Right of property--United States. I. McIntosh, Wayne V., 1950- II. Hatcher, Laura J.

KF562.P7584 2010
346.7304'2--dc22

2010011000

ISBN 9780754678922 (hbk)
ISBN 9780754697602 (ebk)

Mixed Sources
Product group from well-managed forests and other controlled sources
www.fsc.org Cert no. SGS-COC-2482
© 1996 Forest Stewardship Council
FSC

Printed and bound in Great Britain by
TJ International Ltd, Padstow, Cornwall

Contents

List of Figures and Tables

Figures

Tables

List of Contributors

Debbie Becher is a Mellon Post-Doctoral Fellow in the Humanities (2010–2011) and an Assistant Professor (2011–2012) in Barnard College's Department of Sociology. She is preparing a book manuscript from research on property takings in Philadelphia. She has published articles on urban redevelopment in *Poetics* and the *International Journal of Urban and Regional Research*. Debbie earned her PhD in sociology from Princeton University after a decade of professional experience in social work, community development, and housing construction.

Andrea Boggio is an Assistant Professor of Legal Studies at Bryant Research. He is a legal scholar and ethicist interested in questions of law and globalization. He has published a variety of articles on human rights, transnational litigation, and genetic research. Professor Boggio holds a J.S.D from Stanford University.

Darren Botello-Samson is an Assistant Professor of Political Science at Pittsburg State University where he teaches courses on public law and environmental politics. He earned his PhD from Rutgers University and is the author of *Regulatory Takings and the Environment: The Impact of Property Rights Litigation* (forthcoming). He has also contributed articles on regulatory takings law to environmental law reviews, including the *Journal of Natural Resources and Environmental Law* and the *Duke Environmental Law and Policy Forum*, as well as a chapter, titled "Jurisprudence and Environmental Injustices," to a book coming out of the Third Global Conference on Evil, Law and the State.

Richard A. Brisbin, Jr. is Associate Professor of Political Science at West Virginia University. He is the author of *A Strike Like No Other Strike: Law and Resistance during the Pittston Coal Strike of 1989–1990* (2002) and *Justice Antonin Scalia and the Conservative Revival* (1997) and co-author of *Real Law Stories: Inside the Judicial Process* (2010) and *West Virginia Politics and Government* (1996, second edn. 2008). He has published articles in the *American Political Science Review*, *American Journal of Political Science*, *Canadian Journal of Law and Society*, *Political Science Quarterly*, *Publius: The Journal of Federalism*, *Studies in American Political Development*, *Western Political Quarterly*, and several collections of studies.

Gabrielle E. Clark is a PhD candidate at the Institute for Law and Society at New York University. She holds an MA degree in Middle East Studies from NYU and an AB from Harvard College.

Michael C. Evans is Assistant Professor of Political Science at Georgia State University. His current research addresses founding era American political thought, and various aspects of interest group behavior pertaining to the modern US Supreme Court. He received his PhD in government and politics from the University of Maryland in 2009.

Christine B. Harrington is a Professor at New York University, an Affiliate Faculty Member at NYU School of Law, and a Core Faculty Member in NYU's the Institute for Law and Society, which she founded and of which she was the director for 10 years. She is an expert on informal legal orders and the politics of law and legal institutions. In her scholarship on the politics of legal reforms, she argues that dispute processes (mediation and regulatory negotiation) and litigation (federal regulatory and federal appellate civil) are forums for political participation and sites of ideological production about law and legal institutions. In addition to her first book, *Shadow Justice*: *Ideology and Institutionalization of Alternative Dispute Resolution*, she has published articles in the major sociolegal journals (*Law and Society Review*, *Law and Policy*, *Law and Social Inquiry*, and *Social and Legal Studies*) on the politics of reorganizing the labor and dispute processes in trial and appellate courts and in administrative agencies. *Lawyers in a Postmodern World: Translation and Transgression*, with Maureen Cain, examines the role of lawyers and professional power in shaping American political development and state formation. She is currently President-elect of the American Political Science Association's Law and Courts Section.

Laura J. Hatcher is Assistant Professor of Political Science at Southern Illinois University. She received her PhD from the University of Massachusetts at Amherst in 2002. Prior to joining the faculty at SIU, Professor Hatcher was a visitor at the Institute for Legal Studies (with a teaching appointment in Political Science) at the University of Wisconsin-Madison, and a postdoctoral fellow at the Taubman Center for Public Policy and American Institutions at Brown University. Her interests include the cultural production of knowledge through court cases, with a particular focus on the way litigation campaigns construct understandings of property rights. More recently, her research interests have expanded to understanding the way journalists covering property rights and environmental court cases contribute to the construction of individual rights in property through the narratives they create in their reporting.

Victoria L. Henderson is a Doctoral Candidate in the Department of Geography at Queen's University, Kingston, Ontario. In 2007, she was awarded a Canada Graduate Scholarship from the Social Sciences and Humanities Research Council of Canada (SSHRC) to investigate the impact of radio spectrum reform on non-profit community radio in Guatemala. In 2008, she received a four-year SSHRC Doctoral Fellowship, which has allowed her to launch a new research project mapping the spread of libertarian networks in Latin America.

Henderson's articles have appeared in leading journals, including the *Annals of the Association of American Geographers*.

Susan Hunter is Associate Professor of Political Science at West Virginia University. She has published articles in *Policy Studies Journal*, *Political Research Quarterly*, *Policy Studies Review*, *International Studies Quarterly*, *Canadian Journal of Law and Society*, and *PS: Political Science and Politics*, among others. She is co-author of *The EPA's Regulatory Style: The Case of Water Quality Enforcement* (1996).

Kevin M. Leyden is Director of the Institute for Public Affairs and Professor of Political Science at West Virginia University. For 2009–2010 he is Research Professor of Social Science and Public Policy at the Centre for Innovation and Structural Change at the National University of Ireland, Galway. He has published in the *American Journal of Public Health*, *Environmental Health Perspectives*, *British Journal of Political Science*, *Political Research Quarterly*, *Legislative Studies Quarterly*, *American Politics Quarterly*, *American Journal of Health Promotion*, *American Journal of Preventive Medicine*, *Presidential Studies Quarterly*, and *Policy Studies Journal*.

Wayne V. McIntosh is Associate Professor of Government and Politics at the University of Maryland, College Park. His primary interests are in judicial institutions, litigation and politics. He has authored or co-authored four books, with the most recent in 2009 with the University of British Columbia Press.

David Schultz is a Hamline University Professor in the School of Business where he teaches classes in government ethics, public policy, and public administration. He also holds appointments in the Hamline University Department of Criminal Justice and Forensic Science, and at the Minnesota Law School. He is a senior fellow at the Institute of Law and Politics at the University of Minnesota Law School. Professor Schultz is the author of 24 books and over 70 articles on American politics, law, and property rights. In addition, he has authored numerous chapters in *Nichols on Eminent Domain* on property rights and condemnation law. His most recent publications include *Evicted! Property Rights and Eminent Domain in America* and *Constitutional Law in Contemporary America*.

Stephen A. Simon is Assistant Professor of Political Science at the University of Richmond. He received his PhD in Government and Politics from the University of Maryland, and a JD from the NYU School of Law.

Rebecca U. Thorpe is an American Political Science Association Congressional Fellow, and she will be joining the faculty at the University of Washington as Assistant Professor of Political Science in September 2010. She received her PhD in Government and Politics from the University of Maryland in the fall of

2009. She was formerly a Research Fellow at The Brookings Institution, where she completed much of her dissertation research. Her work focuses on national political institutions, business-government relations and constitutionalism.

William R. Wilkerson is Associate Professor of Political Science at the SUNY College at Oneonta.

Introduction

Wayne V. McIntosh and Laura J. Hatcher

Over the course of the last several decades, conservative libertarian and neoliberal groups have put constitutional demands for greater property protection on the agendas of courts in several countries, including the US. In addition to working in national courts and through constitutional processes, property rights activists, pressure groups and social movements have used administrative and regulatory mechanisms in their efforts. Meanwhile, in a range of arenas, lawyers and other advocates have diligently worked to include expropriation clauses in international treaties, such as NAFTA, and to structure the rules of conflict and jurisprudence that, in theory, protect the rights of investors, particularly from government encroachment. Indeed, the US-based Property Rights Alliance, an organization with a considerable record of involvement in litigation, legislative, and regulatory processes, has assembled a world-wide coalition of national affiliates to promote a common political-legal agenda, and has begun publication of an *International Property Rights Index*, rating 115 countries on the degree to which governing regimes recognize the sanctity of private property and its "protection for economic well-being".[1]

Property rights have always held high status on the US political agenda and in many systems featuring a corporate capitalist economy. These rights are included in constitutional designs, debates, and development. Efforts to curb state appropriation of private properties for public purposes also have a long and storied history. The modern libertarian movement in the US (which has a familial relationship with neoliberalism abroad) has coupled animosity toward direct government seizures with resistance against regulatory regimes by attempting to demonstrate specific regulatory effects that allegedly diminish property values. According to this design, whether it is direct or indirect, government policy that penetrates the boundaries of private property violates a basic tenet of fundamental liberty. Ultimately, the effort appears to place cultural demands for property in a new light, both in the US and throughout the world. This collection provides a range of perspectives on these phenomena.

---

1 See http://internationalpropertyrightsindex.org.

Property Rights in Neoliberal Contexts

In the case of property rights, neoliberalism's role matters in part because it has, over the course of the last half of the twentieth century, responded to and been a part of restructuring our notions of property and the institutions that regulate it. "Neoliberalism," however, is notoriously difficult to define and readers should not be surprised to find some tensions in the nuances discussed by the various authors in this volume. Tackling the problem of definition early on in this project, we asked our authors to use a broad understanding from Harrington and Turem's 2006 article, "Accountability in Neoliberal Regulatory Regimes." In it they define neoliberalsm as implying "the (re)emergence of the market and economic rationale as the dominant organizing logic in society" (Harrington and Turem 2006: 204). Part of this process includes "the dismantling of the welfare state, erosion of social provisions, turn to monetarism in fiscal and financial management, tax cuts for business, and increasing disciplining of the state via markets and market mechanisms" (ibid. 204–205). Similarly, David Harvey points out that the role of the state in this process is to "create and preserve" institutional frameworks that are appropriate for these practices (Harvey 2005: 2). Since property rights are fundamental to the market, understanding how property rights are structured as well as wielded to make claims seems an important element of understanding how these institutional frameworks come into being.

Moreover, when property rights are restructured or new forms of property are created, power shifts in a society. Distribution of property, its uses, and whether owners of new forms of property will be granted the same rights as owners of traditional property, all become elements of restructured power. This strongly suggests that when property rights are mobilized by activists, we are seeing not only an attempt to shift societal structures, but also a symptom that structures have already shifted. Sometimes this happens as official actors attempt to regulate new property forms. At other times, this happens as different forms of knowledge (i.e., science, social science, and so on) challenge the way property is traditionally understood either through new forms of property or by highlighting how recognized rights of old forms of property do not work with a new invention or discovery. For example, do we own our own genetic material? Do the scientists who discovered the processes for studying genes (or any other patentable process for studying biology, genetics, and so forth) own the material they can isolate, examine, and convert into marketable commodities? Does their right to the process itself extend to the object of that process? Or is this part of a base of knowledge to which all humans should have access? Most importantly, how does the political struggle that takes place over such issues restructure power and create political claims?

Clearly, no longer is the idea of property tied simply to land or real estate. Instead, we now recognize property in our ideas, our genetic material, bandwidths, as well as in stocks, bonds and various other "things" we claim to own. In the face of scientific innovation, this becomes even more complicated in a context where the free market of ideas is supposed to dominate the way we create and accumulate knowledge. But scientific innovation even places pressure on old forms of property, such as land. Here is an object whose property value we often think we already understand and that its core property meaning has been established. Yet we find that market issues have changed our understanding of ownership, of what can be "owned," and what owners can do with their land. Moreover, scientific developments that challenge old understandings of land use, as well as market forces that push us to redevelop land for new purposes, strain these supposedly settled understandings. The law responds to changing technology and market forces by adapting and attempting to regulate land in new ways. But if law stipulates what uses we can make of our land, and some uses will be more profitable than others, can we claim a property right in the lost value associated with uses that are deemed unacceptable? And how is a right to use land for economic development different from the set of rights that accrue to an owner who uses the land for a home?

As new forms of property are created, it is no wonder that property rights claims become a means of contesting not only their regulation, but their very character. We ask the questions above not as normative political theory, with an eye to what the law *should* say, but rather because we are curious about how law is changing to meet the demands of new technologies and market forces in an era of neoliberal regulatory reform. A close analysis of property rights mobilizations highlights the tensions within concepts such as "the public good" and "private rights." These tensions seem unavoidable in a context where market logics represent the dominant organizing rationales for society. As Laura Hatcher explains in her chapter, such issues make traditional matters of land use planning much more difficult for the state as it also attempts to struggle with demands from property rights owners to develop land for economic use. New technologies also stimulate tensions in part because of the new forms of property they create. Victoria Henderson's chapter presents us with an example of where activists in other countries see private ownership of bandwidth to be troubling because it interferes with public discourse, while Andrea Boggio shows that the discovery of genetic materials and the desire of scientists to pursue their findings raises questions concerning who has control over both the genetic material and cultural heritage. These chapters suggest that when property changes shape or a new form of property is introduced in political contexts where the understanding of property is itself in a state of flux, how to structure the rights of owners and what, if any, regulation is appropriate become matters for mobilization. Authors in this volume highlight that these contests are not merely about gaining a political advantage in a regulatory environment; rather, they remain very much about the way we should understand property and the rights associated with it in the midst of contentious politics concerning neoliberal deregulation and (re)regulation.

Mobilization's Many Forms

Mobilization of law can take a variety of forms, all of which are aimed at creating advantages through the law for a particular policy objective or ideological perspective. It can be part of a strategic plan to promote or enhance a set of strictly parochial interests, or it can be more globally oriented and intended to elevate the likelihood of future benefits. Moreover, mobilization can involve activating legal institutions (courts, agencies, and the like) by placing a set of issues on the agenda for decision, leveraging the process, thus setting the machinery in motion and forcing the other side to face the expensive proposition of mounting a credible formal response, and influencing the language and understanding of law in the books and/or on the street. Indeed, successful litigation leading to a series of reinforcing official decisions and pronouncements can have secondary influences, elevating rights consciousness and casting a shadow over subsequent actions and negotiations. This allows interested parties to leverage the language and meaning of law without a full-dressed show of force.

The most visible mobilization action is to directly engage the process, by leading a litigation effort, joining a coalition to support a case in progress, and related activity. This was among the earliest to attract scholarly attention (e.g., Scheingold 1978, McCann 1994). High profile advocacy, especially that challenging racial segregation, and similar efforts from liberal-leaning organizations and public interest law firms supporting such positions as expansion of women's rights, rights of criminal defendants, and environmental protection, to name a few, seemed to have engineered considerable policy movement, but also gave rise subsequently to counter-advocacy from the right (e.g., Hoover and den Dulk 2003, den Dulk 2006, McCann and Dudas 2006, Southworth 2008, Teles 2008).

We extend this literature on legal mobilizations by presenting a series of case studies that consider, specifically, property rights mobilizations in an era of changing regulatory schemes. Conservative and neoliberal organizations, by the 1970s, gained their legal footing and developed serious strategies to promote private property rights, to offset regulatory interference, and generally to shift political power away from the state and to the market. Among the first to arise, and subsequently most active and influential, was the Pacific Legal Foundation, established in 1973 to promote market-based solutions to public policy issues. The group has also joined forces with other like-minded advocates such as the Institute for Justice, to become a major force in promoting their preferred positions on social policy issues.

We know from past mobilization analyses that rights claims are structured in relation to the law as it is, even when activists are trying to change it. Thus, activists both take advantage of the law as a resource, but also recreate it through various claims concerning both the law's legitimacy and particular rights. The contributors to this volume bring a range of social science perspectives to address three primary issues: 1) the contours and characteristics of property rights mobilization(s); 2) the degree to which property rights movements have influenced development of law in demonstrable ways; and 3) the broader cultural, social and economic implications of modern-era property rights litigation and legal mobilizations.

In Part I, the Schultz, Thorpe-Evans-Simon-McIntosh, Wilkerson, and Becher chapters report a significant presence by these organizations in high-level litigation to advocate for private property rights and pro-market positions in US courts as part of a concerted effort to change the understanding of constitutional "takings" law. David Schultz explains why courts matter to this area of research. Using the US as his case study, Schultz argues that courts are strong and efficient sites for creating legal change. Shifting gears slightly, Rebecca Thorpe, Michael Evans, Stephen Simon, and Wayne McIntosh consider how third-party advocacy in the US system creates unusual coalition patterns, uniting conservative and liberal advocates in ways that change over time and may influence the ways in which justices in the US Supreme Court engage the issues. Focusing upon the famous US takings case, *Kelo v. City of New London*, William Wilkerson describes the legal mobilization by the Institute for Justice on behalf of Susette Kelo. He considers the intertwined political and legal strategies that this public interest law firm uses, and assesses their effectiveness in meeting their goals of legal change, while at the same time, promoting the organization itself. Finally, Debbie Becher moves to the ground level to explore a spirited non-litigation mobilization effort in a Philadelphia neighborhood targeted for an eminent domain development project in the aftermath of *Kelo*. She reports that the way in which the concepts of "home" and "property" were conflated in *Kelo* opinions, ultimately served the agenda of neoliberal organizations who found a receptive audience in the "threatened" community and their supporters.

In Part II Victoria Henderson turns our attention to Guatemala, addressing private property rights in the electromagnetic spectrum as specified in that country's 1996 telecommunications reform. She traces the intellectual roots of neoliberal reform and assesses the impact of the legal change, finding that commodification of this traditionally collectively held resource exacts costs that disproportionately fall upon Guatemala's indigenous population. In the next chapter, Andrea Boggio addresses the question of whether we hold property rights to our genetic code, with research based in a study of indigenous peoples of Papua New Guinea and intellectual property issues arising from commercial exploitation of their DNA samples. In recent years, advocates on behalf of vulnerable populations have demanded that the international community recognize that genetic resources belong to the populations from which the resources are extracted and have mobilized in opposition to a neoliberal biocolonial agenda. Finally, Gabrielle Clark and Christine Harrington find that indeterminacy in the framework of NAFTA has created opportunities to influence domestic as well as international relationships. They argue that government respondents in investors' rights arbitration at the international level have altered the treaty's normative framework through their claims. Taken together, the three papers strongly suggest that the unintended consequences of meaning making in these disputes includes the subversion of the state (while reinforcing the state), as well as undermining the claims made by libertarian and neoliberal activists.

The authors in Part III return to issues arising in the US, beginning with Richard Brisbin, Jr., Susan Hunter, and Kevin Leyden's study of planning commission and zoning board decision making. They report few instances of ideologically charged advocacy in the ongoing series of property issues addressed by local regulatory bodies, although law does set boundaries for discussion and consideration of claims. Their direct observations of board meetings in small cities in West Virginia, Pennsylvania and Maryland, are further supported by a wider-scale survey of commissioners and administrators. This is followed by Darren Botello-Samson's interview-based study of decision-making in federal regulatory agencies, where the balance to be struck is between environmental protection and private property rights associated with surface coal mining. Judge-made law in takings litigation casts a clear shadow in this highly conflictual arena, helping to shape the meaning of language, especially as neoliberal advocates have pressed the courts to make regulation of property more reliant upon market forces and free exchange. Finally, Laura Hatcher looks at state law and policy making regarding regulation of coastal zone properties. The chief protagonist is an individual property owner who became aggressively litigious (Anthony Palazzolo) as he found that his understanding of what he could do with his land varied from the state's. Eventually, he pushed his claims through Rhode Island courts to the US Supreme Court in an uneasy alliance with the Pacific Legal Foundation. Significantly, Hatcher reports that administrative practice changed matters in some ways more than court actions. So we conclude that, while courts matter to the structure of property rights mobilizations, other institutions of government matter as well.

Future Research

When we began this project, we had hoped this volume would contain more comparative work than it currently does. Our original call requested proposals examining facets of property rights mobilizations throughout the world. Alas, we received very few proposals centering upon property rights mobilizations outside of the US. On research within the US, partly because of the high visibility and political saliency of *Kelo v. City of New London*, which had been recently decided, we received an abundance of proposals. We cannot explain the dearth of property rights studies abroad, but future research certainly needs to extend the comparative element of the present volume well beyond where it currently stands. That said, this collection includes work suggestive of other theoretical developments that may matter to research in a range of political-legal contexts (including the US), as well as inquiries addressing activities in international forums.

Taken together, the chapters strongly suggest that understanding the structure of neoliberalist law and politics in particular locations is very important. Even within one country, neoliberal regulatory regimes are subject to considerable variation. Thus, to understand property rights mobilizations, asking first the question of how institutions create the context in which that mobilization occurs seems paramount.

We also see that researchers should be very careful about understanding the structure, motivations, and alliances created during a property rights mobilization. Unusual coalitions do in fact take place, where activists of different ideological perspectives determine that they have the same interest in the rules of ownership. Are these mere alliances of convenience, built to address institutional realities of the moment – or do they represent convergence of political-legal property rights agendas that are longer-lasting and carry through across institutional decision-making arenas? Further, activists may be asking for a strong individual property right that has a familial relationship to the very neoliberal administrative and regulatory forms they contest.

Within the US, it seems imperative that researchers step away from the claims made in the press and/or activists leading the charge in property rights mobilizations to look more deeply at the structure of mobilizations and the responses of official actors to them. More than that, understanding the genesis of property rights mobilizations may require a closer examination of regulatory frameworks and the relationships among various branches of government.

Acknowledgements

Both editors have benefited from the invaluable support of several colleagues, not least of whom are our contributors. We had the wonderful experience of working with a group of authors who were responsive to each other as well as to our comments, and provided a rich set of essays for this volume. It was a pleasure to work with all of them. Other help came from colleagues outside of this volume. We want particularly to thank John Brigham, Richard Brisbin (who is both a contributor to this volume, and served as a critical commentator for us), Tobin Grant, and Tamir Moustafa. We also must thank Joel Olufuwote at Southern Illinois University for his invaluable assistance in preparing the final manuscript, along with Amanda Radke at the University of Maryland. Finally, Robin Paul Malloy, the Law, Property and Society Series Editor has been supportive of this project since the moment he heard about it. We thank him for his guidance and help as well.

PART I
Legal Mobilizations, Social Change, and Property Rights

Chapter 1

Courts Matter: The Supreme Court, Social Change, and the Mobilization of Property Rights Interests

David Schultz

Introduction

Judicial decisions and the law are contextualized within a broader matrix of political power and social control. Both map out an ontology of social relations (Schultz 2002) that define how institutions operate and what groups or individuals have power. The American Constitution, as Dahl (1963) pointed out, was conceived as a document meant to channel political power, premised upon a fear that abuses of authority by any group or institution would threaten the rights of others or popular government. Thus, concepts such as checks and balances, federalism, and even eventually the Bill of Rights were tools for dividing power.

But if the law represents one measure of political power and authority, judicial pronouncements, such as decisions by the Supreme Court, symbolize another. Court decisions can reify and reinforce the status quo, and for many who wish to challenge authority, they bring the potential to enable social change. Litigation, especially declarations of rights, represents one of several ways individuals can seek to alter the matrix or map of political power in society. Scheingold (1978) described the use of litigation to facilitate change as the myth of rights. This myth was "premised on a direct linking of litigation, rights, and remedies with social change" (Scheingold 1978: 5). For Scheingold, the appeals to rights were political symbols (52) and served as agents of political mobilization (148). Groups use a litigation strategy to articulate claims about their rights, hoping that judicial recognition of them will simultaneously facilitate their organization, legitimate their values and interests, and alter the political landscape by giving them increased bargaining power.

Within the public law scholarship there is a significant debate over whether going to court makes sense as a strategy to articulate social change. Specifically, the debate is over whether the courts can facilitate social change on their own. Horowitz (1977), Rabkin (1989), and Rosenberg (1991) all argue that the courts are significantly limited in their capacity to effect social change, while (Cooper 1988), McCann (1994), and Schultz and Gottlieb (1998) describe processes whereby litigation strategies and judicial pronouncements can be successful.

It is not the point of this chapter to resolve this debate. Instead, regardless of the ultimate authority of the courts to bring about social change, two points are true. First, groups act as if this is the case, and they devote significant resources for this purpose. Second, resort to the courts may be one means of furthering organizational interests. Both of the propositions are highlighted when it comes to those organizations interested in property rights.

By the beginning of the presidency of Ronald Reagan in 1981, property rights had long lost their privileged position under the Constitution and the logic of the *Lochner* era jurisprudence (referring to *Lochner v. New York*, 198 U.S. 45 (1905), and an era of jurisprudence committed to the protection of property rights and limited government) had been dismantled by the New Deal Court. Property could be regulated, with legislatures given wide deference to define reasonableness. In the area of eminent domain, in decisions such as *Berman v. Parker*, 348 U.S. 26 (1956), the Court granted legislatures broad deference to define what constitutes a valid public use. This decision facilitated significant authority to take private property. In addition, the Michigan Supreme Court's decision in 1981 in *Poletown Neighborhood Council v. Detroit*, 304 N.W.2d 455 (1981), as well as the Supreme Court's 1984 opinion in *Hawaii Housing Authority v. Midkiff*, 467 U.S. 229 (1984), led many scholars such as Richard Epstein (1985) and Ellen Frankel Paul (1988) to conclude that the public use requirement of the Takings Clause no longer had any serious meaning. Their defense of property rights and a commitment to limiting eminent domain authority must be viewed within a context of part of a *neoliberal* effort to limit state power and promote the free market.

President Ronald Reagan's election in 1980 gave solace to conservatives hoping for renewed support for property rights. His election represented part of a *neoliberal* effort to trim back the welfare state, shift power away from the government, and restore the autonomy of the free market (Bluestone and Harrison 1990, Steger 2002, Yergin and Stanislaw 2002, Kuttner 1999). It was, as Harrington and Turem (2006) describe, an effort to restructure the state in order to make the market the dominant organizing institution in society. All of this was part of a broader project to use the government to enable capital accumulation that had been severely damaged during the fiscal crisis of the 1970s (O'Connor 2001). The rise of *neoliberalism* sets the context for the property rights movement that begins with the election of Ronald Reagan, and it connects to the US Supreme Court's decision in *Kelo v. City of New London*, 545 U.S. 469 (2005), upholding the use of eminent domain to take private property from one owner and give it to another in order to promote economic development. The movement to reinvigorate ownership rights in the United States thus needs to be understood within a broader context of private property mobilization and economic structuring (see Hatcher chapter in this volume).

This chapter examines the road to *Kelo*. It makes three arguments. First, the political mobilization by groups leading up to and after this case are part of a broader neoliberal movement to use the courts and the banner of property rights to shift political power away from the state and to the market. Second, rights talk and the courts can be understood as embedded in a larger political economic battle for political control of the state. More specifically, contrary to most debates in the public law field over whether courts can be efficacious agents of social change, the judiciary is only one of several institutional and cultural playing fields in the battle for political power. The courts represent focal points for legal disputes, galvanize coalitional support, and provide a forum to articulate cultural and political arguments necessary for leveraging political power and building political movements. Finally, as discussion of the reaction to *Kelo* will demonstrate, a legal strategy of using the courts to achieve social change does not necessarily even mean one needs to win a case if the broader aim is using the law to leverage political power or institutional change. In fact, despite the loss in *Kelo*, neoliberals and supporters of property rights achieved significant wins in the legislative and public opinion arenas.

Why Go to Court?

As noted above, a litigation strategy may be employed as one of several efforts by a group to challenge or alter the matrix of power. One can draw upon Antonio Gramsci's (1971: 234–236) concept of hegemony and argue that the law lies at the center of a struggle among contending groups. The courts thus are also one arena in which to articulate demands, or as Schattschneider (1975) contended, one place where there is an effort to mobilize bias and win over bystanders to support one's cause. Courts thus become important institutions that help to define, articulate, and broadcast political interests to a range of audiences and constituencies.

This means also that efforts to describe one's political interests as representing rights are meant to give some legitimacy to one's claims (Muir 1973). Rights then become bargaining tools for Scheingold, or trumps as Dworkin (1984) contends. If successful, declarations of rights bring the courts into play, validating claims that had been articulated. The hope, of course, is to challenge the current balance of power in society.

Poletown and the Origins of the New Property Rights Movement

One of the battle lines over government authority to intervene in the economy centers on the public use justification for the exercise of eminent domain. There is a long history surrounding the question of what constitutes a valid public use, and over a 200 year period eminent domain has been central to many disputes regarding economic development and governmental power (Schultz 2009). However, contemporary battles begin with *Poletown Neighborhood Council v. City of Detroit*, 304 N.W.2d 455 (Mich. 1981), one of the most noted and controversial cases ever involving the use of eminent domain. In *Poletown*, the Michigan Supreme Court upheld the City of Detroit's authority to take a city neighborhood, relocate 1,362 households, and acquire more than 150 private businesses in order to accommodate a General Motors Corporation new assembly plant on 465 acres of land. The City designated the Poletown area as "blighted," and began condemnation proceedings. Several parties facing condemnation challenged the taking under the Michigan Constitution, arguing that it did not serve a valid public purpose, but that instead it was for a private purpose and benefit to one entity, General Motors.

The Michigan Supreme Court upheld the taking as a valid public use under the state constitution, contending that the public would be the primary beneficiary. The Court recognized that the needs that would be served by upholding this use of eminent domain included the alleviation of "the severe economic conditions facing the residents of the city and state, [and] the need for new industrial development to revitalize local industries, the economic boost the proposed project would provide" (456–7).

The *Poletown* decision articulated a broad definition of public use and is a textbook case illustrating how a state court can shape its role in such determinations under its own Constitution. In addressing the meaning of the public use clause in the state constitution, the Court indicated that a "public use changes with changing economic conditions of society, and that the right of the public to receive and enjoy the benefit of the use determines whether the use is public or private" (457). Thus, in order to promote the general economic welfare of the people, the Court approved the municipal taking of private property of some, in order to provide land for the future development and expansion of a General Motors' manufacturing facility.

Poletown was controversial. It angered both political liberals and conservatives. For liberals, such as Ralph Nader, NAACP, and other organizations representing people of color or low-income populations, *Poletown* represented a form of corporate thuggery (Schultz 2007). By that, it joined corporate interests and government to use eminent domain in a way that was both racially exploitive and targeted the poor. It was reference to these concerns which were eventually discussed and seized upon in Justices O'Connor's and Thomas' *Kelo* dissents two decades later. For conservatives, *Poletown* was another example of how small businesses and the market in general were threatened by government authority. From differing perspectives, then, the case was a symbol of racism, constituted plundering the poor, or represented an assault upon personal freedom or the market place. For whatever reason, the decision motivated a host of groups on the political left and right to try to overturn it.

Shortly after *Poletown,* in *Hawaii Housing Authority v. Midkiff*, 467 U.S. 229 (1984), the US Supreme Court equated public use to the scope of a legislature's police power discretion. Justice Sandra Day O'Connor, appointed by President Reagan, wrote the unanimous opinion, upholding a broad construction of public use and eminent domain to take property from large owners and redistribute it to tenants on it. This decision demonstrated a broad redistributive and potentially egalitarian use of eminent domain. Expanding the public use justification to take property for economic development or redistributive purposes represented legal sanction for government intervention in the economy. If neoliberals wished to scale back the state, targeting eminent domain and the public use justification for a taking was one way to do that. Thus, *Poletown*, eminent domain, and property rights served as important symbols in the political battle to secure that purpose.

The First Property Rights Trilogy

Decisions such as *Poletown* and *Midkiff*, coming during the early part of the Reagan era, did not look good to property rights advocates. However, in 1986, Justice Burger retired and President Reagan elevated William Rehnquist to be Chief Justice. Rehnquist was a *bona fide* conservative who had demonstrated that on the Supreme Court. With him as Chief Justice, and with the appointment of Antonin Scalia as a new Associate Justice, the Supreme Court looked poised to be more receptive to the expectations of property rights advocates. Indeed, to conservatives, Rehnquist's ascension to Chief Justice portended a reversal of many of the Warren era precedents, and a renewed concern for the protection of property rights. Three decisions during the 1986–1987 term signaled that hopes for a property rights revival under Rehnquist might actually be realized. As the Thorpe, et al. chapter in this volume pointed out, post 1978, a significant number of groups submitted *amicus* briefs in regulatory takings cases before the Supreme Court, thereby confirming that many interests saw the federal judiciary as a new battle ground regarding property rights.

The first case in the trilogy is *Keystone Coal Association v. DeBenedictis,* 480 U.S. 470 (1987), a regulatory takings case. This case involved the Pennsylvania Bituminous Mine Subsidence and Land Conservation Act (Pa.Stat.Ann., Tit. 52, § 1406.1 *et seq.* Purdon Supp. 1986). Sections 4 and 6 of the act required companies to leave 50 percent of the coal in the ground to preclude flattening and depression of the soil. The act had noted the devastating effects of subsidence to the soil and to structures on the surface, and the 50 percent rule was to allow for enough subsurface soil structure to support surface buildings. Keystone Coal Association filed suit claiming that this act, specifically the sections dealing with the 50 percent rule, was an unconstitutional taking without compensation and also a violation of the Contract Clause because the act had destroyed its leases with other private persons giving it the right to mine. The association argued that this case was no different from *Pennsylvania v. Mahon*, 260 U.S. 393 (1922), where the Court had ruled, in a vaguely worded opinion authored by Justice Holmes, that an earlier version of the Pennsylvania subsidence law effected an unconstitutional taking.

The *Keystone* majority ruled against the association and distinguished it from *Mahon.* Justice Stevens, writing for a majority that included Justices Brennan, White, Marshall, and Blackmun, first stated that in *Mahon* only one private building was to be saved by the Kohler Act. Thus, according to Stevens, it was questionable even in Holmes' mind whether the law served a substantial public purpose. In *Keystone*, many structures, including cemeteries, were involved, and thus a significant public interest was served in saving them.

In dissent, Rehnquist, Powell, O'Connor, and Scalia agreed with the association that *Mahon* was controlling. The regulations here and in *Mahon* served public purposes, but both had placed substantial burdens on private property. Even though the law in *Keystone* served a valid public purpose, the dissenters argued that the 50 percent rule denied association members significant "investment-backed expectations," and was not regulation but a regulatory taking, thus requiring compensation.

Implicit in this dissenting opinion was a desire to return to more heightened judicial scrutiny of legislation affecting property rights. The dissenters questioned the legislative findings of fact and purposes in ways not recently common for the Court. A return to strict scrutiny for economic legislation would mean that the line between regulation and eminent domain would be subject to more acute analysis. This is exactly what happened in the next two cases.

Nollan v. California Coastal Commission, 483 U.S. 825 (1987), was a land development case. The Nollans had a contract to purchase beachfront property, tear down the existing structure, and replace it with a three-bedroom house. The Nollans sought a permit, which was granted on the condition that they provide a narrow public easement along their property allowing people to walk to the public beach. Similar easements had been required for other houses along the beach, on the rationale that such access was necessary to inform the public that the beach was public, because a house obstructing the view of the water could easily lead the public to suspect the beach was private. The Nollans objected to the requirement and brought suit claiming the easement was an uncompensated taking. After a lengthy appeals process that took the Nollans through several administrative and judicial proceedings, the US Supreme Court accepted their case for review.

Justice Scalia, writing for a majority that included Rehnquist, White, Powell, and O'Connor, agreed with the Nollans that the forced easement violated the Fifth Amendment, and that they should be able to exclude the public from their property. Scalia's opinion first pointed out that the right to exclude is one of the most fundamental rights attached to ownership. Second, Scalia argued that past precedent was clear in underscoring a permanent physical occupation of an owner's property to effect a taking. Thus, in requiring the easement across the Nollans' property, the California Coastal Commission demanded a permanent physical occupation of their property, because the public was given unrestricted access and right to "pass to and fro" across it.

The third case in the 1986–1987 property rights trilogy is *First English Evangelical Lutheran Church of Glendale v. County of Los Angeles*, 482 U.S. 304 (1987). After floods destroyed some of First Lutheran's buildings, the County of Los Angeles declared a temporary and total construction ban on properties in the plane. Less than a month after the ordinance was passed denying them the right to rebuild, First Lutheran filed an inverse condemnation suit, claiming that it effectively denied them all use of their property, and took their property without just compensation. They lost efforts to secure declaratory judgments in both in California Superior Court and at the state Court of Appeals, with the California Supreme Court declining to hear the case.

In a majority opinion authored by Rehnquist that included Scalia, White, Brennan, Marshall, and Powell, the temporary but total ban on the use of property was ruled a taking. According to the Court, for the time the ban was in effect, total use of the property was enjoined. For the Court, then, the question was whether "the Just Compensation Clause requires the government to pay for 'temporary' regulatory takings" (313). The Court ruled that it did.

Evaluating the First Trilogy

What do these rulings in the first trilogy say about the Court, property rights, and eminent domain at the start of the Rehnquist Court era? First, the cases do not represent a revival of property rights to the status of the Lochner era. The protections that the Court seemed to want to extend to property interests in *Nollan* and in *First Lutheran* (and for the minority in *Keystone*) were compensatory rights. They do not suggest a return to substantive due process, which involved widespread judicial review and limitation of the police power to protect private property (Schultz 2006: 961–2).

In assessing the first property rights trilogy, what else do we learn? First, property interests won two of three cases, with the decisions, such as in *Nollan*, hinting at increased scrutiny for these types of interests that had not been used since perhaps before the New Deal. Moreover, a breakdown of the votes in the three cases also reveals an interesting pattern.

Whatever revival property rights enjoyed, it did not come solely as a result of support from the conservatives. In some cases Brennan and Marshall supplied critical votes.

However, the significance of the 1986 trilogy was that it suggested to property rights advocates that the Court had become more receptive to their arguments. But after 1986, except in *Lucas v. South Carolina Coastal Council*, 505 U.S. 1003 (1992), and *Dolan v. City of Tigard*, 512 U.S. 374 (1994), the Rehnquist Court proved to be less interested in property rights and eminent domain issues. Both of those cases attracted large numbers of *amici* briefs from property rights organizations, who nonetheless continued to press their case for changes in eminent domain law. These decisions, as well as *Poletown*, worked together to encourage pro-property rights groups to continue to find the right fact pattern to challenge an expanded view of eminent domain authority.

Victory in Michigan

As noted above, the 1981 Michigan Supreme Court decision in *Poletown Neighborhood Council v. Detroit* was detested by both liberal and conservative groups, with both seeking to overturn the holding. One of the groups formed to address property rights was the Institute for Justice. As Wilkerson describes elsewhere in this book, the Institute for Justice was a major player in property rights and other conservative causes, with a track record of success before the Court. The Institute was a critical player in supporting the Kelos as they moved their cause to the Supreme Court. There were other conservative groups active in the eminent domain and property rights movement. Thorpe points out that the Pacific Legal Foundation filed more *amicus* briefs (19) in the regulatory takings cases than any other group. But the Institute combined an impressive litigation and public relations strategy together, especially in *Kelo*, which as Wilkerson describes, distinguished its activity from others. Thus, arguably in *Kelo* and in other recent property rights cases, the Institute deserves particular attention.

The Institute for Justice is a great example of a neoliberal group. It is a conservative libertarian organization that describes its mission in part "to secure economic liberty, school choice, private property rights, freedom of speech and other vital individual liberties, and to restore constitutional limits on the power of government" (Institute for Justice 2009). The group took upon itself the task of addressing what it considered to be eminent domain abuse. In 2003, it issued a report with the Castle Coalition (a group essentially indistinguishable from the Institute and sharing the same address)—*Public Power, Private Gain: A Five Year, State-By-State Report Examining the Abuse of Eminent Domain*—declaring that from 1998 to 2003 there were "10,000 cases where homes, businesses, churches and private land were seized or threatened with seizure over the past five years—not to be used for public use, but instead for private for-profit development" (Berliner 2003). They claimed that the government was strong-arming individuals to sell their property or else face eminent domain and eviction. They sought to dispel notions that the use of eminent domain was a last resort or that owners voluntarily sold their property to the government in most cases. Of course, to strengthen their claims, the report and their Web page featured profiles of individuals whom they believed were victims of eminent domain abuse. The Institute also litigated and sponsored a number of cases, including *County of Wayne v. Hathcock*, 471 Mich. 445, 684 N.W.2d 765 (2004). It also provided some technical support to the protestors that Becher describes in her chapter on the American Streets project.

In *Hathcock*, the Michigan Supreme Court declared that the taking of property from one private owner and transferring it to another in order to encourage economic development or alleviate unemployment was not a valid public use under Article X, Section 2 of the Michigan Constitution. In reaching this decision, the Michigan Supreme Court overruled its landmark *Poletown* holding. *Hathcock* imposed a significant limit upon the ability of Michigan's state and local governments to use eminent domain as an economic development tool and, potentially, a tool to address business plant closings. Moreover, in reversing *Poletown*, the Michigan Supreme Court also invalidated a major legal precedent cited in many jurisdictions across the United States to support the use of eminent domain for economic development purposes.

Hathcock attracted a significant amount of legal attention for a state case, with 13 *amicus* briefs filed. The case was a major victory for property rights advocates. The decision appeared to be the first step toward constricting the scope of eminent domain law and declaring a more narrow reading of what constitutes a valid public use. In the wake of this opinion, the US Supreme Court, merely a few weeks later, announced that it would accept an eminent domain economic development takings case from Connecticut, *Kelo v. City of New London,* which raised similar issues. Property rights advocates hoped that *Kelo*, coupled with the Michigan court's *Hathcock* opinion, would be the one-two knockout they had been looking for. As it happens, *Kelo* was part of a second trilogy of property law cases that the Rehnquist Court would examine.

The Second Property Rights Trilogy

In the 2004–2005 term the Supreme Court heard three cases that held considerable promise to property rights advocates. Since 1987, several Justices had been replaced—most notably the liberals Brennan and Marshall—and new, supposedly more conservative, Justices such as David Souter and Clarence Thomas had taken their seats. In addition, Lewis Powell, who voted for the property owners in all three of the first trilogy cases, was replaced by Anthony Kennedy, another supposed conservative, and Harry Blackmun, who voted against the owners in all three cases, was also now gone. Moreover, in cases such as *Dolan v. City of Tigard*, and *Lucas v. South Carolina Coastal Council*, the Rehnquist Court had imposed new protections for owners, suggesting the Court was poised to complete a property rights revolution. However, in *Kelo v. City of New London*, 545 U.S. 469 (2005), *Lingle v. Chevron, U.S.A. Inc*, 544 U.S. 528 (2005), and *San Remo Hotel v. San Francisco*, 545 U.S. 323 (2005), the Court ruled against property interests in all three cases, unambiguously stating that promoting economic development is a valid public use, that the judiciary should not ordinarily second-guess legislatures in the area of economic policy, and that there was no exception to the Full Faith and Credit Clause that would allow owners to sue in federal court after their claims had been heard at the state level. Legally, these cases represented major defeats for property rights advocates, but politically, *Kelo* became a significant rallying symbol for a public relations campaign to mobilize support for their cause.

Of the three cases, *Kelo* was the most important. *Lingle* addressed a Hawaii rent control law that limited the amount that an oil company may charge a lessee-dealer. Chevron contended that the rent control law constituted a taking. *San Remo Hotel* addressed simple procedural questions growing out of a very complex litigation history that involved land use permits. In both cases property rights advocates lost, but these two cases were never highlighted by the Institute for Justice or other ownership groups. Indeed, the legal issues were not as salient as those in *Kelo*, but more importantly, the plaintiffs, an oil company and a hotel, were not as sympathetic "victims" as the Kelos. Moreover, for the Kelos, they lost their home—something with which most Americans could identify, whereas with the other two plaintiffs, the cases involved regulatory takings—the acquisition of property interests and not the physical appropriation of a home.

Kelo v. City of New London raised the hope of many conservatives that eminent domain authority would be trimmed. In part, aspirations were high because *certiorari* was granted on September 28, 2004, less than two months after the Michigan Supreme Court had issued its *Hathcock* decision and ruled that the taking of private property for economic development purposes violated the state constitution. In overturning *Poletown*, one case that many had described as the requiem for property rights had been dismantled. This raised anticipation that the decision to review *Kelo* would lead to new limits on eminent domain under the federal Constitution.

In *Kelo v. City of New London*, the United States Supreme Court affirmed a decision of the Connecticut Supreme Court which held that the taking of unblighted private property for economic development purposes constituted a valid public use under both the state and federal constitutions.

At issue in this case was an attempt by the City of New London, a municipal corporation, and the New London Development Corporation, to exercise eminent domain to build and support economic revitalization of the city's downtown. Elsewhere in this volume, Wilkerson provides more detail on the *Kelo* case, but some facts here still need to be noted. In its plan, New London divided the development into seven parcels, with some of these parcels including public waterways or museums. However, one parcel, known as Lot 3, would become a 90,000 sq. ft. high technology research and development office space and parking facility for the Pfizer Pharmaceutical Company. Several plaintiffs in Lot 3 challenged the taking of their property, claiming that the condemnation of unblighted land for economic development purposes violated both the state and federal constitutions. The Kelos lost in the state courts, and for a bare majority, Justice Stevens agreed with the Connecticut Supreme Court, finding that the taking did not violate the public use requirement of the Fifth Amendment.

First, Stevens reaffirmed the proposition that a taking for a purely private benefit would be unconstitutional. In this case, it was not a private taking because the decision to acquire the property was part of a "'carefully considered' development plan" indicating that neither the real nor hidden motive was to convey a private benefit (478).

Second, the Court rejected argument that, because the property would eventually be transferred to a private party, it failed the public use requirement because the land would not be used by the public. Stevens stated that the "Court long ago rejected any literal requirement that condemned property be put into use for the general public" and that instead, this narrow reading of public use had been discarded in favor of a broader public purpose reading of the public use doctrine (479). Thus, as Stevens defined the issue, the case turned on whether the taking served a valid public purpose, and he ruled that the Court should adhere to the long-established judicial tradition of deferring to legislative determinations on this matter, as evidenced by its decisions in *Berman v. Parker* (1954), and *Hawaii Housing Authority v. Midkiff* (1984). In short, given the broad and flexible meaning attached to the public use stipulation, and past judicial deference to legislative definitions of public purpose (use), Stevens and the majority concluded that the taking of private property for economic development purposes was a valid public use.

Finally, Stevens rebuffed arguments that the Court carve out an economic development exception to the broad public use doctrine that it had created. He rejected this new rule as unworkable, stating that it would be impossible, principally, to distinguish economic development from other valid public purposes. He also dismissed assertions that the taking-for-economic-development purposes blurred the distinction between a public and a private taking.

In many ways, *Kelo* really did not make new law. *Berman*, *Midkiff*, and a host of cases going back to the nineteenth century had established ample precedent for this result. As Stevens pointed out, the City could not take private property for another private party's benefit. He also noted that the more narrow conception of public use had long since been abandoned, and governments have long had the power to convert private property to a variety of public welfare purposes, including economic development. *Kelo* really simply reaffirmed existing takings law. Overall, *Kelo* seemed to cap a recent line of jurisprudence, giving governments broad authority in this domain.

But in anticipating that his opinion might be controversial, Stevens and the majority made it clear that their holding did not prevent states from imposing greater restrictions on eminent domain projects. Specifically, the Court stated:

> We emphasize that nothing in our opinion precludes any State from placing further restrictions on its exercise of the takings power. Indeed, many States already impose "public use" requirements that are stricter than the federal baseline. Some of these requirements have been established as a matter of state constitutional law, while others are expressed in state eminent domain statutes that carefully limit the grounds upon which takings may be exercised (483).

While the Fifth and Fourteenth Amendments permit the taking of unblighted private property for purely economic development purposes, states, under their own constitutions, or by statute, can impose more restrictive conditions upon what constitutes a valid public use. The Court cited *Hathcock*, the recently-decided Michigan Supreme Court case, as such an example where a state did precisely that. This means that *Kelo* did not overrule state decisions that had already placed more restrictions on takings, if decided on their own constitutional or statutory grounds.

Dissenting, Justice O'Connor, joined by Rehnquist, Scalia, and Thomas, acknowledged that there are three situations in which the Court has upheld the taking of private property under a broad public use doctrine. The first is when the property is transferred to public ownership to construct a hospital, road, or military base. Second, transfers of private property to another private owner are permitted when common carriers such as railroads take possession, because ultimately the public does get to use the property. However, O'Connor also identifies a third category of takings—when current use of property is deemed harmful—as being sanctioned by the Court as a valid public use. In reaching this conclusion, O'Connor examines both *Berman* and her own opinion in *Midkiff*, arguing that in the former, removal of blight; and in the latter, concentrated ownership that skewed the real estate market, were the "bads" that the legislatures were seeking to abate, and which the Court had been willing to affirm. O'Connor did not see the New London condemnation as one seeking to alleviate some detriment that the Kelo property was inflicting upon others. Instead, O'Connor argued that in moving "from our decisions sanctioning the condemnation of harmful property use, the Court today significantly expands the meaning of public use" (501). Hence, because the taking of the Kelos' property did not fit into one of the three designated categories, she concluded that it should not be permitted.

O'Connor's dissent also makes two other notable points. First, she acknowledges the broad deference that generally should be given to legislatures to make public use decisions. Second, conspicuously absent from her opinion is a clear indication that she wished to increase the level of scrutiny of public use decisions. Granted, O'Connor identifies three types of takings as permitted public uses, while excluding others; however, nowhere does her opinion really suggest heightened scrutiny of legislative motives.

The lone Justice willing to move toward more substantive property protection is Thomas. In his solo dissent, he argues for a return to the original meaning of the "public use" clause. For Thomas, public use is not the same as public welfare or purpose. Indeed, property may only be taken to further an expressly enumerated power. Singularly among the Justices, he would not afford deference to legislatures to define public use. In addition, Thomas goes further, concluding that, contrary to the Court's previous decisions, the *Berman* and *Midkiff* precedents are wrong, and the Constitution imposes a substantive limit on the power of the government to take private property. In fact, he invokes *Carolene Products*' Footnote 4 logic, and the protection it affords to minorities and to those subjected to eminent domain.

Explaining the Second Trilogy and the Failed Property Rights Revolution

On one level, property rights advocates struck out big in the 2004 term. They lost all three cases, and more significantly, among the three cases, a total of only four votes were cast for owners. Except for *Kelo*, even the most ardent defenders of property interests, such as Scalia and Rehnquist, based upon their support in 1986, did not consistently support new limits or remedies in eminent domain action. There seemed to be little sympathy for heightened scrutiny of property rights claims, with Thomas alone supporting this position in *Kelo*. In many ways, 2004 was a retreat from the legal possibilities hinted at in 1986–1987.

Yet, while property rights lost in court, advocates seized on *Kelo*, using it as a major political symbol to push their agenda to narrow eminent domain law across the country. Property rights advocates lost the legal battle in *Kelo* but they did not lose the war over eminent domain. Instead, one of the most surprising aspects of the *Kelo* decision was the public reaction to it. The Supreme Court's decision upholding the use of eminent domain to take private property from one owner and give it to another in order to promote economic development evoked widespread anger. The titles, alone, of countless articles appearing in the press, are symptomatic of the broad public reaction. For example, Timothy Egan (2005), *Ruling sets off Tug of War over Private Property*, Michael Corkery and Ryan Chittum (2005), *Eminent Domain Uproar Imperils Projects*, Joi Preciphs (2005), *Eminent Domain Ruling Knits Rivals*, and Adam Karlin (2006), *Property Seizure Backlash*, in the national press, were just a few of the many headlines signaling negative responses to the *Kelo* opinion.

Reaction to *Kelo* was not confined to reporting and editorializing. On June 27, 2005, Senator John Cornyn (R-TX) introduced legislation, the "Protection of Homes, Small Businesses, and Private Property Act of 2005," to limit the use of eminent domain in economic development projects. A year later President George Bush issued an Executive Order restricting the use of eminent domain "for the purpose of benefitting the general public, and not merely for the purpose of advancing the economic interest of private parties to be given ownership or use of the property taken" (Executive Order 13406). States and local governments across the country similarly adopted laws to address the *Kelo* decision, following, perhaps, Stevens' admonition that they could take action to further limit eminent domain beyond what the Constitution permitted. Within two years of the *Kelo* decision, more than 20 states adopted laws that prohibited takings for economic development reasons, or to make use of eminent domain more difficult. Some of these laws required more hearings before a taking could occur; some banned the taking of private homes; some required more evidence before a taking could occur; and others instituted rules to award legal fees to owners if they successfully challenged a taking.

The Kelos and the Institute for Justice

Why was the *Kelo* decision a big deal? First, the Kelos were sympathetic plaintiffs. Susette Kelo was a 40-year-old nurse who by 1997 had finally saved enough money to buy a house. It was a cottage in the blue-collar neighborhood of New London; it was older, modest in size and it needed work. But to Ms. Kelo, like for many others, her home was her castle. Her effort to save her home pitted her against Pfizer Pharmaceuticals and the City of New London who, together, wanted to take her home in order to build a parking faciltity and an industrial park for the drug company. Her battle to save her home was clearly reminiscent of those in Poletown, Michigan in 1981, who unsuccessfully fought against Detroit and

General Motors. She also became the poster child for other movements, as Becher notes in her chapter on the American Streets project, and served as a rallying symbol for those individuals in Philadelphia. But here, unlike with the residents in Poletown, Ms. Kelo did not stand alone. The Institute for Justice came to her defense, offering her up as a sympathetic average person facing the threats of big bad government and big bad business who wanted to screw her out of her home. But besides property rights advocates, the Kelos were also supported by groups such as the NAACP, who saw direct parallels between her battle (even though she was white) for her home and similarly situated people of color who had fought to protect neighborhoods targeted by eminent domain projects. Liberals also supported her because of her working class roots and again saw this as a battle to avenge Poletown residents against the fat cats.

Second, unlike with the *Poletown* decision, there was an enormous public relations and media campaign, accompanying the political movement supporting the Kelos' battle. If the *Poletown* decision was the beginning of the property rights and ownership movement, *Kelo* was the culmination of nearly a quarter-century of mobilization.

One of the more important weapons in the eminent domain propaganda and public relations wars was an April 2003 report by the Institute for Justice's Castle Coalition entitled *Public Power, Private Gain: A Five Year, State-By-State Report Examining the Abuse of Eminent Domain.* Written by Dana Berliner, it asserted that from January 1, 1998, until December 31, 2002, there were at least 10,282 examples of eminent domain abuse across 41 states. Eminent domain abuse was defined as "the number of condemnations for private use or benefit. We break those down into filed, threatened, total, and development projects with private benefit condemnations." Among its 10,000 plus examples of abuse included 3,722+ properties with condemnations filed for the benefit of private parties, 6,560+ properties threatened with condemnation for private parties, and 4,032+ properties currently living under threat of private use condemnation.

The report received wide circulation and discussion, with the Institute and the Castle coalition astutely using the media and the web to circulate their findings. In many ways the report was highly flawed and methodologically suspect (Schultz 2009). The report passed over many facts about who was benefitting from the eminent domain, how the benefits were distributed, and what it meant to be living under the threat of a taking. It suggested that the condemnations were all directed at residential properties and small business properties. However, most of the highlighted case studies profiled in the report emphasized individuals similar to Susette Kelo—a single family home owner. This is how the 10,000+ was defined.

There are many other problems with the *Public Power, Private Gain* study that question its methodology and conclusions. But it did not matter. It received wide publicity across the traditional and new media. The *Kelo* decision only made the arguments by the Institute more salient. Now there was a Supreme Court decision that had in fact represented all that it had deplored in *Public Power, Private Gain.* Ms. Kelo was the single family, blue-collar home owner who refused to sell her property. The City wanted to condemn it and give it to a drug company. This was good versus evil, David versus Goliath. Everyone cheers for David even if he loses. Post *Kelo*, the Institute continues to document eminent domain abuse. In particular, it has prominently noted that the project for which Ms. Kelo's house was taken went bust, and its website features more stories like Ms. Kelo's. It also continues to press its case that eminent domain is abused and that the *Kelo* opinion was unprecedented, again without challenge.

Overall, supporters of eminent domain reform had done a terrific job highlighting Ms. Kelo's story as well as many others. In addition to the good public relations and sponsorship, there did appear to be some momentum toward Kelo's side. The Michigan Supreme Court, as noted previously, had reversed the *Poletown* decision and that created the sense that when the Supreme Court accepted the *Kelo* case for appeal, it too was ready to act. But the decision did not go the way many expected, even if legal scholars were not surprised by the decision.

Support for the Kelos came from two directions, as indicated by the total of 41 *amicus* briefs filed in the case. First, traditional neoliberal, conservative, libertarian or pro-property rights groups filed briefs in her support; but surprisingly, liberal and left-leaning individuals and organizations such as Jane Jacobs and the National Association for the Advancement of Colored People, also supported the Kelos. Briefs supporting the City of New London generally came from other governmental units. In part, the political and public relations success of the conservative neoliberals resided in co-opting the liberals to join them in an "us versus them" battle to defend property rights and limit governmental authority. The *Poletown* decision a generation earlier had enraged political interests of all stripes, but it was the conservatives who deployed a myth-of-rights and fear-of-eminent-domain-abuse strategy to marshal support for their version of the political and legal battle.

Another distinguishing factor was that the *Kelo* decision was very different from either the *Berman* or the *Midkiff* rulings. For one, the facts in the case revolved around someone losing their single family home. In *Berman* the plaintiffs (Berman) owned a department store, while in *Midkiff* the challenge to the Hawaiian law was an owner of a large tract of land—essentially a land baron. Neither party makes for a very sympathetic poster child for property rights. Second, in both *Berman* and *Midkiff*, the Supreme Court issued unanimous opinions. *Kelo* was a fractured 5-4 decision along liberal/conservative lines punctuated with two very strong dissents. Moreover, Stevens' majority opinion seemed cold and antiseptic. He recounted the law and expressed little sympathy for the Kelos, except for saying states could impose more restrictions on eminent domain if they wished—not much consolation or comfort for Susette Kelo. In fact, Becher points out that the choice of language used by Stevens versus the dissenters revealed a difference in how they spoke about the taking. Stevens opted to use the word "property" regarding what was being taken, whereas O'Connor and the dissenters preferred the terms "house" and "home." The latter words clearly conveyed more emotion with which the public could connect.

Justice O'Connor, who had written the majority opinion in *Midkiff*, and who was, by now, one of the most popular Justices on the Court, wrote in emotional terms expressing concern for the Kelos and their home. She suggested that the majority's decision would threaten the safety of anyone who owned a home: "Any property may now be taken for the benefit of another private party, but the fallout from this decision will not be random. The beneficiaries are likely to be those citizens with disproportionate influence and power in the political process, including large corporations and development firms" (505). Similarly, Clarence Thomas spoke of how, in the past, eminent domain had targeted racial minorities and the poor. The *Kelo* holding surely would mean this would continue. O'Connor spoke to the homeowners and working class; Thomas to the poor and people of color. Stevens looked like he was the executioner for big business.

But as noted earlier, the immediate reporting of the *Kelo* opinion added fuel to the combustible, if incorrect, perception that the majority holding was unprecedented. The Associated Press, in reporting on the decision, headlined the story "Cities Can Bulldoze Homes for Development" (Main 2007: 174). Similar headlines appeared across the country as newspapers, wire services, cable television, talk radio, and the Web ran news of the *Kelo* opinion. The *Houston Chronicle* editorialized that the decision sanctioned something no different from what the communists did in the Soviet Union and China when they seized private property.

Post-*Kelo*, the Institute for Justice also did an excellent job in shaping the *Kelo* opinion, even several years later. It declared *Kelo* as symbolic of "eminent domain" abuse, a symbol of all that is wrong with big government. At the heart of the *Kelo* criticism, there seems to be an argument that eminent domain abuse exists and that property rights are insecure. This suggested in part that the government—especially local government—is running roughshod over homeowners and property owners, and that both are left defenseless. The fear of eminent domain abuse also seems to suggest that the courts are incapable or unwilling to come to the aid of property owners, and that they are unable to protect individual rights. The solution? Pass more laws and enhance the legal status of property so that the courts can afford it more protection. The criticism of the courts and the solution were contradictory, as was the overall strategy of asserting that homes were more than market property, but that did not matter. The contradictions had been glossed over in the ideological and political battle to limit state power, perhaps even that of the courts, to interfere with the marketplace.

Conclusion

Viewed in isolation, the Court's decision in *Kelo* was a singular loss for property rights. However, that decision stands midstream in a river of political controversy over government regulation and the marketplace. Neoliberal groups seeking to limit the power of the government to regulate the marketplace began a mobilization in the 1970s and 1980s around the issue of property rights and eminent domain.

Their ostensible goal was to place boundaries on the public use justification for the exercise of eminent domain. Decisions such as *Poletown* and *Midkiff*, and individual property rights stories, became important symbols that help rally supporters to their side. Pro-property rights groups, such as the Institute for Justice, have litigated with multiple purposes. If they prevail in court, they advance the cause, gaining legitimacy, recognition, and articulation for their positions. On the other hand, an adverse court decision can be used to exemplify the plight of the powerless against an abusive government. Finally, one could also view the litigation and other support strategies by the Institute and other groups as part of an organizational maintenance process. By that, they were also in competition with other neoliberal groups seeking to define their own hegemonic role vis-à-vis them. Thus, *Kelo* should thus be examined not in isolation in terms of whether the decision itself brought about social change, but instead in terms of how a group or groups can mobilize around an issue and make turns to the judiciary part of a broader hegemonic battle for political power. It is this Gramscian notion of a power struggle that implicates property rights in a battle over state and market sovereignty.

Chapter 2
Legal Mobilization and US Supreme Court Decision Making in Property and Civil Rights Cases, 1978–2003[1]

Rebecca U. Thorpe, Michael C. Evans, Stephen A. Simon, and Wayne V. McIntosh

Introduction

Political elites, as well as the general public, perceive property rights and civil rights issues differently. While "culture war" cleavages typically divide mainstream America on civil rights policies, economic issues consistently tap into fundamental questions of property rights and the ends and means of economic activity. As early as 1840, Alexis de Tocqueville recognized a unique American penchant for economic property rights (1969, vol. 2: 638–639). Tocqueville's assessment of American reverence for the right of ownership quietly resounds today, and recent scholarship shows that within an otherwise divided electorate public sentiments typically converge (or at least fail to diverge) on economic issues (Gerring 1999). As such, judicial determinations of the constitutional status of private property rights have traditionally received little attention. While legal scholars generally agree that the case law addressing property rights is confusing and possibly inconsistent (Peterson 1989, Meltz et al. 1999),[2] to date no prominent theories exist to explain how the Supreme Court addresses these questions.

Judicial scholarship is not only largely silent on how the Supreme Court has addressed economic regulatory conflicts.[3] Most scholars have gone so far

1 This research was supported by the National Science Foundation (Law and Social Sciences, SES-0416455 and SES-0519157, and Behavioral and Cognitive Sciences, BSC-0624067). In addition to the contributors to this collection, we would like to thank Paul Herrnson, Douglas Grob, Frances Lee, and Geoffrey Layman for their helpful support, suggestions, and criticism.

2 As one legal article notes, the Court evaluates regulatory takings claims with a cost-benefit, "balance-all-the-commensurate-factors test" that "even it admits is 'ad hoc'" (Barr, Weissman, and Frantz 2005, quoting *Penn Central Co.* 1978).

3 But see Schubert (1962), Spaeth (1963), Rhode and Spaeth (1976), Hagle and Spaeth (1992) for several attempts to analyze Warren and Burger Court business decisions;

as to dismiss or ignore Supreme Court decision-making on economic questions concerning property rights. Some suggest that such issues do not capture national public attention and are therefore relatively impervious to empirical modeling (Segal and Spaeth 2002: 304). Both Hagle and Spaeth (1992) and Dudley and Ducat (1986, 1987) elaborate at length on the difficulty in modeling economic decisions. As such, researchers have focused attention almost exclusively on judicial behavior in a long-standing jurisprudence regarding publicly salient civil rights and liberties cases (Pritchett 1948, 1954, Schubert 1959, 1965, 1974, Ulmer 1960, Rhode and Spaeth 1976, Segal and Spaeth 1993, 2002).

From the New Deal era until the late Burger Court, this academic disregard also reflected the Supreme Court's plenary docket. While early judicial statements primarily concerned individual property rights and contract requirements,[4] a judicial distinction between economic and social regulations guided the Court's treatment of each issue throughout the New Deal and postwar eras. As first introduced in Justice Stone's famous Footnote 4 of *U.S. v. Carolene Products Co.*, 304 U.S. 144 (1938), the mid-late twentieth century Court applies heightened scrutiny to social regulations infringing on "discrete and insular minorities," while relaxing judicial standards in decisions regarding economic regulations.

Although this "double standard" continues to characterize judicial approaches to social and economic regulations, the Burger and Rehnquist Courts deviated from the long-standing practice of deferring to elected branches of government on federal regulatory policy and to lower courts and local governments on issues concerning local land-use. Indeed, property rights have been a focal point of significant political movements, especially that of neoliberal think tanks and legal advocacy groups that began to flower in the 1970s (see e.g., Teles 2008). Nonetheless, little work has examined the political processes behind Supreme Court decisions on property rights.

To address this gap in the literature, we focus on regulatory takings and affirmative action cases from 1978 to 2003. By juxtaposing these issues, we exploit a "natural experiment" conveniently suited for an exploratory study of variation across legal questions. While these two issues alone do not provide a comprehensive account of judicial decision-making across property rights and civil rights decisions generally, we believe that this assessment offers a useful starting point from which to formulate broader theories on interest group mobilization and judicial behavior in different types of cases, based on several conditional factors that we introduce.

---

also see Mendelson (1964) for a piercing critique of Spaeth's (1963) Business-Scale ("B-Scale") analysis.

4 For two particularly prominent examples, see *Fletcher v. Peck*, 9 Cranch 87 (1810); *Dartmouth College v. Woodward*, 4 Wheat 518 (1819) (citing the Guarantee Clause, Article IV, Section 4).

Data for Natural Experiment

In 1978, the Court made decisions on regulatory takings and affirmative action that are currently regarded as paradigmatic judicial precedents. *Penn Central Transport Co. v. New York City*, 438 U.S. 104 (1978), and *Regents of the University of California v. Bakke*, 438 U.S. 265 (1978), both initiated a new line of analysis within regulatory takings and affirmative action doctrine respectively.

Between 1978 and 2003, by our count, the Court decided 40 regulatory takings and 15 affirmative action cases on the merits. The common time span in these developments holds the composition of the Court and societal/contextual dynamics equal, allowing us to control for those factors while gaining insight into the influence of the unique characteristics of each issue on observed behavior. If, for example, significant interests align differently and the level of justices' internal agreement and ideological consistency also differ markedly, then this might illuminate divergent judicial treatment across issues. Accordingly, this study details several structural discrepancies between an economic and civil rights issue area. The work also addresses how issue-based mobilization influences Supreme Court decision-making and provides a useful starting point for future empirical research.

For our data, we first identified every decision in regulatory takings and affirmative action cases from 1978 to 2003. To do so, we drew upon Supreme Court databases generated at the University of Maryland, cross-checking each case manually by reviewing the full opinion text.[5] We eventually settled on 15 fully-argued affirmative action[6] and 40 regulatory takings cases decided on the merits.

We used Westlaw and Lexis Nexis to acquire judicial opinions and *amicus* briefs, and whenever possible, we included *amici* briefs from both the *certiorari* and merits stage.[7] To assess interest group participation, we first generated an exhaustive list of every group that participated as *amicus curiae* in the selected cases. We isolated 961 groups. Of these, 486 submitted briefs in regulatory takings cases, and 564 participated in affirmative action cases. To assess the representation of the groups participating across issues, we coded each group that submitted at least one brief to two or more cases. Hereinafter, we refer to these groups as "repeat participants."

---

5 With support from the National Science Foundation (Law and Social Sciences, SES-0416455 and SES-0519157, and Behavioral and Cognitive Sciences, BSC-0624067).

6 A sixteenth case, *Minnick v. California Dept. of Corrections,* attracted nine *amicus* briefs and was orally argued before being dismissed as improvidently granted. We therefore only include it in computations focused solely on third party participation.

7 *Lexis*, unlike Westlaw, only provides briefs from the merits stage. We therefore relied mostly on Westlaw's briefs collection. However, for an unknown reason, Westlaw does not list *amicus* briefs under its "Briefs and Other Related Documents" section in two affirmative action and four regulatory takings cases. Consequently, for six cases our dataset only includes groups participating at the merits stage.

Overall, there were 148 repeat *amicus* participants in regulatory takings and 147 in affirmative action cases. Additionally, 88 groups submitted at least one brief to both issue areas. In our analysis of group participation, we only include cases that attracted at least one *amicus* brief. There were 36 regulatory takings and 16 affirmative action cases that met this condition.

While most of our measures are well-understood, two of our variables warrant brief explanation. First, "*amicus* conflict" is calculated by multiplying the overall level of *amicus* participation (i.e., number of briefs submitted) by what we call a "conflict ratio." The "conflict ratio" is defined as the ratio of the smallest number of groups declaring support for one side to the number of groups declaring support for the other side. The conflict ratio therefore ranges from 0 to 1, with 1 representing balanced representation (perfect conflict) or completely one-sided representation (no conflict). Second, to compare judicial voting behavior at the individual level, we used the ideological direction variable from Spaeth's "US Supreme Court Database." For each justice, we calculated the percentage of liberal votes for each issue area.

Legal Mobilization

The most common mode of interest group participation has become the filing of *amicus curiae* briefs (O'Conner and Epstein 1982), and these briefs have a substantial impact on justices' agenda setting (Caldeira and Wright 1988). Consequently, it is held to be in the mutual interest of lawyers, interest groups and government actors to build coalitions with one another in order to maximize influence on judicial decision-making (McGuire 1994). Because participant resources are not infinite, however, interest organizations must reserve time, money, energy and other assets for cases that are of primary importance to the broader public membership and other groups with whom organized interests might pool resources (Caldeira and Wright 1988: 112). Therefore, *amicus* participation indicates groups' priorities and issue targets.

We assess three aspects of legal mobilization: (1) the overall level of *amicus* participation, (2) the overall level of "*amicus* conflict," and (3) the relative diversity of mobilized interests. A reasonable preliminary assumption is that affirmative action, given its widespread and emotionally charged appeal, inspires greater legal mobilization than regulatory takings, which has remained an obscure, technical, and mostly particularized issue. Therefore, we expect that;

> Mobilization Hypothesis 1: On average, fewer *amici* briefs are filed in regulatory takings cases than in affirmative action cases.

Looking at overall interest group participation and the Court's decisional outcomes, we find strong support for Mobilization Hypothesis 1[8] and Judicial Hypotheses 1(a)[9] and 1(b).[10] As reported in Table 2.1, on average, affirmative action cases

Table 2.1 *Amicus* participation/conflict and court disagreement descriptive statistics

Variable	Mean	Stand. Dev.	Min.	Max.
***Amicus* Participation/Conflict**				
# Amici Submissions	16.3	20.0	0	112
Regulatory Takings	10.4	8.1	0	30
Affirmative Action	31.9	31.6	6	112
Affirmative Action (-3 outliers)[a]	17.7	7.3	6	30
# Amici Weighted by Conflict[b]	8.0	8.0	0	43.1
Regulatory Takings	6.4	6.4	0	24
Affirmative Action	12.1	10.4	1.5	43.1
Affirmative Action (-3 outliers)	8.2	4.5	1.5	16.7
Court Disagreement				
Size of Winning Opinion Coalition	6.6	2.1	1	9
Regulatory Takings	7.3	1.8	5	9
Affirmative Action	4.6	1.4	1	6
# Opinions	3.3	1.5	1	7
Regulatory Takings	2.7	1.1	1	5
Affirmative Action	4.9	1.2	2	7

Notes: [a] For each column, the first entry represents the given statistic for both issue areas combined (n=55), the second is only for regulatory takings decisions (n=40), the third is only for affirmative action (n=15), and the fourth, when applicable, is for affirmative action less the statistical outliers *Bakke, Grutter, and Gratz* (n=12).

[b] For each decision, a "conflict ratio" was calculated by dividing the lowest number of briefs submitted from either (declared) side by the number of briefs submitted by the other side. Values thus range from 0 to 1, with 0 meaning briefs were submitted to support only one side and 1 meaning both sides were represented by an equal number of briefs. We interpret values closer to 1 as indicating greater conflict. The conflict ratio is then multiplied by the number of *amici* submitted to generate a value that we use as a proxy for overall degree *amicus* conflict for each case.

8 Mobilization Hypothesis 1: On average, there were fewer *amici* briefs filed in regulatory takings decisions than in affirmative action decisions.

9 Judicial Hypothesis 1(a): All else held equal, there will be fewer opinions per case in regulatory takings decisions than in affirmative action decisions (we discuss this hypothesis a bit later in the chapter).

10 Judicial Hypothesis 1(b): All else held equal, winning opinion coalitions will be larger in regulatory takings decisions than in affirmative action decisions (we discuss this hypothesis a bit later in the chapter).

attracted far more *amicus* briefs, generated more opinions, and resulted in smaller winning opinion coalitions than did regulatory takings cases. No affirmative action decision attracted fewer than six third party briefs, and one (*Bakke*) attracted 112. By contrast, interest group participation in regulatory takings cases ranged from 0 to 30 *amicus* briefs per case. Indeed, the average level of *amici* participation in affirmative action cases (31.9 briefs per case) outnumbered regulatory takings (10.4) three to one. Even if three outlier affirmative action cases – *Bakke* (112 briefs), *Grutter v. Bollinger* (92 briefs), and *Gratz v. Bollinger* (63 briefs) – are removed, average third party participation in affirmative action cases (17.7 briefs/case) was still 1.7 times greater than in regulatory takings cases.

However, we are interested in more than just the overall level of *amicus* participation. On the one hand, we assess the relative balance of participation on behalf of the opposing sides in each issue area. On the other hand, we also would like to know something about the diversity of interests involved.[11] We have no preliminary expectations about the relative balance of participation for one side or the other. However, for the same reasons we expect higher levels of participation in affirmative action, and we do expect to find support for;

> Mobilization Hypothesis 2: Groups participating as *amicus curiae* in affirmative action cases represented a broader cross-section of society than those in regulatory takings controversies.

Figures 2.1 and 2.2 summarize group participation across issue areas among cases that attracted at least one *amicus* brief. Figure 2.1 depicts the proportion of cases in which at least one repeat participant from each group type submitted at least one brief. Figure 2.1 reports the average number of groups per case of each group type that submitted briefs regarding each issue area. This analysis provides mixed support for Mobilization Hypothesis 2. On the one hand, it is not exactly true, as the hypothesis states, that groups participating as *amicus curiae* in affirmative action cases represent a broader cross-section of society than those in regulatory takings cases. In fact, nearly all of the group categories are represented in both issue areas. If anything, according to our classification scheme, regulatory takings cases attracted a greater diversity of interests than affirmative action. While "Higher Education" groups only submitted briefs to affirmative action cases, two types of organizations – "Environmental/Conservation" and "Retirees" – participated solely in regulatory takings decisions. On the other hand, however, there is a critical difference in the degree of participation by each group type across issues. All but one of the group categories represented in both issues ("Private/Commercial/Agriculture")

11 By diversity of interests, we mean the range of group types aligned on either side of the issues. We understand that there can be diversity of positions among, for example, public interest organizations. Indeed, the Pacific Legal Foundation and the Institute for Justice generally support the same side in property law cases, but they do not always present the same rationale (see, e.g., Teles 2008, Southworth 2008).

participated in a higher proportion of affirmative action than in regulatory takings cases. Furthermore, at least one "Conservative Public Interest/Law" group, one "Liberal Public Interest/Law" group, and one "Government Group/Association" group submitted one or more brief(s) to *every* affirmative action case. By contrast, regulatory takings[12] claims generated group participation in 62, 81, and 19 percent of cases among these respective categories. There is also a stark gap in issue-based participation among the "Racial/Religious/Ethnic" and "Sex/Gender" categories. At least one group per category participated in 93.8 percent and 81.3 percent of affirmative action cases, respectively. By contrast, representation among those group types falls to 8.3 percent and 2.8 percent of regulatory takings cases. Finally, the participation gap was very small (75 percent vs. 68.8 percent) for the only group with representation in both issue areas *and* a higher participation rate in regulatory takings ("Private/Commercial/Agriculture").

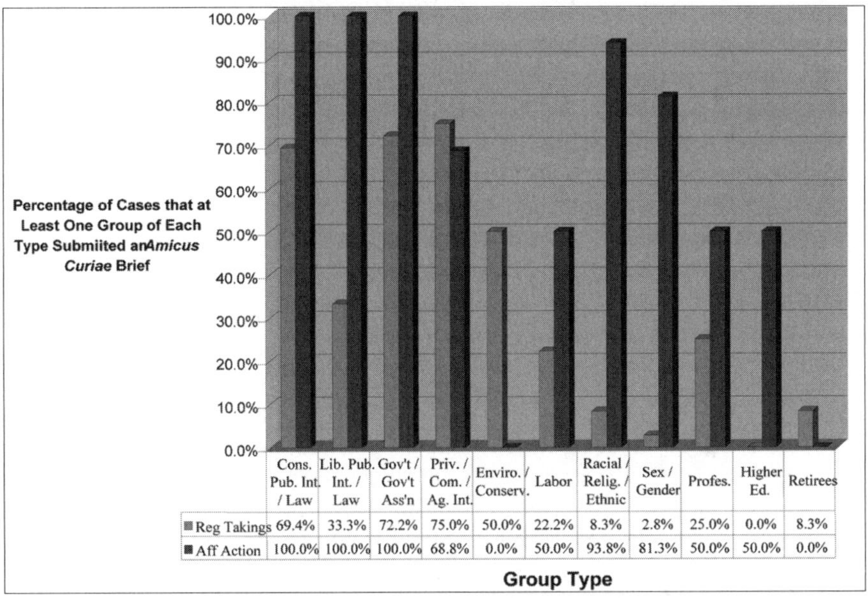

	Cons. Pub. Int. / Law	Lib. Pub. Int. / Law	Gov't / Gov't Ass'n	Priv. / Com. / Ag. Int.	Enviro. / Conserv.	Labor	Racial / Relig. / Ethnic	Sex / Gender	Profes.	Higher Ed.	Retirees
Reg Takings	69.4%	33.3%	72.2%	75.0%	50.0%	22.2%	8.3%	2.8%	25.0%	0.0%	8.3%
Aff Action	100.0%	100.0%	100.0%	68.8%	0.0%	50.0%	93.8%	81.3%	50.0%	50.0%	0.0%

Group Type

Figure 2.1 Cross-issue comparison of group participation as *amicus curiae* by group type

The average level of group participation per case was also higher in affirmative action cases. Every group type (with the exception of "Environmental/Conservation" and "Retirees") was represented, on average, at least once per case in affirmative action decisions. By contrast, only four group types – "Conservative

12 That is, among the regulatory takings cases that received at least one *amicus* brief.

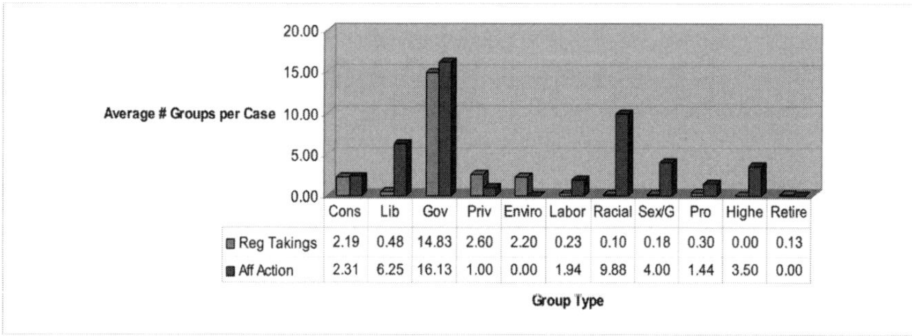

Figure 2.2 Cross-issue comparison of average *amicus* participation per case by group type

Note: Charts only include "repeat participant" groups. Out of 486 groups submitting *amicus curiae* briefs to regulatory takings decisions, 148 were repeat participants. Of the 564 groups that submitted *amicus curiae* briefs to regulatory takings decisions, 147 were repeat participants. Eighty-eight groups submitted at least one brief to both issue each issue area. Charts only include cases that attracted at least one *amicus* brief. There were 36 regulatory takings and 16 affirmative action cases that met that condition.

Public Interest/Law," "Government Group/Association," "Private/Commercial/ Agriculture," "Environmental/Conservation" – participated at a rate higher than 0.5 groups per case in regulatory takings cases. Furthermore, groups of every category – with the exception of "Private/Commercial/Agriculture" and "Environmental/ Conservation" – participated more times per case on average in affirmative action than in regulatory takings cases. Taken together, these findings suggest that while a wide array of group types are represented in both issue areas, a substantial cross-section of society generally participates in a higher proportion of affirmative action than in regulatory takings cases.

Figures 2.1 and 2.2 also reveal an unanticipated difference between "conservative" and "liberal" public interest legal associations. Even if "Racial/ Religious/Ethnic" and "Sex/Gender" groups are counted as "liberal" groups, the conservative participants appear to cast a wider net in terms of issue involvement. Put another way, liberal groups are far more specialized than their conservative counterparts.[13] While there is virtually no presence by ("non-Labor Environmental/ Conservation") liberal groups in regulatory takings cases and a dominant presence by these groups in affirmative action, conservative groups participate at a very high level in both issue areas. The individual group-level data in Appendix B suggests

13 This difference may be related to group age. Most now active neoliberal groups did not appear on the scene until at least the 1970s, while organizations on the other side preceded them, sometimes by decades (see, e.g., Nielsen and Albiston 2006: 1611–1615).

that this is in no small part due to heavy lifting by the Pacific Legal Foundation, which is the highest ranked third party participant on both issues.

We also can expect variation in mobilization behavior associated with the two issues over time. Although *Bakke* was a path – breaking decision on affirmative action, the issue associates with long-established national political cleavages and organizations dating back to the beginning of the century. We therefore should not expect a substantial increase in interest group participation or conflict in affirmative action from 1978 to 2003. *Penn Central*, by contrast, involved an issue that was predominantly local in impact for 50 years, and largely divorced from established national political cleavages. The legal theory behind the recent surge in "regulatory takings" case law emanated from conflict between environmental group mobilization in the 1960s and a counter-response spearheaded by neoliberal public law interest groups in the early to mid 1970s (Epstein 1985, Coyle 1993). Perhaps most notably, groups such as the Pacific Legal Foundation led a new movement for heightened property rights protections in reaction to an increasing environmental regulatory policy (see especially, chapters by Schultz and Wilkerson, also, Teles 2008, Hatcher 2005, Epstein 1985). As the issue became better known within the broader legal/political community (due in large part to increased Court attention to the issue) and the interested parties became better organized and coordinated, we would expect increases in both overall third-party participation and *amicus* conflict over time. Therefore, we expect that;

> Mobilization Hypothesis 3(a): *Amicus curiae* participation will increase at a greater rate in regulatory takings cases than in affirmative action cases; and

> Mobilization Hypothesis 3(b): *Amicus* conflict should increase at a greater rate in regulatory takings cases than in affirmative action cases.

Our final pair of mobilization hypotheses posit expectations about change in *amici* activity over time. Figures 2.3 and 2.4 illustrate issue-specific changes in the overall level of *amicus* participation and conflict, respectively, from the initial emergence of each legal issue from 1978 to 2003. Two versions of each set of observations are presented; one includes the *Bakke* decision (a statistical outlier) (Figures 2.3.A and 2.4.A) and the other does not (Figures 2.3.B and 2.4.B). Because this analysis is based on running averages over time, the second figure is necessary in order to account for the effect of a statistical outlier. Given the low number of affirmative action observations, combined with the extraordinary number of *amici* submitted to the *Bakke* case at the beginning of the series, including *Bakke* leads to the erroneous appearance of a drastic downward trend among affirmative action cases in both overall third party participation (Figure 2.3.A) and conflict levels (Figure 2.4.A). When the case is excluded, the time series exhibits a more constant rate of change (Figure 2.3.B).

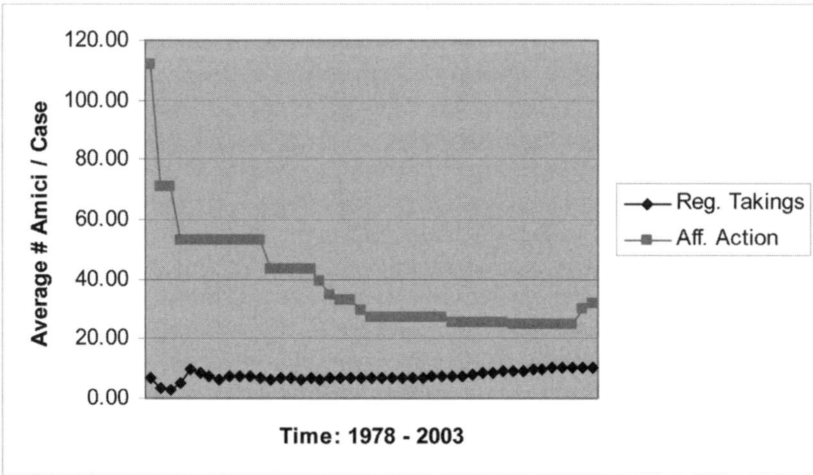

2.3.A All cases included.

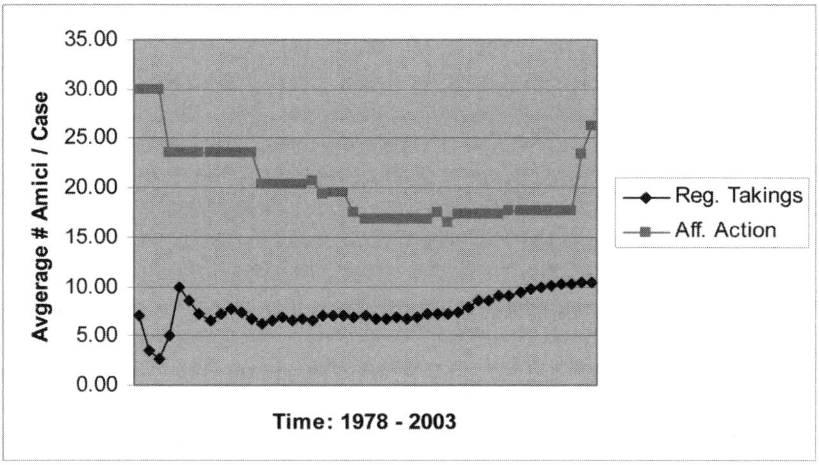

2.3.B Outlier *Bakke* decision excluded.

Figure 2.3 Cross-issue comparison of change in the average number of *amici* submissions per case from 1978 to 2003 (running averages)

As illustrated, participation descended from 30 briefs per case (after *United Steelworkers v. Weber* 1979), to a rate of 20 per case at the time of the *Wygant v. Jackson Board of Education* decision (1986), and then stabilized around 17 briefs per case. This trend met a sharp increase (26 briefs) with the *Grutter* and *Gratz* "twin bill" in 2003. Overall, *amicus* conflict in affirmative action cases fluctuated steadily around 8.0 for nearly the entire series (when *Bakke* is excluded). Thus,

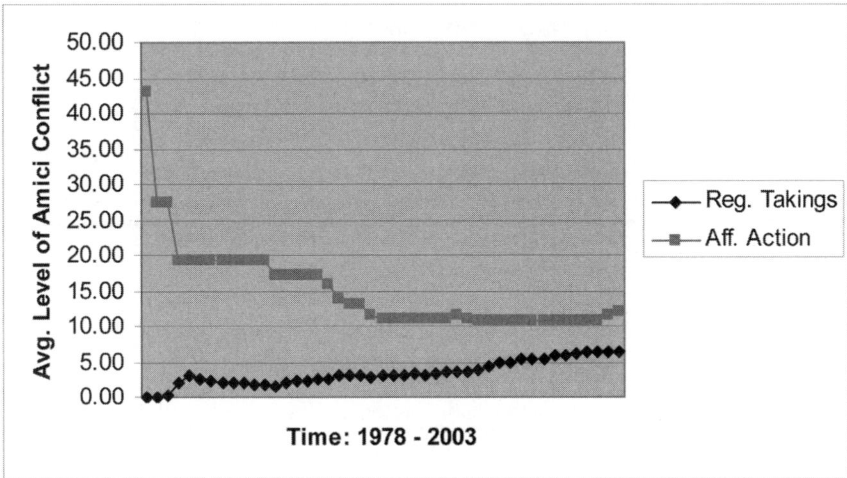

2.4.A All cases included.

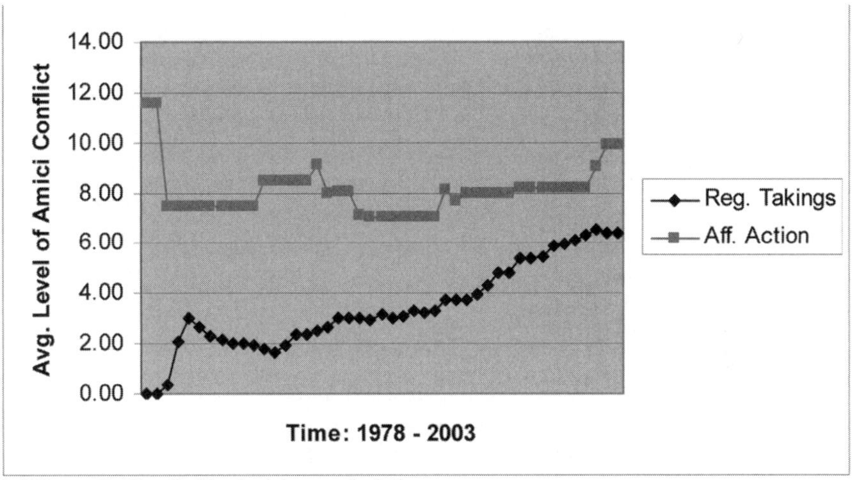

2.4.B Outlier *Bakke* decision excluded.

Figure 2.4 Cross-issue comparison of change in the average level of *amici* conflict per case from 1978 to 2003 (running averages)

the trend in both *amicus* participation and the level of conflict in affirmative action cases either held constant or declined over this time period. By contrast, in regulatory takings cases, third party conflict increased markedly, and the average level of participation either increased or remained constant. These results strongly support Mobilization Hypotheses 3(a) and 3(b).

Judicial Values and Policy Making Processes

Perry (1991, p. 278) suggested that justices generally operate from one of two basic "modes" when deciding whether to grant *certiorari*. If a justice feels strongly about the ideological outcome of a case, he will adopt an "outcome mode," casting his *cert* vote with an eye toward the anticipated policy consequences of granting or not. On the other hand, if a justice does not care much about the policy outcome on the merits, he will operate from "jurisprudential mode," allowing legal considerations to predominate. With Perry, we see little reason to think this distinction applies only to the *cert* stage. Whether they are bargaining over opinion language or casting their final vote on the merits, it makes sense that justices will operate in an outcome-oriented mode when issues relate to deep value commitments, and in a different mode for less value-laden issues. When issues relate to justices' deepest value commitments, we argue, their merits decisions will often conform to the expectations of the attitudinal model (Segal and Spaeth 2002). Likewise, the process of opinion assignment, bargaining, and accommodation will operate according to justices' institutionally structured strategic pursuit of opinions that best advance their policy preferences (Epstein and Knight 1997, Maltzman, Spriggs, and Wahlbeck 2000). We argue that judicial decision-making in affirmative action cases exemplifies this outcome-oriented decision mode.

Following Schattenschneider on the socialization of conflict, we assume that the conflict surrounding affirmative action policies generates greater contagion – or more widespread public disagreement – than regulatory takings cases. Since justices, like most American citizens, not only carry deep-seated values concerning the status of affirmative action programs but also bitterly disagree, we should expect justices to carry a hard bargain in order to optimize legal and policy outcomes. Assuming an even distribution of judicial values, this should result in a high degree of separate opinion writing and a preponderance of small winning decision coalitions.

Given a narrower scope of conflict surrounding regulatory takings claims, in addition to the justices' legal and political backgrounds – only Justices Brennan, Scalia, and Breyer first approached regulatory takings cases with any previous experience that might include property policies[14] – cues in their environment, such as third party participation, leadership from other justices, the policy preferences of other governmental actors, and so on, may well take on greater importance. Justices have typically lacked both a strong value commitment to the consequences of alternative positions on what constitutes a "taking" in the regulatory context and clear beliefs about what those consequences in fact might be.

14 Justice Brennan was a known specialist in labor law, Justice Scalia was a close colleague of Richard Epstein at the University of Chicago, and served on the DC Circuit during the early Reagan years when property rights issues experienced re-birth (see e.g., Brisbin 1997), and Justice Breyer came to the bench with considerable experience in regulatory law.

One indicator of the relative degree of justices' value commitments to disparate issue areas is the relative un/willingness of justices to expend scarce resources bargaining with one another over opinion language, and the corresponding un/willingness of majority opinion authors to accommodate their colleagues. If, as we expect, the justices' value commitments are significantly stronger in affirmative action, then we should find support for;

> Judicial Hypothesis 1(a): There were fewer opinions per case in regulatory takings decisions than in affirmative action decisions; and
>
> Judicial Hypothesis 1(b): On average, winning decision coalitions were larger in regulatory takings decisions than in affirmative action decisions.

Another indicator of disparate value commitment is the extent to which voting polarization varies across issues. We expect, therefore, that;

> Judicial Hypothesis 2: Individual justices more consistently voted in a liberal or conservative direction in affirmative action than in regulatory takings decisions.

The data reflecting patterns of judicial decisions is rather striking. The mean coalition size for affirmative action cases (4.6 justices) actually falls below a "minimum winning" coalition majority, reflecting disproportionately large numbers of split opinions and internal judicial fractures. In fact, the Court fell short of a five-member majority opinion in 2/5 of the affirmative action cases (6 of 15) and produced a minimum winning coalition in all but three of the remaining cases. No affirmative action decision exceeded a six-member majority. By contrast, the Court secured *at least* a minimum winning coalition in all regulatory takings decisions and averaged more justices per majority opinion (7.3) than the maximum number from any affirmative action case. Additionally, affirmative action decisions generated two more opinions per case than regulatory takings cases (4.9: 2.7). While every affirmative action case provoked some judicial disagreement – and one case (*Bakke*) resulted in seven opinions – regulatory takings cases met with far greater judicial consensus and unanimity (ranging from one to five opinions/case).

In Table 2.1, we show that the Court produced more opinions (Judicial Hypothesis 1) and smaller winning opinion coalitions (Judicial Hypothesis 2) in affirmative action than in regulatory takings cases. These findings are consistent with the expectation that justices have stronger, more divisive value commitments at stake in the former than in the latter. Further support for this is provided by conducting individual-level analysis of the justices' voting behavior (Figure 2.5/Appendix C). This indicates that the justices have indeed been more polarized in affirmative action than in regulatory takings cases. Of the 16 members who sat on the Court during this time period, six justices (Brennan, Marshall, White, Blackmun, Souter, and Ginsburg) voted in a liberal direction 91–100 percent

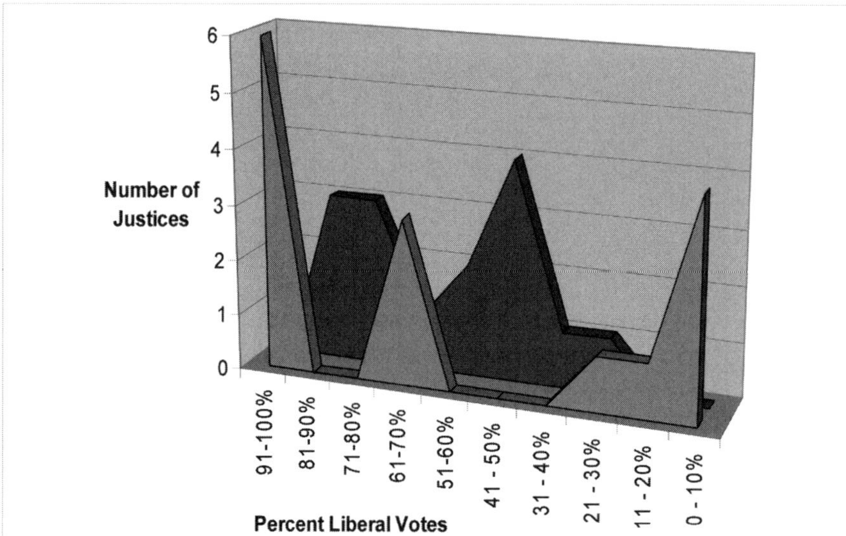

	91-100%	81-90%	71-80%	61-70%	51-60%	41 - 50%	31 - 40%	21 - 30%	11 - 20%	0 - 10%
Aff. Action	6	0	0	3	0	0	0	1	1	4
Reg. Takings	0	3	3	1	2	4	1	1	0	0

Figure 2.5 Cross-issue comparison of the distribution of justices' liberal voting percentages

of the time, and four (Rehnquist, Scalia, Kennedy, and Thomas) did so in 0–10 percent of decisions for affirmative action cases. However, no justice behaved as consistently liberal or conservative in regulatory takings decisions. The three most *liberal* justices (Souter, Ginsburg, and Breyer) voted in a *conservative* direction 10 to 19 percent of the time in regulatory takings cases, and the most conservative justice (Thomas) voted in a liberal direction no less than 21 percent of the time on that issue (Schultz reports similar patterns of voting in the property rights cases he assesses in his chapter). While no justice voted "moderately" – within the 31–60 percent liberalism range – in affirmative action cases, seven justices balanced their regulatory takings votes within that very range. All of this further supports the conjecture motivating Judicial Hypothesis 2[15] that justices have stronger value commitments at stake in affirmative action cases than in regulatory takings cases.

However, in both decision-making modes, justices very well may pay attention to outside participants. A body of scholarship demonstrates why justices in an outcome-oriented mode may look beyond the bench to gauge the interests of

15 Judicial Hypothesis 2: Individual justices will more consistently vote in a liberal or conservative direction in affirmative action than in regulatory takings decisions.

external parties: "rational" judicial actors who seek to influence policy must pay at least some attention to the political interests at stake in order to become better informed about certain policy consequences and to deliver a feasible political outcome (Murphy 1964, Eskridge 1991, Epstein and Knight 1998). These scholars contend that justices utilize information transmitted by *amici* to maximize *efficacious* policy by tempering their doctrine in light of the preferences of other actors and the institutional context in which they act (Epstein and Knight 1998).

Sophisticated voting implies that case facts, externally mobilized interests, and judicial attitudes may be weighed differently on a case-by-case basis, depending, in part, on the *level of attention* and *perceived reactions* of external political players. Cases drawing less (or more consensual) legal mobilization – or issues that attract participation limited to a narrow category of interest groups – indicate low levels of public salience. Conversely, high levels of conflictual legal mobilization that attract participation from a wide range of interests carry a greater level of policy information and indicate high public salience, which is something rational policy oriented justices are unlikely to ignore. Such external considerations very well may exacerbate internal divisions on the Court, creating yet another source of separate opinions and small winning coalition sizes. If regulatory takings cases do not attract as many repeat players (Galanter 1974) providing justices with reliable information, or petitions from the Solicitor General whose compliance is often necessary for policy enactment (Segal 1988),[16] then justices are not made as expressly aware of significant audience members anticipating policy results (Baum 2006).

However, even when justices are not engaged in outcome-mode – due, for example, to a lack of familiarity with and/or deep value commitment to an issue – external actors may still exert an influence. As mentioned above, some justices may use *amicus* participation as an information cue to help them decide a case about which they lack strong conviction, which also could create internal dissension among justices. Therefore, we expect that;

> Judicial Hypothesis 3(a): The greater the level of *amicus* conflict in a case, the more opinions the case will generate, *regardless of issue area*.

> Judicial Hypothesis 3(b): The greater the level of *amicus* conflict in a case, the smaller the size of the winning decision coalition, *regardless of issue area*.

Table 2.2 presents the results of our OLS tests of Judicial Hypotheses 3(a) and 3(b). As expected, regardless of issue area, the level of *amici* conflict is negatively associated with the size of the winning opinion coalition (Model A) and positively

16 Segal's study demonstrates that between 1954 and 1982, the Court adopted the position of the Solicitor General (SG) in 72 percent of 691 cases in which the Presidential administration participated as *amicus* (see Epstein and Knight, id., 225 (citing Segal 1991, Puro 1981). Moreover, Collins (2008: 106) reports that SG participation in a case moves the outcome in either ideological direction, depending on which side the SG supports.

Table 2.2 OLS regression results demonstrating relationship between issue area, *amicus* conflict/participation and two measures of court disagreement

Independent Variables	Model A: Dependent Variable Size of Winning Opinion Coalition	Model B: Dependent Variable Number of Opinions
	Coefficient (Robust SE)	**Coefficient (Robust SE)**
(1) *Amici* Participation Weighted by Conflict	-0.10** (0.03)	0.06** (0.02)
(2) Issue Area 0 = Regulatory Takings 1 = Affirmative Action	-2.72*** (0.56)	1.64*** (0.47)
(3) Interaction of (1) and (2)	0.05 (0.43)	0.02 (0.03)
Constant	8.00*** (0.36)	2.35*** (0.22)
	F (3, 51) = 16.24 Prob > F = 0.00 R-squared = 0.44	F (3, 51) = 61.85 Prob > F = 0.00 R-squared = 0.54

Note: N = 55; *** P < 0.001; ** P< 0.01; * P< 0.05.

associated with the number of opinions (Model B). Interestingly, the results also provide further support for the *independent influence* of issue on Court conflict. Even controlling the impact of third party participation (or another causal factor prior to *amicus* activity), affirmative action cases, on average, are expected to result in winning coalitions with 2.72 fewer justices and to generate 1.64 more opinions than regulatory takings.

Finally, just as we expect to find variation across issues in changes in *amicus* activity over time, we also suspect that changes in judicial behavior will not be uniform across the two issue areas over time. We posit that the distribution of the *degree* (although not direction) of value commitment toward affirmative action remained fairly constant on the Court between 1978 and 2003, despite the nearly complete turnover of membership over the period (only Rehnquist and Stevens served the entire time). The well known increase in the level of conservatism on the Court over this time period should not alter the degree of conflict over affirmative action, since the justices would each continue to harbor strong opinions on the issue, and stake out positions distinct from even those with whom they share general ideological affinity. With regulatory takings, however, we might expect a significant amount of *adaptation* on the part of the justices. This developmental process might involve coming to understand how the issue relates to prior value commitments, developing new (secondary) value commitments in light of the issue, and/or gaining stronger beliefs about the consequences of alternative decisions. Moreover, as increased information will have a cumulative effect, creating greater possibilities for judicial divergence, this should enhance position taking and, thus, conflict. For these reasons, we posit that;

> Judicial Hypothesis 4(a): Over time, the number of opinions per regulatory takings decision will increase at a higher rate than will the number of opinions per affirmative action decision; and
>
> Judicial Hypothesis 4(b): Over time, the average size of winning regulatory takings decision coalitions will decrease at a higher rate than will the average size of winning affirmative action decision coalitions.

We find very modest support for Judicial Hypotheses 4(a) and 4(b). As with the analysis of change in *amicus* participation over time, we present the judicial conflict results both including (Figures 2.6.A and 2.7.A) and excluding (Figures 2.6.B and 2.7.B) the *Bakke* decision. The trend for affirmative action varies considerably depending on whether *Bakke* is included. If included, there appears to be a decrease in the average number of opinions per case (from 7 to 5) and an increase in average winning coalition size (from 1 to 6) over time. When *Bakke* is excluded, the average number of opinions increases immediately before stabilizing around 4.5 opinions per case. The average winning opinion coalition size stabilizes around 5 after an early drop from 5 to 4. Thus, when *Bakke* is excluded, the Court has demonstrated either constant or increased levels of conflict in affirmative action decisions over time. With *Bakke*, the level of conflict has either remained constant or decreased over time. For regulatory takings, Figure 2.6 demonstrates a modest increase in the average number of opinions from about 2 to just over 2.5. Depending on which affirmative action series is chosen, the regulatory takings trend either contrasts with a decrease in affirmative action opinions over time (Figure 2.6.A) or closely parallels a slight increase in affirmative action opinions from 4 to just over 4.5 (Figure 2.6.B). Figure 2.7 demonstrates a change in regulatory takings opinion coalition size from an average close to eight in the first half of the series to almost seven in the last half. Affirmative action coalition sizes, by contrast, either increased over time (Figure 2.7.A) or remained constant (Figure 2.7.B). This suggests that regulatory takings cases generated slightly higher levels of judicial disagreement over time, while affirmative action cases met with a decrease in judicial disagreement after *Bakke* was decided.[17]

17 The high level of *amicus* attention and considerable judicial divisions that *Bakke* drew are also consistent with the theory that, like the broader American public, justices approach affirmative action cases with strong values in mind.

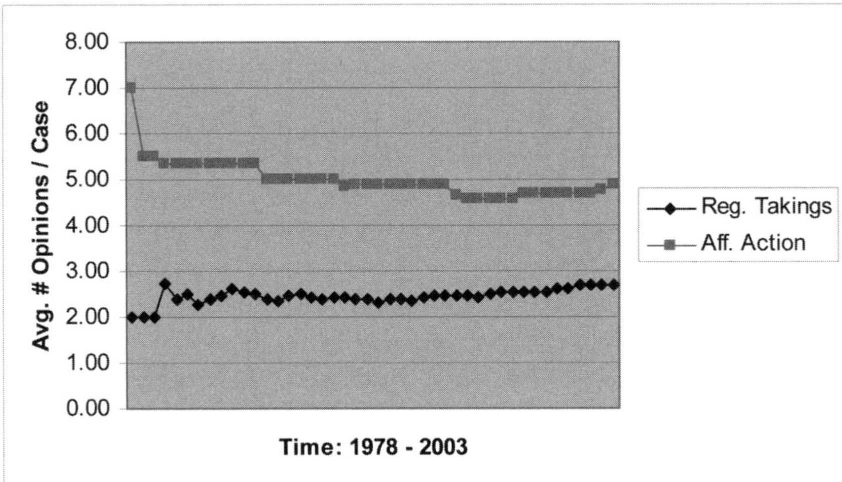

2.6.A All cases included.

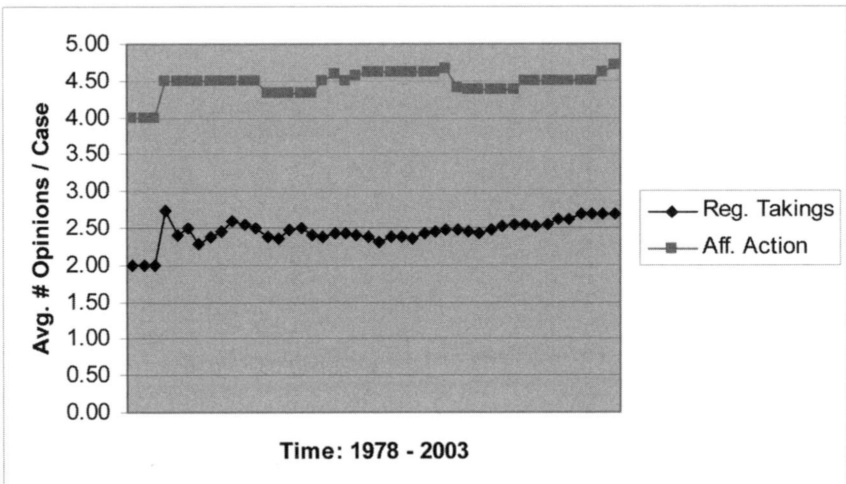

2.6.B Outlier *Bakke* decision excluded.

Figure 2.6 Cross-issue comparison of change in the average number of opinions generated per case from 1978 to 2003

Conclusions

We have introduced a framework for investigating the impact of legal mobilization on judicial decisionmaking, specifically assessing the degree of participation by third-parties in property rights and civil rights litigation before the US Supreme Court. We find that judicial processes and behavior vary according to differences

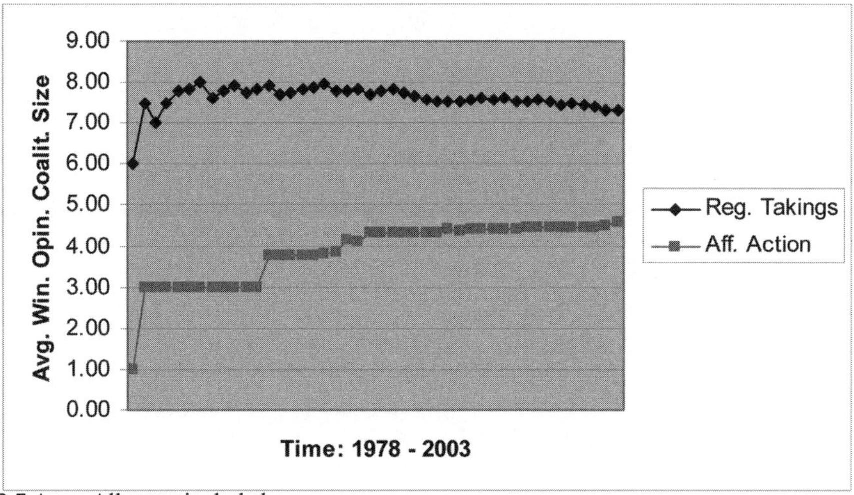

2.7.A All cases included.

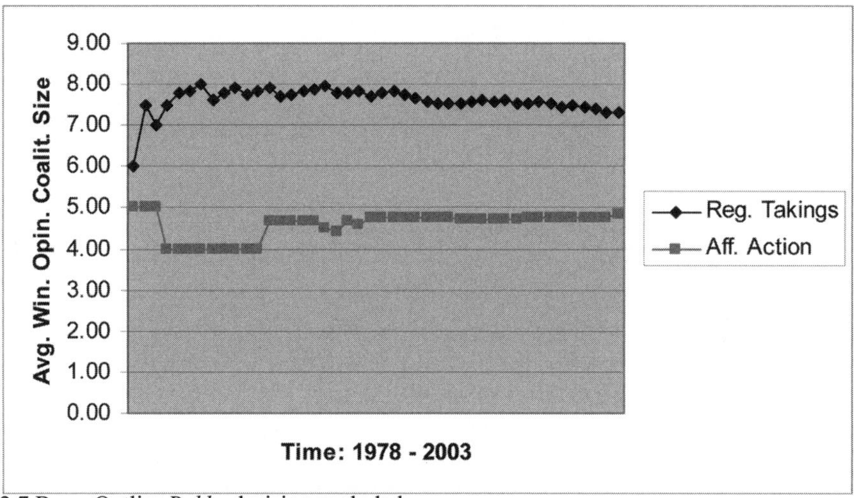

2.7.B Outlier *Bakke* decision excluded.

Figure 2.7 Cross-issue comparison of change in the average winning opinion coalition size from 1978 to 2003

in external (interest group mobilization) and internal (intensity of justices' value commitments and instrumental beliefs) factors. Affirmative action, an extension of the civil rights era struggles, consistently draws large numbers of interested parties on both sides of the issue and is met with highly splintered results on the Court, multiple opinions and small winning coalitions. The once quiescent issue of regulatory takings (marked both by few external participants and a Court in general agreement) became a focus of neoliberal organizations in the early 1980s as part of their effort to reign in the regulatory state in the interest of unleashing private markets, and to hold government agencies more accountable (see e.g., Harrington and Turem 2006). Their mobilization effort succeeded in driving up the level of conflict evident in cases before the Court and, although we did not investigate wins and losses, in encouraging voting and opinion divisions among the justices.

Our analysis points to considerable fertile territory for scholars interested in exploring longitudinal variation within and across issues in Supreme Court litigation. Methodologically, future studies might construct models with a greater number of observations in order to test for more systemic, issue-based mobilization effects. Substantively, what does an increasing multiplicity of organizations add to the decisional context beyond providing clear evidence of conflict? Some parties engage the system far more often than others, such as the Pacific Legal Foundation and the American Civil Liberties Union. Do their arguments evolve over time, or do they recycle their position in case after case? In our study period, we see the emergence of neoliberal groups in property rights cases. Did they focus primary attention on a small number of justices, with the intent of splintering off a few members from a relatively consensual Court, thus creating a base of opinions (even if minority ones) upon which they could build? Do the neoliberal organizations always agree, or do they present the Court with a range of options? Such questions warrant much further investigation.

Appendix A Regulatory takings and affirmative action cases

Citation	Case	Date of Decision	*Amici* Submitted?	Decided on Merits?
Regulatory Takings Cases				
98 S.Ct. 2646	*Penn Cent. Transp. Co. v. City of New York*	06/26/78	Y	Y
100 S.Ct. 318	*Andrus v. Allard*	11/27/79	N	Y
100 S.Ct. 383	*Kaiser Aetna v. U.S.*	12/04/79	Y	Y
100 S.Ct. 2035	*Prune Yard Shopping Center v. Robins*	06/09/80	Y	Y
100 S.Ct. 2138	*Agins v. City of Tiburon*	06/10/80	Y	Y
100 S.Ct. 2716	*U.S. v. Sioux Nation of Indians*	06/30/80	Y	Y
101 S.Ct. 446	*Webb's Fabulous Pharmacies, Inc. v. Beckwith*	12/09/80	N	Y
101 S.Ct. 1287	*San Diego Gas & Elec. Co. v. City of San Diego*	03/24/81	Y	Y
101 S.Ct. 2376	*Hodel v. Indiana*	06/15/81	Y	Y
101 S.Ct. 2352	*Hodel v. Virginia Surface Min. and Reclamation Ass'n, Inc.*	06/15/81	Y	Y
102 S.Ct. 3164	*Loretto v. Teleprompter Manhattan CATV Corp.*	06/30/82	Y	Y
103 S.Ct. 407	*U.S. v. Security Indus. Bank*	11/30/82	N	Y
104 S.Ct. 2187	*Kirby Forest Industries, Inc. v. U.S.*	05/21/84	Y	Y
104 S.Ct. 2862	*Ruckelshaus v. Monsanto Co.*	06/26/84	Y	Y
105 S.Ct. 3108	*Williamson County Regional Planning Com'n v. Hamilton Bank of Johnson City*	06/28/85	Y	Y
105 S.Ct. 3325	*Thomas v. Union Carbide Agr. Products Co.*	07/01/85	Y	Y
106 S.Ct. 455	*U.S. v. Riverside Bayview Homes, Inc.*	12/04/85	Y	Y
106 S.Ct. 1018	*Connolly v. Pension Ben. Guar. Corp.*	02/26/86	Y	Y
106 S.Ct. 2561	*MacDonald, Sommer & Frates v. Yolo County*	06/25/86	Y	Y
107 S.Ct. 1107	*F.C.C. v. Florida Power Corp.*	02/25/87	Y	Y
107 S.Ct. 1232	*Keystone Bituminous Coal Ass'n v. DeBenedictis*	03/09/87	Y	Y
107 S.Ct. 1487	*U.S. v. Cherokee Nation of Oklahoma*	03/31/87	N	Y
107 S.Ct. 2076	*Hodel v. Irving*	05/18/87	Y	Y
107 S.Ct. 2378	*First English Evangelical Lutheran Church of Glendale v. Los Angeles, CA*	06/09/87	Y	Y
107 S.Ct. 3008	*Bowen v. Gilliard*	06/25/87	Y	Y
107 S.Ct. 3141	*Nollan v. California Coastal Com'n*	06/26/87	Y	Y
108 S.Ct. 849	*Pennell v. City of San Jose*	02/24/88	Y	Y
109 S.Ct. 609	*Duquesne Light Co. v. Barasch*	01/11/89	Y	Y
110 S.Ct. 914	*Preseault v. I.C.C.*	02/21/90	Y	Y

Appendix A continued Regulatory takings and affirmative action cases

112 S.Ct. 1522	*Yee v. City of Escondido, Cal.*	04/01/92	Y	Y
112 S.Ct. 2886	*Lucas v. South Carolina Coastal Council*	06/29/92	Y	Y
113 S.Ct. 2264	*Concrete Pipe and Products of California, Inc. v. Construction Laborers Pension Trust For Southern, CA*	06/14/93	Y	Y
114 S.Ct. 2309	*Dolan v. City of Tigard*	06/24/94	Y	Y
117 S.Ct. 1659	*Suitum v. Tahoe Regional Planning Agency*	05/27/97	Y	Y
118 S.Ct. 1925	*Phillips v. Washington Legal Foundation*	06/15/98	Y	Y
118 S.Ct. 2131	*Eastern Enterprises v. Apfel*	06/25/98	Y	Y
119 S.Ct. 1624	*City of Monterey v. Del Monte Dunes at Montere, Ltd.*	05/24/99	Y	Y
121 S.Ct. 2448	*Palazzolo v. Rhode Island*	06/28/01	Y	Y
122 S.Ct. 1465	*Tahoe-Sierra Preservation Council, Inc. v. Tahoe Regional*	04/23/02	Y	Y
123 S.Ct. 1406	*Brown v. Legal Foundation of Washington*	03/26/03	Y	Y
Total			36	40
Affirmative Action Cases				
98 S. Ct. 2733	*Bakke*	06/28/78	Y	Y
99 S. Ct. 2721	*United Steelworkers of America, AFL-CIO-CLC v. Weber*	06/27/79	Y	Y
100 S. Ct. 2758	*Fullilove v. Klutznick*	07/02/80	Y	Y
101 S. Ct. 2211	*Minnick v. California Dept. of Corrections*	06/01/81	Y	N
104 S. Ct. 2576	*Firefighters Local Union No. 1784 v. Stotts*	06/12/84	Y	Y
106 S. Ct. 1842	*Wygant v. Jackson Bd. of Educ.*	05/19/86	Y	Y
106 S. Ct. 3019	*Local 28 of Sheet Metal Workers' Intern. Ass'n v. E.E.O.C.*	07/02/86	Y	Y
106 S. Ct. 3063	*Local No. 93, Intern. Ass'n of Firefighters, AFL-CIO C.L.C. v. City of Cleveland*	07/02/86	Y	Y
107 S. Ct. 1053	*U.S. v. Paradise*	02/25/87	Y	Y
107 S. Ct. 1442	*Johnson v. Transportation Agency, Santa Clara County, Cal.*	03/25/87	Y	Y
109 S. Ct. 706	*City of Richmond v. J.A. Croson Co.*	01/23/89	Y	Y
109 S. Ct. 2180	*Martin v. Wilks*	06/12/89	Y	Y
110 S. Ct. 2997	*Metro Broadcasting, Inc. v. F.C.C.*	06/27/90	Y	Y
115 S. Ct. 2097	*Adarand Constructors, Inc. v. Pena*	06/12/95	Y	Y
123 S. Ct. 2325	*Grutter v. Bollinger*	06/23/03	Y	Y
123 S. Ct. 2411	*Gratz v. Bollinger*	06/23/03	Y	Y
Total			16	15

Appendix B All repeat *amicus* participants, by group type and level of participation

Group	Cases in Which Group Submitted at Least One Brief		
	Either Issue	Affirmative Action	Regulatory Takings
Conservative Public Interest/Law Groups			
Pacific Legal Foundation	34	15	19
Washington Legal Foundation	14	6	8
Defenders Of Property Rights	7	***	7
Institute For Justice	6	***	6
Mountain States Legal Foundation	6	2	4
Allied Educational Foundation	5	***	5
Mid-America Legal Foundation	4	2	2
Southeastern Legal Foundation	4	3	1
Alliance For America	2	***	2
Citizens For Constitutional Property Rights	2	***	2
Edison Electric Institute	2	***	2
Georgia Public Policy Foundation	2	***	2
Northwest Legal Foundation	2	***	2
Texas Justice Foundation	2	***	2
Trans Texas Heritage Association	2	***	2
Competitive Enterprise Institute	2	1	1
Mid-Atlantic Legal Foundation	2	1	1
Liberal Public Interest/Law Groups			
American Civil Liberties Union	18	15	3
Lawyers' Committee For Civil Rights Under Law	14	14	***
Center For Constitutional Rights	7	5	2
National Urban League	7	7	***
National Lawyers Guild	6	6	***
Affirmative Action Coordinating Center	5	5	***
Municipal Art Society Of New York	4	***	4
American Civil Liberties Union Of Northern California	4	3	1
National Legal Aid And Defender Association	3	1	2
Coalition For Economic Equity	3	3	***
Employment Law Center	3	3	***
National Employment Law Project	3	3	***
Illinois South	2	***	2
American Public Health Association	2	1	1
National Association Of Social Workers	2	1	1

Appendix B continued All repeat *amicus* participants, by group type and level of participation

American Association For Affirmative Action	2	2	***
Center For Urban Law	2	2	***
Southern Regional Council	2	2	***
Government/Government Associations			
National League Of Cities	23	5	18
The United States Of America	21	9	12
National Association Of Counties	20	5	15
The State Of New York	20	8	12
The State Of Minnesota	18	9	9
The State Of California	17	8	9
The State Of Maryland	16	6	10
The State Of Oregon	16	6	10
The State Of Wisconsin	16	9	7
The State Of Florida	15	2	13
The State Of New Jersey	15	5	10
The State Of Louisiana	15	6	9
The State Of Hawaii	14	1	13
The State Of Vermont	14	2	12
The State Of Washington	14	4	10
Council Of State Governments	13	2	11
National Conference Of State Legislatures	13	2	11
The State Of Illinois	13	4	9
The State Of Massachusetts	13	4	9
International City Management Association	12	5	7
The State Of Michigan	12	5	7
The State Of New Mexico	12	5	7
American Planning Association	11	***	11
The State Of Iowa	11	2	9
The State Of Connecticut	11	4	7
The State Of Nebraska	11	5	6
The State Of West Virginia	11	6	5
The State Of South Dakota	10	***	10
The State Of Maine	10	1	9
The State Of Nevada	10	1	9
The State Of New Hampshire	10	1	9
The State Of North Carolina	10	2	8
The State Of Oklahoma	10	2	8
The State Of Rhode Island	10	2	8
Los Angeles	10	6	4
The State Of Alaska	9	***	9

Appendix B continued All repeat *amicus* participants, by group type and level of participation

The State Of Utah	9	***	9
National Governors' Association	9	1	8
The State Of Texas	9	1	8
The State Of North Dakota	8	***	8
National Institute Of Municipal Law Officers	8	1	7
The State Of Wyoming	8	2	6
The State Of Ohio	8	4	4
District Of Columbia	8	7	1
The State Of Missouri	7	1	6
The State Of Arizona	7	2	5
The State Of Indiana	7	2	5
The State Of Montana	7	2	5
City Of Detroit	7	7	***
California Coastal Commission	6	***	6
The State Of Tennessee	6	***	6
City Of San Francisco	6	1	5
The State Of Kansas	6	1	5
The State Of Idaho	6	2	4
The State Of South Carolina	6	2	4
New York City	6	3	3
The State Of Delaware	5	***	5
The State Of Arkansas	5	1	4
The State Of Colorado	5	1	4
The State Of Pennsylvania	5	1	4
National Conference Of State Historic Preservation Officers	4	***	4
Puerto Rico	4	***	4
San Jose	4	***	4
County Of San Francisco	4	1	3
The State Of Kentucky	4	1	3
The State Of Virginia	4	1	3
The State Of Alabama	4	2	2
Guam	3	***	3
Monterey	3	***	3
San Diego	3	***	3
San Francisco Bay Conservation And Development Commission	3	***	3
Tahoe Regional Planning Agency	3	***	3
The State Of Mississippi	3	***	3
The State Of Georgia	3	1	2
Virgin Islands	3	2	1
California Fair Employment And Housing Commission	3	3	***

Appendix B continued All repeat *amicus* participants, by group type and level of participation

Pennsylvania Human Relations Commission	3	3	***
Congressional Black Caucus	3	3	***
American Samoa	2	***	2
Broward County	2	***	2
City Of Oakland	2	***	2
Conference Of Chief Justices	2	***	2
County Of Los Angeles	2	***	2
County Of Santa Barbara	2	***	2
Board Of Governors	2	2	***
City Of Cleveland	2	2	***
Sunnyvale	2	0	2
California Tahoe Regional Planning Agency	2	0	2
Private/Commercial/Agriculture Interest Groups			
National Association Of Home Builders	11	***	11
Equal Employment Advisory Council	11	11	***
American Farm Bureau Federation	7	***	7
California Building Industry Association	6	***	6
National Association Of Realtors	6	***	6
California Association Of Realtors	5	***	5
American Mining Congress	4	***	4
International Council Of Shopping Centers	4	***	4
National Cattlemen's Association	4	***	4
National Coal Association	4	***	4
National Association Of Manufacturers	4	1	3
Building Industry Association Of Washington	3	***	3
National Association Of Reversionary Property Owners	3	***	3
National Apartment Association	3	***	3
Chamber Of Commerce Of United States Of America	3	1	2
California Farm Bureau Federation	2	***	2
Nevada Farm Bureau Federation	2	***	2
American Loggers Solidarity	2	***	2
Building Industry Legal Defense Foundation	2	***	2
California Business Properties Association	2	***	2
Fairness To Land Owners Committee	2	***	2
Hill Country Landowners' Coalition	2	***	2
Drexel Chemical Company	2	***	2
Griffin Corporation	2	***	2

Appendix B continued All repeat *amicus* participants, by group type and level of participation

National Multi Housing Council	2	***	2
New York State Cable Television Association	2	***	2
Real Estate Board Of New York	2	***	2
Environmental/Conservation Groups			
National Trust For Historic Preservation	11	***	11
National Wildlife Federation	10	***	10
Sierra Club	10	***	10
National Audubon Society	9	***	9
Natural Resources Defense Council	8	***	8
Conservation Foundation	4	***	4
Environmental Defense Fund	4	***	4
Preservation Action	4	***	4
Environmental Conservation Organization	3	***	3
National Parks And Conservation Association	3	***	3
Coast Alliance	2	***	2
Appalachian Coalition	2	***	2
League For Coastal Protection	2	***	2
National Center For Preservation Law	2	***	2
Save Our Cumberland Mountains	2	***	2
Tahoe Sierra Preservation Council	2	***	2
Labor			
American Federation Of Labor And Congress Of Industrial Organizations	13	7	6
United Mine Workers Of America	4	2	2
National Education Association	4	4	***
United Automobile Aerospace And Agricultural Implement Workers Of America UAW	3	3	***
Racial/Religious/Ethnic			
National Association For Advancement Of Colored People	13	13	***
National Conference Of Black Lawyers	8	7	1
Mexican American Legal Defense And Educational Fund	8	8	***
American Jewish Congress	5	4	1
League Of United Latin American Citizens	5	5	***
Puerto Rican Legal Defense And Education Fund	5	5	***
American Jewish Committee	4	4	***
Asian American Legal Defense And Education Fund	4	4	***

Appendix B continued All repeat *amicus* participants, by group type and level of participation

National Jewish Commission On Law And Public Affairs	3	3	***
Asian Law Caucus	3	3	***
National Black Police Association	3	3	***
Indian Law Resource Center	2	1	1
National Council Of Jewish Women	2	1	1
Coalition Of Bar Associations Of Color	2	2	***
California Association Of Black Lawyers	2	2	***
Keweenaw Bay Indian Community	2	2	***
Little River Band Of Ottawa Indians	2	2	***
Little Traverse Bay Bands Of Odawa Indians	2	2	***
Match-E-Be-Nash-She-Wish Band Of Pottawatomi Indians Of Michigan	2	2	***
Michigan Indian Legal Services	2	2	***
Nottawaseppi Huron Band Of Potawatomi	2	2	***
Oneida Tribe Of Indians Of Wisconsin	2	2	***
Bay Mills Indian Community	2	2	***
Grand Traverse Band Of Ottawa And Chippewa Indians	2	2	***
Hannahville Indian Community	2	2	***
Anti Defamation League Of B'nai B'rith	2	2	***
International Association Of Black Professional Firefighters	2	2	***
League Of Martin	2	2	***
National Alliance Against Racist And Political Repression	2	2	***
National Association Of Black Owned Broadcasters	2	2	***
National Association Of Minority Contractors	2	2	***
North Carolina Association Of Black Lawyers	2	2	***
Office Of Communication Of United Church Of Christ	2	2	***
National Black United Fund	2	2	***
Incorporated Mexican American Government Employees	2	2	***
Latino Organizations	2	2	***
National Council Of La Raza	2	2	***
New Jewish Agenda	2	2	***
Order Sons Of Italy In America	2	2	***
Unico National	2	2	***
United Methodist Church	2	2	***
Central Conference Of American Rabbis	2	2	***

Appendix B continued All repeat *amicus* participants, by group type and level of participation

Sex/Gender Groups			
Women's Legal Defense Fund	8	9	1
National Women's Law Center	9	9	***
Now Legal Defense And Education Fund	6	7	1
Women Employed	6	7	1
Women's Law Project	4	5	1
League Of Women Voters Of United States	5	5	***
Northwest Women's Law Center	3	4	1
Women's Equity Action League	3	4	1
National Organization For Women	4	4	***
California Women Lawyers	3	3	***
Wider Opportunities For Women	3	3	***
Women's Equal Rights	1	2	1
National Bar Association Women Lawyer's Division Greater Washington Area Chapter	2	2	***
Federally Employed Women Legal And Education Fund	2	2	***
Women's Law Fund	2	2	***
Professional Associations			
National Bar Association	7	7	***
International Municipal Lawyers Association	6	***	6
Charles Houston Bar Association	4	4	***
American College Of Real Estate Lawyers	3	***	3
American Bar Association	3	1	2
Hellenic Bar Association Of Illinois	2	2	***
Higher Education Groups/Associations			
Society Of American Law Teachers	4	4	***
Howard University	3	3	***
Kappa Alpha Psi	3	3	***
University Of Pennsylvania	3	3	***
Alpha Kappa Alpha Sorority	2	2	***
American Association For Higher Education	2	2	***
American Educational Research Association	2	2	***
Association Of American Colleges And Universities	2	2	***
Association Of American Law Schools	2	2	***
Association Of American Medical Colleges	2	2	***
Columbia University	2	2	***

Appendix B continued All repeat *amicus* participants, by group type and level of participation

Committee On Academic Nondiscrimination And Integrity	2	2	***
Harvard University	2	2	***
Law School Admission Council	2	2	***
Law Students Civil Rights Research Council	2	2	***
National Association For Equal Opportunity In Higher Education	2	2	***
National Association Of Scholars	2	2	***
National School Boards Association	2	2	***
Sigma Pi Phi Fraternity	2	2	***
University Of Chicago	2	2	***
Retirees			
American Association Of Retired Persons	2	***	2
Legal Counsel For Elderly	2	***	2

Appendix C Individual justice's voting records by issue area

Justice	Affirmative Action Votes	Affirm. Action % Liberal Votes	Z-Score	Regulatory Takings Votes	Reg. Takings % Liberal Votes	Z-Score
Stevens	15	66.7%	0.288	40	75.0%	0.626
Rehnquist	15	0.0%	-1.263	40	45.0%	-0.889
Stewart	3	33.3%	-0.488	10	60.0%	-0.131
Burger	7	14.3%	-0.931	19	57.9%	-0.238
Powell	8	62.5%	0.191	25	48.0%	-0.737
Brennan	12	100.0%	1.063	29	75.9%	0.670
Marshall	12	100.0%	1.063	29	72.4%	0.496
White	4	100.0%	1.063	30	63.3%	0.037
Blackmun	12	100.0%	1.063	32	84.4%	1.100
O'Connor	12	25.0%	-0.681	30	50.0%	-0.636
Scalia	8	0.0%	-1.263	21	33.3%	-1.478
Kennedy	6	0.0%	-1.263	13	46.2%	-0.831
Souter	3	100.0%	1.063	10	90.0%	1.384
Thomas	3	0.0%	-1.263	11	27.3%	-1.784
Ginsburg	3	100.0%	1.063	8	87.5%	1.258
Breyer	3	66.7%	0.288	7	85.7%	1.167
		Mean 54.3% Std Dev. 43.00%			Mean 62.6% Std Dev. 19.80%	

Chapter 3
Kelo v. New London, the Institute for Justice, and the Idea of Economic Development Takings

William R. Wilkerson[1]

The June 22, 2005 US Supreme Court decision in *Kelo v. New London, Connecticut* broke no new ground in the constitutional law of takings. The neoliberal activists who financed and argued the lawsuit were not successful on behalf of their clients. Rather, the Court followed a clear path indicated by earlier Supreme Court decisions. The decision was uncontroversial among mainstream legal analysts who had anticipated the decision beforehand (Mahoney 2005, citing Ackerman 1977, Merrill 1986, and Tribe 2000).

Traditional scholarship argues that litigation, even if successful in court, is unlikely to create legal change and could in fact harm the very ideas and political movements it hopes to promote (Rosenberg 1991, Scheingold 1974). Using resources and losing is almost certainly counterproductive. The opportunity costs, it is argued, can be high, discouraging more productive activities such as organizing social movements. Despite questions by academics about the efficacy of such efforts, the belief in creating legal and social change through litigation, what Scheingold calls "the myth of rights" is widespread (1974). Liberal groups have long sought to use the courts to expand existing rights and to create new ones—prominent examples include the NAACP's efforts to break down the barriers of racial segregation, and Jehovah's Witnesses' efforts to expand religious liberty—establishing a now well-worn path for others to follow. Since 1980, conservative legal activists have grown in number and breadth to challenge the roles played in law and politics by well-established liberal groups and roll back earlier decisions and establish new rights through litigation (Southworth 2008, Teles 2008).

More recent scholarship on the law and social movements led by Michael McCann (1994, 2008) has reexamined the role of litigation in social movement and legal change. Rather than seeing litigation as unlikely to succeed and even harmful to efforts elsewhere, a hollow hope, McCann showed in his study of labor unions

1 An earlier version of this chapter was presented at the 2009 annual meeting of the Midwest Political Science Association, April 2–April 5, Chicago, Illinois. Thanks to SUNY Oneonta student Kaitlin Jewell for research assistance on this paper. A grant from the SUNY Oneonta Provost's Fund partially paid for the research in this work.

that it is possible for a social movement with access to the necessary resources—legal expertise, time, and money—to succeed in part by using litigation as an integral part of a larger strategy (1994). Litigation does not necessarily dissipate a movement; rather it can encourage rights—or legal—consciousness, encourage mobilization, and strengthen efforts before other government entities (McCann 2008). These advantages, as was the case with the equal pay movement, can accrue even to groups who have not won in Court. While many scholars have looked at traditional liberal groups, "[t]he use of courts by conservatives and economic libertarians, however, still requires further evaluation, particularly as it related to liberal legalism" (Hatcher 2005: 116, McCann 2008, Teles 2008).

Have conservatives been successful in using the strategies that McCann notes? With *Kelo v. New London*, the Institute for Justice (IJ), who brought the dispute to the nation's highest court, has had such a success. In referring to *Kelo* Steven Teles notes, "that what Michael McCann has argued about the comparable worth movement also appears true of conservative litigation: it is possible to win, in the sense of encouraging popular mobilization and inducing action in venues other than the courts by losing" (2008: 243).

In bringing *Kelo* to the US Supreme Court, IJ was able to recast and reinvigorate historic criticism about "urban renewal" and "community redevelopment" in constitutional terms that had their genesis in the neoliberal ideology that emerged in American politics with the election of Ronald Reagan. Neoliberalism emphasizes limiting the welfare state and governmental power in general, and also emphasized individualism and the importance of property rights (Harrington and Turem 2006. See also Schultz for a longer discussion of these ideas). In recasting the debate, IJ and others—for example, the Pacific Legal Foundation and the Mackinac Center for Public Policy—argued that the "public use" provision of the US Constitution's Fifth Amendment Takings Clause placed real limits on the use of the eminent domain power. Notably, they urged that "public use" provided protections to property owners against what they described as "economic development takings": the use of eminent domain by public entities for the purpose of handing property over to private developers for the public purpose of raising more tax revenue than current property use provides. IJ argued economic development takings went unconstitutionally beyond the historic use of takings to redevelop truly blighted areas. In contrast with traditional liberal notions of community renewal and development, IJ emphasized the notion of the home as a personal castle, personal property, possessing real government protections from invasion. If the homes of New London, Connecticut residents could be taken and given to a developer, no property was safe from economic development takings (see Becher for a longer discussion of the idea of "home").

Despite losing before the US Supreme Court, IJ managed to put the use of eminent domain for private development on the political map as an issue of import. The decision was a major news story in the summer of 2005 (Wolf 2008), and reactions to the decision led directly to changes in the law of over 40 states (National Center for State Legislatures 2007a, 2007b, 2008. See also Schultz). *Kelo* continues to make news more than four years after the decision was handed down (Lithwick 2009).[2] This did not happen by chance. The libertarian public interest law firm IJ took over the case with the idea of both setting precedent *and* bringing the takings issue to the public, changing the way the public viewed a common use of eminent domain with the ultimate goal of changing the state of the law. While the goal was to win expanded eminent domain protections under the Constitution, IJ President and Founder William H. (Chip) Mellor was aware the loss before the US Supreme Court had helped their efforts to redefine property rights. As Mellor noted in a post-*Kelo* interview:

> A defeat with the kind of dissent that we got, is as good as it could possibly be. Not only has this ignited outrage across the country that will transform the debate for a long time to come, it will demonstrate the power of citizen activism on this issue. That's good for property rights and the democratic process … (Teles 2008: 242).

This chapter examines how IJ was able to both capture the public's attention and spark an existing political movement from the not uncommon actions of a small city and a loss in the legal arena with *Kelo v. New London*. Why was *Kelo* more successful in this instance in meeting the goals of mobilization and legal change compared with previous property rights cases? The sections that follow will: (1) review the development plans in New London, Connecticut that led to the dispute; (2) examine *Kelo*; and (3) investigate the aftermath of the case: how IJ has used the *Kelo* decision to promote legislative and judicial changes in economic development takings law at the state-level and look at the impact that the decision has had on IJ as an organization.

The Setting and the Dispute

The *Kelo* dispute arose out of an effort by a small, depressed city to revitalize itself with the help of a multinational corporation and state aid. Neither New London's problems, nor their efforts to better their situation are unusual. The dispute that arose is typical of events that take place in American cities and towns every year. As with many Supreme Court decisions, what is remarkable is that it went so far.

New London

Settled in 1646, New London sits at the head of the Thames River on the Long Island Sound. Blessed with a deep natural harbor, much of the City's economic life was tied to the sea and to national defense (Decker 1976, Ruddy 2000). Like many areas dependent on the defense industry, the end of the Cold War was hard

2 The early 2009 publication of *Little Pink House* by Jeff Benedict has generated many reviews and news stories about the dispute.

on New London (Hamilton 2001). Thousands of defense workers were laid off, Fort Trumbull closed, and in 1996 the Naval Undersea Warfare Center, a Navy research lab located in the Fort Trumbull area, closed (Moran 2004b).

These economic disruptions along with the middle class flight from the city to the suburbs that began in the 1960s left a depleted city: by 2000 the population declined to 1920 levels (US Census 2008), the residents were poorer than the surrounding community and the state as a whole, and the housing stock was in decline (New London Development Corporation 2001). The decline was exacerbated by the lack of developable land; according to the New London Development Corporation in the mid 1990s there were 53 acres of developable land in the entire city (New London Development Corporation 2001: 23). In addition New London has a high percentage—56 percent—of non-taxable property. Finally, New London has suffered from poor political leadership for decades making concerted efforts to change difficult.[3] Problems like this are all too common in the upper Midwest and the Northeast.

The Plan

In early 1998, New London had what most agreed was a remarkable stroke of good fortune. Pfizer, Inc.—the large, multinational pharmaceutical firm—decided to build a new research facility. This project would bring over 1,400 white collar jobs to the city (Wong 2001). They chose to build on a 24 acre site near the vacant Fort Trumbull along the Thames River. The selection of the site was surprising: it was smaller than they were looking for and was located on the long abandoned, environmentally problematic New London Mills (Hathaway 1998). Pfizer saw itself as helping a depressed area where it was already a major economic presence (Benedict 2009). Pfizer was hailed regionally as an outstanding corporate citizen. As a *Hartford Courant* editorial put it, the project was, "good medicine for Connecticut in many fronts" with "the potential to cure many economic ills" (1998).

The state provided support. It agreed to clean up contamination at the site, to clean up a nearby scrapyard, and to upgrade the neighboring wastewater treatment plant. These incentives cost $26 million. In addition, Pfizer was given significant tax breaks (Lagnado 2002).

Seeking to use the project as a centerpiece for turning around New London's declining economic fortunes, the city selected the Fort Trumbull area adjoining Pfizer's planned lab as a location for a large-scale multi-use redevelopment. As Pfizer's local executive George Milne noted later, "It was an opportunity to do something really transforming (Lagnado 2002)." From the city's perspective, Fort Trumbull was a declining area ripe for change. The fort was unoccupied as was the former naval research center. In 1998 Fort Trumbull had a 20 percent residential

3 There have been several efforts to change the structure of the city government. Each referendum failed.

vacancy rate and, according to a city survey, the housing stock was largely substandard. Over 80 percent of the commercial properties were vacant; many buildings were in disrepair. The area produced only modest property tax revenue. For Pfizer, redevelopment of Fort Trumbull would improve the area adjoining their new office campus as well as provide services for their business—including offices for related businesses, a hotel, and restaurants—and potential homes for their employees.

The New London Development Corporation (NLDC) was charged by the City with shepherding the project to reality. Recently revitalized with a new board, New London's City Council provided NLDC with eminent domain power to acquire property as was allowed under Connecticut law. In all, 90 acres of the Fort Trumbull area—115 residential and commercial properties—were designated for redevelopment. For a city that claimed only 53 acres of open, developable land, this was a major project, the type of large-scale development that rust belt city leaders dream about. Richard Brown, New London city manager and NLDC vice-chairman saw a very different Fort Trumbull in the offing: "I envision people working here, shopping here, and coming for recreation" (Hathaway 1998).

Republican Governor John Rowland sought to benefit as well. As with the Pfizer project, the state was the financial force behind the plan. By funding the Fort Trumbull project, he hoped to make inroads into staunchly Democratic New London as his run for a second term approached. The State accelerated plans to create a $25 million state park at Fort Trumbull, and agreed to spend up to $75 million to ready the Fort Trumbull area for development (Lagnado 2002).

The Pfizer project proceeded quickly. Ground was broken in late-August 1998 and the research facility was opened in June 2001. Pfizer instantly became New London's largest property taxpayer and a major employer. The new facility had a positive impact on the economic climate of New London (Hamilton 2001).

In contrast, NLDC's redevelopment of Fort Trumbull was to run into a major problem. A comprehensive plan for the entire 90 acres was quickly developed and the plan gathered the necessary approvals in January 2000 (*New London Day* 2004). It called for a state park highlighting the historic fort, a hotel, retail and office space, a shoreline walkway, upscale housing, and possibly a Coast Guard museum. But even after significant efforts to persuade them otherwise, the owners of 15 residences—owner-occupants and rental property owners—refused to sell their properties. The negotiation process became acrimonious, with claims of intimidation by some of the property owners. For example, New London was bulldozing property as it acquired it, leaving increasingly large areas of cleared land around the holdout's property (*Voices of American Law: Kelo* 2006).

Believing they needed the entire 90-acre site to make the project a reality, NLDC began eminent domain proceedings in November 2000 to acquire the 15 remaining properties scattered throughout Fort Trumbull. Still hoping to move quickly, NLDC designated a private developer for the project, the large Boston firm, Corcoran Jennison (Moran 2004a).

The Dispute Goes to Court

The plaintiffs filed their initial lawsuit on December 20, 2000, seeking an injunction that would bar NLDC from taking their properties through eminent domain. The lawsuit came after efforts by the Fort Trumbull property owners, led by Susette Kelo, who worked with a series of community groups—including New London Landmarks, Friends of Fort Trumbull, and the Fort Trumbull Conservancy—to save their properties and the neighborhood more broadly. These groups generated publicity about the cause and spoke before City Council meetings (*Voices of American Law: Kelo* 2006, Benedict 2009). The Fort Trumbull organizations, too, filed a series of lawsuits to stop the project.[4]

The property owners eventually enlisted the support of the neoliberal public interest law firm, IJ. Based on a first contact by a historic preservation activist and additional research, IJ attorney Scott Bullock agreed to visit New London. Kelo and her colleagues placed a report of the visit in the local press (Benedict 2009).

Upon visiting the Fort Trumbull neighborhood, Bullock was excited about the prospects of the lawsuit. Rather than a dilapidated neighborhood, Bullock found modest, well kept houses. "This is depressed?" he was quoted as thinking to himself (Benedict 2009: 167). He was also impressed with the potential plaintiffs, a group of committed middle and working class property owners. Once he was convinced that the group was not simply after more money, rather they wanted to keep their homes in their original locations even in the face of new development, he agreed to accept the case (Benedict 2009).

The Institute for Justice was interested in challenging current law and publicizing the plight of the plaintiffs, not settlement. Founded in 1991 by William Mellor and Clint Bolick, veterans of both the first wave of conservative, neoliberal public interest law firms established in the 1970s as well as the Reagan Administration, IJ litigated neoliberal issues: protection of free enterprise, property rights as well as education reform including school choice. Initial funding came from Charles Koch, CEO of the privately held Koch Industries, who also funded the Cato Foundation (Teles 2008).

The Institute for Justice has a penchant for highly publicized cases. Mellor and colleagues had successfully argued the Cleveland school voucher case, *Zelman v. Simmons-Harris*, before the Court in 2002. Earlier in the 2004 term IJ had won before the Supreme Court again in *Swedenburg v. Kelly*, where the Court struck down a ban on interstate wine shipments. Unlike Philadelphia's American Street campaign (Becher), who sought to protect their homes through elected officials, IJ sees litigation as the primary catalyst of change. For IJ, legal disputes also serve as a catalyst for wide dissemination and discussion of their neoliberal agenda. Their earliest cases established a pattern they have continued

4 These lawsuits concerned both procedural issues and environmental concerns. The last of these cases, finally resolved in New London's favor when the Fort Trumbull Conservancy was found to lack standing, was not resolved until 2008.

since: find disputes highlighting neoliberal ideals by pitting the little guy against oppressive government that will catch the eye of the media and the public. For example, IJ's first case was a challenge to the District of Columbia's Cosmetology Code on behalf of the African-American owned Cornrows & Co. in which they argued that DC's code was not relevant to current hair styling, and was entirely irrelevant to the work that Cornrows & Co. did, making the license unnecessary and the licensing system unconstitutional. The suit generated news reports in both Washington newspapers and *Business Week*. The pattern of the case would also be similar to what happened in *Kelo*, the lawsuit failed (Williams 1991, French 1992, Smart 1992), but within a year the DC City Council had repealed the law (Institute for Justice 2009).

Connecticut Courts

In *Kelo*, IJ argued that New London's action violated the public use provision of the Takings Clause of the Fifth Amendment, claiming that government can use eminent domain only when government itself wishes to directly use the property.[5] The Constitution allows government to acquire property for a public use, for example to build a road or a school, but not as proposed here where New London intended to hand the properties over to private developers with the single goal of increasing the economic value of the land. Much of the original filing detailed the ties of the plaintiffs to the community, the longtime ownership of some of the residents, and described in detail the condition of each home. The plaintiffs sought to establish these properties as "homes". Bullock, IJs lawyer, was willing to stipulate the facts and instead wished to focus on constitutional issues (Institute for Justice 2000). The City countered that the eminent domain action was well within established Connecticut law. The plan was thorough; the action was an effort to build a strong, economically vibrant city (City of New London 2001). Rather than focusing on individual rights, the City focused on collective rights and responsibility, the good of the City as a whole.

Superior Court Judge Corradino issued a 100-plus page decision on March 13, 2002, generally finding for the City. New London had authority to exercise eminent domain, and could turn property over to a private developer; but based on the specific facts in this case, the judge granted a permanent injunction for four of the property owners who were located in an area designated for park support near the proposed Fort Trumbull state park. Corradino determined that the plan for this area was not specifically detailed to meet the threshold for public use.

In a 4-3 decision, the Connecticut Supreme Court reversed in part and upheld the takings in their entirety. The majority agreed economic redevelopment by a private party was an acceptable public use under the Takings Clause. It found that the development plan was detailed, and while private interests would profit from

5 The clause reads in full "nor shall private property be taken for public use without just compensation."

development, the public too would benefit from the economic growth and increased tax revenue the project would bring to the community. The dissenters agreed that in principle the City could take the properties at issue, but because they saw the development plan as vague—no contracts had been signed and the economic climate was uncertain—NLDC had not provided the "clear and convincing evidence" needed to insure that the public would benefit from the development plan.

Supreme Court of the United States

By the time the case reached the nation's highest court, it had generated interest beyond New London. More than three dozen *amicus curiae* briefs were filed with many on both sides. Support for Kelo cut across ideological lines and included libertarian groups like the Pacific Legal Foundation among others, while on the ideological left, briefs were filed on behalf of the NAACP, AARP, and the Southern Christian Leadership Conference. State and local governments as well as planners such as the American Planning Association supported New London.

By a vote of 5-4, the Supreme Court upheld the Connecticut High Court, agreeing that economic development was an acceptable "public use" supporting the use of eminent domain. Justice Steven's straightforward Opinion of the Court noted that the New London action was well supported by a series of earlier decisions, most notably *Berman v. Parker* (1954) and *Hawaii Housing Authority v. Midkiff* (1984) that broadly defined the public use provision to mean "public purpose". Further he argued that economic development was a constitutional goal of government. In this instance, New London had developed a sufficiently detailed plan to proceed with the entire project. Finally, Justice Stevens noted states are free to increase protections to property owners through their state laws or state constitutions:

> [W]e do not minimize the hardship that condemnations may entail, notwithstanding the payment of just compensation. We emphasize that nothing in our opinion precludes any state from placing further restrictions on its exercise of the takings power. … As the submissions of the parties and their *amici* make clear, the necessity and wisdom of using eminent domain to promote economic development are certainly matters of legitimate public debate (489, footnotes omitted).

Mainstream legal observers saw *Kelo* as unsurprising and a natural extension of the earlier cases.

The decision also included sharp dissents by Justices O'Connor and Thomas. Both clearly bought into the idea of "home". As Becher notes, each used the term numerous times in their opinion. O'Connor argued that the Court had deferred too much to government in this case. Under this standard, government could take any property it wishes, even if the primary beneficiary is a private entity, thus placing all property at risk. As Justice O'Connor put it: "who among us can say she already makes the most productive or attractive possible use of her property? The specter of condemnation hangs over all property. Nothing is to prevent the state from replacing any Motel 6 with a Ritz-Carlton, any home with a shopping mall, or any farm with a factory (503)." This quotation came almost directly from an oral argument exchange between O'Connor and IJ attorney Bullock. Thomas would go even further, finding that any public purpose that did not allow for total public access—such as a road or school—to be constitutional. Unlike the rest of the Court, he would also overturn *Berman* and *Midkiff.*

The Aftermath

The Fort Trumbull property owners were ultimately unsuccessful in the courts. Their homes were eventually purchased and leveled, or moved to another location, but does not end with the June 2005 decision. The Institute for Justice is a successful litigator, but they are more: IJ is a notably media savvy organization with a full-time public relations staff who use their attorneys and lawsuits to promote their ideas to the wider public.

A review of its website—www.IJ.org—shows an impressive presentation. Their work includes clear discussions of the goals and work using a variety of media, including everything from court filings to You Tube video. On their website they note articles and interviews in major newspapers (*Washington Post*, *New York Times*, *Los Angeles Times*, *USA Today*, *Boston Globe*, and the *Wall Street Journal*), business publications (*Investors Business Daily*, *Forbes*), and conservative journals (*Reason* and *National Review*). Radio and television activities include appearances on National Public Radio, the three major networks and news channels, including *60 Minutes* and the *Today Show* (Institute for Justice 2009).

The Institute for Justice is explicit about wanting to win in both court and in the broader public policy arena as a *New York Times* story about *Zelman v. Simmons-Harris* (2002) made clear. Then IJ vice president Clint Bolick noted, "One of our strategies was to distill the message, not only for the Court but in the court of public opinion[.]" Furthermore, "[s]uccess in shaping public policy, Mr. Bolick said, often requires 'translating complex issues into compelling themes (Greenhouse 2002).'"

Raising the Profile of Economic Development Takings

Using their well-established model, *Kelo v. New London* provided an outstanding medium to promote the issue of economic development takings from a neoliberal perspective. As IJ President Mellor noted in an interview, much of the work was raising the profile of eminent domain: "All along the way in *Kelo* [and in other litigation in the area], we had the challenge to take an issue that we thought was vitally important, but by its very nature conducted in a way that it was not on the radar screen of most Americans. … We had to figure out ways to mobilize people and public outrage around the people" (Teles 2008: 241).

Work in this area did not begin with the *Kelo* decision, rather IJ's work on eminent domain began at least half a decade earlier. Legal scholars connected to IJ sought to redefine the issue of public use to a more compelling one to be used in its court proceedings. Based on the work of University of Chicago Law Professor, Richard Epstein (1986), George Mason Law Professor Ilya Somin first used the term "economic development taking" in a 2004 *Michigan State Law Review* article on the *Hathcock* decision (see Schultz for more on *Hathcock*). While not precisely defined, it was described in a 2005 *Policy Analysis* article as "many state courts have read 'public use' more broadly to allow government to transfer property from one private owner to another simply because the latter is expected to make a greater contribution to the local economy (1)."

The Institute for Justice has framed its legal arguments in this way. For example, in *Kelo* before the Superior Court of Connecticut IJ was willing to stipulate the facts of the taking: they did not challenge the price offered by the NLDC, the process, or New London's right to use eminent domain for a traditional public use; rather they wished only to argue that using eminent domain for economic development and increasing tax revenue was unconstitutional (Institute for Justice 2000). Their efforts are similar to those of pay equity reform advocates in the 1970s and 1980s who distilled complicated arguments into "comparable worth" and "equal pay" that helped motivate workers to advocate for change and build public support (McCann 1994). Judges in each of the Connecticut courts took the ideas seriously. In the trial court IJ was partially successful and the Connecticut Supreme Court dissenters used the ideas IJ presented as well. Importantly, Justice O'Connor used the term in her *Kelo* dissent, and both O'Connor and Justice Thomas portrayed stark examples of the little guy losing their home or small business to government and developers.

By selecting litigants carefully, as they did in *Kelo*, IJ has been able to translate this in ways that courts, the general public, and legislators, easily understand. Kelo and her fellow litigants were middle class and working class people, connected to their community. They were consistently portrayed in litigation and public pronouncements by IJ in this way.

Grassroots Organization

Beyond the courts, IJ formalized its grassroots organizational efforts in March 2002 under the name the Castle Coalition to make their case in other venues (Keeney 2002, Teles 2008). This group was formed in the wake of IJ's first effort in this area, a November 2000 success in saving 64 residences and 125 businesses in downtown Pittsburgh, Pennsylvania from plans to replace them with a shopping mall. IJ supported the effort by purchasing anti-eminent domain billboards. Both before and since *Kelo*, IJ has been active in many communities and as of August 2009 lists 56 success stories in 16 states (Castle Coalition 2007a). Among their successes before the *Kelo* decision are Gardena and Martinez, California; Brooklyn Park, Crystal, and Duluth, Minnesota; Lincoln, Nebraska; as well as Camden and

Evendale, New Jersey. The Castle Coalition also produced *Public Power, Private Gain*, a study of eminent domain use in each of the 50 states (Berliner 2003). IJ and the Castle Coalition were well placed to take advantage of the *Kelo* decision when it was handed down. Susette Kelo's pink house was to become a symbol of a growing movement.

The Castle Coalition website today provides numerous resources for those interested in the issue (Castle Coalition 2009b). Among them are information on how to organize—a "Rally in a Box"—success stories and information on current efforts; a survival guide for those who face condemnations; and information on past and current efforts.

News and Editorial Coverage of the Kelo Decision

Kelo v. New London was notably well covered by the media in the days and weeks after the decision (Wolf 2008).[6] IJ had begun to prime major media outlets for the decision upon filing their *cert* petition with the US Supreme Court in July 2004. They hosted a luncheon and members of the IJ staff met individually with other reporters and editors (Benedict 2009). George Will (2004), the influential conservative columnist, dedicated a column to *Kelo* shortly thereafter.

This groundwork paid off. News coverage of *Kelo* was in stark contrast to earlier eminent domain decisions (Wolf 2008, Nadler, Diamond, and Patton 2008). News coverage began shortly after the decision was announced on the morning of June 22, 2005 and continued to build in the days after. Web coverage on major news sites CNN.com and Foxnews.com began at noon. MSNBC quickly supplemented their wire story with a video report by NBC correspondent Pete Williams. The web story would include a photo of Kelo and the pink house that became the center of the dispute. The companion cable news channels also covered the case throughout the day. CNN for example included a news report, commentary by their legal affairs analyst Jeffrey Toobin, a story that included an interview with IJ attorney Scott Bullock, and an interview with George Washington University Law Professor Jonathan Turley. Fellow IJ attorney Wesley Horton was to appear in the evening on MSNBC. ABC began their "World News Tonight" with the story, as did the NBC "Nightly News." CBS covered the story later in their newscast.

Newspapers continued the powerful publicity of the case in the days that followed, and the *Chicago Sun-Times* headline "Court Shows Homeowners Door; Development Trumps Property Rights" was typical, if more restrained than some. By Sunday of that week editorial coverage was widespread in large and small papers across the country. With the exception of the *Washington Post* and *New York Times* whose editorial was titled "The Limits of Property Rights," papers across the nation came out strongly opposed. Headlines such as the *Chicago Tribune*'s "Is Your Home Safe?" and the *Providence Journal*'s "The Little People Get Hit" were typical. Opposition came from conservative and liberal editorial pages alike.

---

6 The section that follows is largely based on Wolf's work.

Popular conservative radio host Rush Limbaugh took up the cause as well. The case continued to be a story in the conservative media in the days and weeks to come. IJ was clearly successful in putting the issue of economic development takings on the political map through the news media once the decision was handed down.

Public Opinion

Little pre-*Kelo* polling was done on eminent domain questions (Nadler, Diamond, and Patton 2007). The limited polling done during this period showed notable interest in the issue by the public and indicated strong support for limiting economic development takings. In July 2005, an NBC News/*Wall Street Journal* poll found that Americans identified the case as presenting the most recognizable issue that came before the Court during the term—more important than parental notification of abortion by minors, public display of the 10 Commandments, and the constitutionality of right to die laws. The one national poll on *Kelo* showed over 80 percent disapproval of the decision (Nadler, Diamond, and Patton 2007). State polls in New Hampshire, Ohio, Florida, and Connecticut all showed strong support for eminent domain reform and opposition to *Kelo* (Somin 2007, Nadler, Diamond, and Patton 2008).[7]

State Government Actions

Justice Stevens urged that state governments were free to change their own laws providing more protection than the US Constitution guaranteed. Using *Kelo* as a catalyst, change came remarkably quickly.[8] The day after the decision, IJ pushed these efforts in motion with a $3 million "Hands off My Home" campaign (Teles 2008). The campaign included rallies, advertising, and an IJ-run workshop for activists (Kingsley 2005, Price 2005).

Four states—Alabama, Delaware, Ohio, and Texas—passed laws by the end of 2005 (NCSL 2007a). In 2006, another 23 states passed eminent domain legislation in response to *Kelo*, while Alabama passed a second law strengthening its 2005 effort (NCSL 2007b). Michigan's legislature passed a constitutional amendment

---

7 An August 2008 survey jointly sponsored by the Associated Press and the National Constitution Center showed strong support for property rights (National Constitution Center 2008). For example 87 percent of those surveys did not think government should have the power to "Take people's private property in the interests of redeveloping an area." Seventy-five percent continued to agree even if the project "creates many jobs." Eighty-eight percent of those surveyed agreed with the idea that "private property rights are just as important as other rights like freedom of speech and religion."

8 As the Court noted, change had already begun. Several states already had laws on the books limiting the use of eminent domain and the Michigan Supreme Court overturned its earlier decision in the *Poletown* case in 2004.

that was confirmed by voters in November 2006. By the end of 2006 each of the 46 legislatures that held sessions since the *Kelo* decision at least considered a bill related to economic development takings reform. Ten more states legislatures passed laws in 2007 (NCSL 2008). Citizens too enacted laws in response to *Kelo*. In 2006 voters in 10 states approved ballot measures protecting property owners from eminent domain, while voters in three states rejected such measures (NCSL 2006). After rejecting a referendum in 2006, California passed an eminent domain proposition in 2008. All told, by the end of 2008, 42 states established changes in their state law through statute or constitutional amendment.

The substance and significance of state actions varies considerably. Some provide procedural guarantees before a taking can occur, including improved notice and comment and requirements that local government entities vote before condemning public property. Some states placed moratoria on condemnations while task forces studied the problem. More significant revisions include stringent definitions of "public use," limiting eminent domain by defining the idea of blighted areas targeted by economic development takings projects, and restricting more generally the use of eminent domain for economic development and increasing tax revenue (NCSL 2007a, 2007b, NCSL 2008). Commentators, including IJ (2007), have found some changes to be of limited value (Sandefur 2006, Somin 2007). Somin (2007) found laws passed in 18 states to be effective in limiting economic development takings. Seven states—Florida and New Mexico by legislative enactment, and Arizona, Louisiana, Nevada, Oregon, and North Dakota through ballot actions—banned economic development takings post-*Kelo*. They joined Utah, which had passed similar legislation earlier in 2005. Eight states—Alabama, Georgia, Idaho, Indiana, Michigan, New Hampshire, Virginia, and Wyoming—established definitions for "blight" that limit eminent domain use. Minnesota and Pennsylvania passed laws similar to the above states, but these laws included exemptions to at least some urban areas in the state. Two additional states—Kansas and South Dakota—ban the transfer of property acquired through eminent domain to another private owner.

While neoliberal commentators have been disappointed that more states have not passed substantial limits on economic development takings, most states passed laws and a plurality of them have created the type of meaningful limits that libertarians have advocated.

Federal Government Action

The House of Representatives held hearings in the summer of 2005, and the House later passed the Private Property Rights Protection Act of 2005 (PPRA) in November. The Senate never formally acted on the proposal. The PPRA would have precluded a state or local government from using economic development takings if it receives federal economic development funding. The bill included a broad definition of economic development takings and would have punished violations of the law with the loss of two years of economic development funds.[9]

President Bush signed Executive Order 13406 on the one-year anniversary of the *Kelo* decision, but it has been criticized for lacking substance. The policy reads:

> It is the policy of the United States to protect the rights of Americans to their private property, including by limiting the taking of private property by the Federal Government to situations in which the taking is for public use, with just compensation, and for the purpose of benefiting the general public and not merely for the purpose of advancing the economic interest of private parties to be given ownership or use of the property taken.

Because of language that allows for takings "benefiting the general public" libertarian advocates were disappointed in the action. In addition the law includes numerous exceptions (Somin 2007).

Litigation

The Ohio Supreme Court (*City of Norwood v. Horney* 2006) and the Supreme Court of Oklahoma (*Board of County Commissioners v. Lowery* 2006) explicitly sided with the dissenters in *Kelo* and the Michigan's *Hathcock* decision. Lower federal courts have thus far followed the *Kelo* decision. Those who decide on US Circuit Courts of Appeals-level are panels on the Second (*Goldstein v. Pataki* 2008), Third (*Carole Media LLC v. N.J. Transit Co.* 2008), Fourth (*Presley v. City of Charlottesville* 2006), Sixth (*Western Seafood Co. v. United States* 2006), and Ninth (*United States v. 14.02 Acres* 2008) circuits.

The Institute for Justice has continued to litigate cases in this area since *Kelo* was decided. Most prominent was *Norwood* representing a group who lost their homes to a mall expansion. It was the first case heard by a state high court after *Kelo*. They have been active in economic takings litigation in St. Paul Minnesota; Port Chester, New York; Long Branch, New Jersey; and other locations (Institute for Justice 2009). They filed an *amicus curiae* brief in the Brooklyn, New York Atlantic Yards (*Goldstein v. Pataki*) dispute that unsuccessfully challenged the use of eminent domain for a $4 billion downtown Brooklyn commercial development (Chan 2008) as well as in the *Western Seafood* and Lowery cases.

9 Section 8, clause 1 reads: "from one private person or entity to another private person or entity for commercial enterprise carried on for profit, or to increase tax revenue, tax base, employment, or general economic health".

Conclusion

What made *Kelo* so successful as a mobilizer of neoliberal ideas? The proposed development in New London was in many ways a dream scenario for any rust belt city. As Schultz notes, the efforts to elevate takings in the minds of jurists and the public was not new—"the takings project" (Tushnet 2006)—and heretofore had had only limited success. The property owners lost at every level in the courts. Yet, the case generated intense publicity, moved public opinion, and more importantly, moved state government officials across the nation to act on an issue that is not usually on the front burner of public policy discussions.

One key element was IJ's skill at selecting cases, at crafting legal arguments, and at moving legal disputes into the broader political arena. They had honed their skills in earlier disputes and had the resources to act on economic development takings. In *Kelo*, IJ found litigants who as Justice Scalia noted in oral argument didn't want "just compensation" from New London: "[Y]ou're giving the money to somebody who doesn't want the money, who wants to live in the house that she's lived in her whole life".

The Institute for Justice was able to transform abstract neoliberal goals into ideas that would find a sympathetic hearing in court, on editorial and news pages, and with the general public. Their consistent promotion of their plaintiffs as middle class martyrs was important. Susette Kelo's modest dream house with a view of the ocean and her neighbors, the Derys, who had lived in the same modest Fort Trumbull house for nearly a century, are consistent stories told from the first court filing onward. These stories are still used by IJ and resonate with people everywhere. As Becher and others (Barros 2005, Fee 2006) have noted, the concept of "home" is a profound one. Both Justices O'Connor and Thomas agreed with this in their opinions. O'Connor's comment about every house being at risk was widely referred to in editorials.

The Institute for Justice further showed their skill by having a grassroots organization in place well before *Kelo* got to the US Supreme Court. The Castle Coalition would serve to help mobilize the foment generated by the decision. While it seemed at the time that the reaction to *Kelo* came out of nowhere, in fact it had not. It was part of a well planned effort to maximize the impact of the decision, regardless of the result in court. In addition, no similar effort to promote the other side of the argument to the public existed. The City of New London, planners, and developers had a victory in court and were seemingly satisfied with the result.

Even so, the enormity of the backlash cannot be explained by IJ's organizational skill alone. While IJ clearly hoped that their ideas and plaintiffs would resonate, they could have only hoped for the reaction to the "little pink house" that was to result. Experimental research by Nadler and Diamond (2008) has attempted to understand why sentiment was so powerfully opposed to the decision. They found that people reacted negatively to private development; their experiment found that reactions to takings for building a children's hospital were less negative than reactions to a mall or unspecified development, but that long time home ownership loomed larger in the assessment that individuals had about hypothetically losing their homes to development. More of their subjects who hypothetically owned their homes for a long time were opposed to selling at any price and those who would sell expected greater compensation above the market value of their home. The notion of the house as home is also centrally important. According to Nadler and Diamond the legal terms of the dispute—the nature of the public use—was not the strongest part of the story for the public. IJ did well in not only emphasizing constitutional interpretation in their court filings and media efforts, but their emphasis of the idea of "home" was critical.

Not touched on by Nadler and Diamond is the fact that these homes were characterized as being modest, but well maintained. This was not a case of a poor neighborhood as in Philadelphia's American Street (Becher). The homes in Fort Trumbull were not blighted. Some of the support generated by *Kelo* is likely the result of the fact that every homeowner, or potential homeowner, can sympathize with the idea that their house can be taken simply to generate more tax revenue.

In *Kelo* we see that the well intended actions of government officials to improve the economic prospects of a depressed city were overwhelmed by the powerful attachments that Americans have to the idea of home. This is an attachment shared by the overwhelming majority of people from across the political spectrum and from many demographics. It was this well orchestrated effort to tap into this previously untouched public emotion that led to changes to the laws in more than 40 states in such a short period of time. Rather than dissipating mobilization efforts, IJ showed that a legal dispute could be expanded beyond the courthouse to other arenas, including state capitols.

Addendum: In November 2009 Pfizer Inc. announced that it would close the New London research facility as part of its merger with Wyeth Pharmaceuticals. Employees are expected to be moved out of the facility by the end of 2011. Efforts to find a new tenant or owner for the facility have thus far been unsuccessful.

Chapter 4
The Rights Behind Eminent Domain Fights: A Little Property and a Lot of Home

Debbie Becher[1]

A popular belief in property rights propelled a national movement to reform eminent domain laws in 2005. To what extent was that popular commitment to property rights aligned with neoliberal goals? The mobilization was sparked by the US Supreme Court decision in *Kelo v. City of New London*, Connecticut (545 U.S. [2005] 469), which denied a request to save several properties taken for economic development. The public backlash was almost visceral. How could the Court sanction the dislocation of Susette Kelo, the lead plaintiff, from her well-cared-for, pretty pink house? Especially when local government had planned to replace it with a commercial complex to bring economic development. According to national opinion polls, the disapproval rating for the *Kelo* decision was extremely high, between 80 and 90 percent (see Nadler, Seidman, Diamond, and Patton p. 298). Reflecting public sentiment (or creating it), four of five newspaper editorials voiced opposition to the Court opinion (Sagalyn 2008). Public anger at the decision, fear of growing government abuses nationwide, and adept political organizing catalyzed legislative-reform efforts. In 2007, just two years after the *Kelo* decision was announced, the Castle Coalition (a project of the Institute for Justice, itself an arm of the libertarian Cato Institute, dedicated to "Citizens Fighting Eminent Domain Abuse") claimed to have ushered new statutes through 42 state legislatures. How do we understand the widespread support for the libertarian agenda that emerged and helped secure these reforms?

---

1 Thanks to government agencies for information access: Redevelopment Authority of the City of Philadelphia, and the City of Philadelphia Office of the Neighborhood Transformation Initiative and Empowerment Zone. Support for this research provided by the American Association of University Women, Brookings Institution, Hauser Center for Nonprofit Organizations, Horowitz Foundation for Social Policy, National Science Foundation (Grant Number SES-0648083), US Department of Housing and Urban Development (Grant Number H-21536SG), and the Arthur Liman Public Interest Law Project. A version of this chapter was presented at the 2009 Law and Society Association Annual Meeting in Denver, Colorado, where Dick Brisbin and several audience members made key contributions. My gratitude goes to Wayne McIntosh and Laura Hatcher for being supportive and attentive editors. Thanks to them and my fellow contributors for collecting an important group of essays.

Media coverage made the public reaction to *Kelo* seem quite straightforward. The majority of news headlines related to *Kelo* suggested that the American public objected to government power expanding too far, endangering property rights and homes (Sagalyn 2008). Many of the pictures and articles published about the case suggest at first glance that the public reaction was right in line with what has been critically labeled a neoliberal ideology, defending the private real estate market from government intervention. A *Parade* magazine article began, "Across the country, Americans fight to protect their property," and pictured a young woman marching with a sign "YOUR HOME MAY BE NEXT!" (Flynn 2006). The cover photo pictured a mother, father, and their three children in front of their house with a title "Will the Government Take Your Home?" (Moser 2006). The Institute for Justice posed plaintiff Susette Kelo in front of her pretty pink house with a "Not for Sale" sign posted on it (Castle Coalition 2007b). Were these images in the media and by the Castle Coalition reflecting or reinventing popular sentiment? (See Wilkerson's contribution to this volume for a detailed analysis of the Castle Coalition's use of *Kelo* to mobilize support for property rights). Beyond simply stopping this case of eminent domain, what did the widespread public rejection of *Kelo* signal public support for?

To answer these questions, I studied Philadelphia's version of *Kelo*. The American Street Takings is my phrase for three large-scale property acquisitions pursued by Philadelphia's eminent domain authority. All three land assembly efforts were officially initiated between 2001 and 2002 and rested along a one-mile strip of a road called North American Street (its real name). Like in *Kelo*, American Street's anti-eminent domain activists publicized stories of government stripping rightful owners of their houses for economic development (Webb 2003). These owners demanded that the takings be stopped, but they used very little litigation to defend their cause. How closely did this local, grassroots mobilization against eminent domain reflect a broader neoliberal agenda?

Scholars have used the term neoliberalism to mean many things, but there are some fairly central tenets: demands to increase private powers to pursue gain through markets, in exchange for more limits on government power. The various contributions in this volume attest that the last few decades have witnessed several environments where governments have increased, or at least attempted to increase, private property rights, which may seem to mean an expansion of a neoliberal agenda. Whether or not property rights support market activity and limit government power at the policy level, how well does an increased public faith in property rights represent neoliberal sentiments? Does the American popular mobilization for property rights, against eminent domain, indicate widespread appeal for a neoliberal ideology? Through the analysis of mobilization against the American Street Takings, I argue in this chapter that popular demands for protection of property and home represented claims for respect for three distinct ideas: property possession, emotional investments in houses, and community self-determination. Though there is some overlap with the kinds of property rights defended in other legal mobilizations termed neoliberal, the particular demands here seem either unrelated or at odds with a neoliberal agenda.

In what follows, I first elaborate on why we should be curious about ideas represented by the terms "home", "house", and "property". I then explain why the American Street Takings are an ideal case study for the questions I have posed and give an abbreviated history of them, ending with the protests against the takings. Finally, I interpret citizen mobilization against eminent domain on American Street as making three different kinds of demands for property and home rights, each moving further away from a neoliberal ideology.

The Difference a Word Makes: Property, House, and Home

The *Kelo* dissenting opinions used the words "property" and "home" much more than the majority opinions. What might this choice of words reflect about the popular appeal of post-*Kelo* anti-eminent domain mobilizations? How might "property" and "home" represent what Americans found so distasteful about the story of eminent domain they read about *Kelo?* What is commonly referred to as the Takings Clause of the Fifth Amendment has one of two direct references to property in the US Constitution, stating "nor shall private property be taken for public use, without just compensation." It is not surprising that the *Kelo* dissenters, arguing that this Amendment was violated, used the word "property" more than twice as often as the majority opinion upholding the government actions (see Table 4.1). Opinions on both sides also used the word "house," though much less often and in fairly equal numbers. Justice Stevens used the word "house" to refer to improvements Susette Kelo had made, where petitioner Wilhelmina Dery was born, and where her husband Charles has lived. Justice O'Connor used the word similarly: to refer to where Dery lives and was born, where Dery's husband lives with her, and where their son lives (next door). Houses (and the land on them) were the real property at stake in the *Kelo* case.

The reaction to *Kelo* may have clarified a public sentiment that not all property deserves the same kind of security and that property rights may not fully represent what inspired popular reactions. Legal scholars were generally unsurprised by the *Kelo* decision; they did not think it had created any new property law. If we treat property as the only issue that ignited the *Kelo* backlash, we miss this important fact. An owner-occupied house – not a car, a garage, a lot, a gadget, or even a rental home or a business – was at stake. Home ownership is a special kind of property ownership in the American psyche and American public policy, whether or not the law should and does recognize it as such (Perin 1977). Recognizing that home ownership in particular was at issue in *Kelo*, some recent law review articles argue for legal recognition of the special status of home ownership or housing (Fee 2005–2006, Godsil and Simunovich 2008). (For a study acknowledging this as existing practice, and arguing normatively against it, see Stern 2009.) Recognition that a house, not just any kind of property, was the issue suggests part of what was at stake in the *Kelo* backlash. But the more startling differences are in the use of "home" in the *Kelo* opinions.

Table 4.1 Word choice in *Kelo* opinions

Author	Type of Opinion	Counts of Words Used[a]			
		Total Words	"Property"	"House"	"Home"
Stevens	Of the Court	4,150	17	3	1
Kennedy	Concurring	1,132	1	0	0
O'Connor	Dissenting	3,808	44	4	9
Thomas	Dissenting	5,498	44	0[b]	8

Notes: [a] Words in footnotes not included in the count, [b] Thomas' opinion uses the word "house" three times, but as "light-houses," "custom-houses," and "court-houses" when he quotes another opinion.

Justice O'Connor's now famous *Kelo* dissenting opinion opened the description of the facts with an emphasis on home, "Petitioners are nine resident or investment owners of 15 homes in the Fort Trumbull neighborhood of New London, Connecticut …To save their homes, petitioners sued New London and the NLDC [New London Development Corporation], to whom New London has delegated eminent domain power." Justice O'Connor's and Justice Thomas' dissents mentioned "home" nine and eight times respectively. They used the word mostly to refer to what the petitioners were asking to be protected, but they also used it to quote directly or to paraphrase other court opinions dealing with homes. By contrast, Justice Stevens' majority opinion used the word just once, to defend the use of eminent domain in the case brought in *Hawaii Housing Authority v. Midkiff* (467 U.S. [1984] 242) for creating home-ownership opportunities.

The similar, and somewhat spare, use of the word "home" in the dissenting and majority opinions suggests that there was something in the difference between the connotations of "house" and "home" that captured the imagination of those protesting the decision. One difference between "house" and "home" is that talking about a property as a "home" implies an emotional investment and/or a sense of identity more than "house." In protests to eminent domain, descriptions of the time someone has lived in a home and the memories one has there refer, at least in part, to one's emotional investments that deserve respect and protection. A second difference between "house" and "home" is that the latter term can refer to a community, rather than to an individual or single family. Residents of the Philadelphia's American Street neighborhood, and perhaps residents of New London's Fort Trumbull neighborhood, asked government for some help with change, not protection of the status quo. Under the banner of "property" and "home," they claimed rights that are not well reflected by an ideology that reveres markets and limits government power. The demands I uncovered in Philadelphia were of three kinds: to have individual rights to possess property, to have the emotional investments in their houses respected, and to enjoy collective rights to control neighborhood change.

Studying American Street

Thirteen of the several thousand properties Philadelphia government has condemned in the last 15 years for urban redevelopment have become locally infamous (Becher 2009). These 13 properties were the privately owned, occupied homes, out of 109 privately owned properties targeted by eminent domain for large-scale assembly projects on three blocks of North American Street in 2001 and 2002 (See Table 4.2.) Public testimony at City Council hearings about what I call the American Street Takings looks similar to what we know about how nine New London property owners became plaintiffs in *Kelo*, but only a few of the American Street owners turned to the courts, and they did so individually. Most of American Street's homeowner-occupants were asking government to stop the use of eminent domain. Government officials argued they had been working on a long-term plan of urban revitalization, and these takings were necessary for that plan. According to protesting residents, condemnees (owners and occupants of property taken by eminent domain) were left in the dark while government and business had been planning their demise in the name of economic development. As in *Kelo*, despite resistance, the condemnations along American Street in Philadelphia moved forward, although delayed and with more attention to relocating homeowners. The condemnations eventually galvanized activism that built widespread resistance in Philadelphia to government taking of property, between 2002 and 2004, just as *Kelo* was making its way to the US Supreme Court. Philadelphia's anti-eminent domain activists have continued to tell the American Street story in videos and news stories to mobilize support against city redevelopment plans.

What can the fight against eminent domain on American Street tell us about property rights? The American Street Takings involved a particular kind of mobilization around rights related to property, outside of court. Scholarship on legal mobilization attends to how people use the law in ways other than litigation (McCann 2008). Mobilization of three kinds can be distinguished: mobilization of courts, of public support, and of legal concepts. This case allows me to look at what happens when only public support and legal concepts are in play, and courts have very little immediate impact. It is extremely important to look at the subgroup of cases of legal mobilization that fail to involve the courts but successfully use legal ideas to garner public support. On the one hand, these are likely to involve the most radical or creative of ideas. They are likely to occur in the exact moments when courts will not settle disputes in the claimants' favor. And claimants can frame their arguments without envisioning a judge adhering to the written law as an audience. On the other hand, to be successful, they must appeal to a different audience; some segment of public opinion will both provide an opportunity and limit how they frame their appeals (Snow and Anderson 1987, Snow and Benford 1988).

I investigate the Philadelphia case of American Street, rather than the New London history of *Kelo*, precisely because the takings on American Street raised similar issues but did not make their way through the courts. Resident advocates crafted messages about American Street to gain public support, but they focused very little attention on litigation. Nevertheless, conflict was evident as both sides argued their cases as they testified at City Council hearings, wrote reports, talked to reporters, created videos, spoke at meetings, and shared with their friends and neighbors. I study the American Street Takings by reading the testimony to a legislative rather than a judicial body. Nationally, legislatures are much more likely to be the sites of debate; discussions here happen during, rather than after, the decision-making process. (The courts have repeatedly given legislatures authority to decide which economic development projects fit the "public use" requirement of the US Constitution's Fifth Amendment.) I also investigate what happened that led to the testimony at those hearings. To understand what caused the public conflict, I draw largely on private communications: in-person interviews and personal communications (with me and others) rather than only news articles, policy papers, or public meetings.[2]

A Concise Recounting of Events

American Street circa 1970 to 2000: Unofficial Daily Land Management and Invitations for Official Help

Any description of a neighborhood in eminent domain debates is highly charged. The decision to attach the label of "blight" focuses on failure and often confers power on a government authority to condemn property, therefore raising suspicions in the impacted neighborhoods. Government supporters of an eminent domain project often describe the place as if nothing there were of value. In the late twentieth century, that kind of depiction of American Street was possible. By the 1970s, what had been the main thoroughfare of Philadelphia's former textile industry was full of contaminated lots and empty buildings. Through the 1980s and 1990s, much of the vacant land became dumping sites and urban weed farms. Its reputation for lawlessness and vacant property had earned it the nickname with outsiders of the "Badlands."

Whatever an area's problems are, some neighborhood stakeholders argue that a space that is cared for and inhabited cannot and should not be called blighted. One former American-Street-area resident explained, "Many years ago, there used to be a lot of drugs on every corner, but as years have gone by, now it is good." She had preceded the comment about drugs in the neighborhood by saying,

2 I reviewed government records on the development project and on individual properties, and I conducted over 30 in-person interviews with residents, business owners, community leaders, and government representatives who were heavily involved in the project. Files accessed were at the Redevelopment Authority of the City of Philadelphia, the Department of Commerce of the City of Philadelphia, and the Philadelphia Mayor's Office of the Neighborhood Transformation Initiative and Empowerment Zone.

"It was nice. It was a small block, like six houses, and the neighbors, they were all almost family. There was like four of them that were all related, and it was nice growing up there." Residents of the American Street area against eminent domain talk about their neighborhood as paradise rather than disaster. Community leader Rosemary Cubas tells one videographer she tours around the neighborhood, "We have beauty. We have comfort. We have safety" (McCollough 2005) and another that it "used to be a beautiful neighborhood" (Community Leadership Institute, Philadelphia Folklore Project, and Dornfeld 2004). A resident in a third video explains, "It was well maintained and pretty and everything." "All these houses were perfectly conditioned" before "everybody is just like asked to move" (Community Leadership Institute 2008: Tata speaking).

To some extent, pride in the area's local beauty has been all the sweeter because it was often the result of hard work. Many residents of the area in the 1990s share a history of the neighborhood as a place of struggle, strength, and refuge from a city that denied them resources. The land situation was not completely dire because an active informal management system emerged. The lack of security and care in the neighborhood forced residents to be vigilant around their homes. Residents who were there largely watched out for each other, and the vacant space actually made some of them feel safe, for it served as a barrier that anyone attempting to harm them would have to cross. Individual residents cleaned up, fenced off, and used abandoned land; business owners cleaned trash as well. "At the end of the block, people come and dump and dump … They come at night and just dump it. So this is a never-ending fight" (Interview 2008). "When I first moved in this area, that park was full of needles and glass and everything was dirty around this area. And neighbors start chipping in and cleaning up, you know cleaning up the neighborhood" (Interview 2007).

They even breached private property boundaries to care for land abandoned by its legal owners. It was very common for residents to begin caring for lots they did not own. It was obvious no one else was going to do it. It also became clear that caring for property, and fencing it, was a crucial way to prevent dumping and the other nuisances that followed. A group of lots commandeered by a large family living to the south of them, catty corner to one of the blocks discussed in this chapter. When I was walking there in 2008, the area looked like it had been well used for some time. The width of about five row homes side by side, the dirt lot was fenced in, had a large vegetable garden, a chicken coup, and several yard chairs. You would have to either look up the titles or ask the people using the lot (and living in the house adjacent to it) to find out that they did not own it. The yard they had cultivated was even featured in a local paper, and they were proud of it.

Eventually, community leaders encouraged a strong government presence to help bring the neighborhood additional security and development. One group of women organized to fight the influx of drugs in the 1980s and solicited help from law enforcement and their City Councilperson; several other groups formally organized in the 1970s and 1980s, either to pursue lawsuits against government and banks for neighborhood neglect, or with other goals related to empowering local community members and improving the area. These organizations have grown immensely since then, and by the 1990s several of them had created or become community development corporations, contributing significantly to housing and business construction with government financing. A core group of small business owners founded the American Street Business Association in 1979, and in the 1990s, lobbied for and won $25 million in state money for a land assembly program along the strip to be overseen by the city's Commerce Department (Dougherty 2007). In the early 1990s, residential and business leaders together convinced Mayor Ed Rendell to include them as one of three communities on a national application for federal Empowerment Zone funds, which was successful in 1994, and dedicated another $29 million in federal dollars to the American Street area. The Empowerment Zone would be one of the organizations that helped push forward on the use of eminent domain to pursue large parcels for commercial development.

Moving Forward on Takings and Meeting Resistance

In the late 1990s, staff in several government departments and leaders of different community organizations considered using eminent domain to consolidate large (three-acre) parcels along American Street. In the mid 1990s, the American Street Site Assembly Project (a multi-agency committee led by the City of Philadelphia Department of Commerce) had purchased what properties they could privately, and forced tax delinquent-parcels to go to sheriff's sale to buy them there. As early as 1993, they suggested the west side of block 1 of North American Street as a potential parcel for acquisition, but they held back because this and other sites, though mostly vacant, were dotted with occupied private properties. In general through the 1990s, government workers worried about the negative political fallout that could result from taking occupied properties and avoided doing it. A few things changed that reluctance. A business interested in signing a contract for the land, and the Mayor's office's willingness to use its power to push interagency cooperation, gave people on the inside reason to think government could indeed pull this off. In late 2000, three major government programs (the American Street Site Assembly Project, the American Street Empowerment Zone, and the Mayor's anti-blight initiative[3]) coalesced around the plan to acquire the full block 1 of North American Street for Reline Brakes, and plans to acquire properties on two nearby blocks (blocks 2 and 3) shortly thereafter. There would be 109 privately owned properties subject to eminent domain in total, to help the city piece together two three-acre and one half-acre site for industrial development. Of those properties, 92 were lots, one a vacant building, 13 occupied residences, and three occupied businesses (See Table 4.2).

3 At that time it was called the Blight Elimination and Neighborhood Transformation program, but it would later become the Neighborhood Transformation Initiative or NTI.

Table 4.2 Use of private properties in large-scale land assemblages of American Street Takings

	Area (acres)	Use 2001–2002				Total
		Lots	Vacant Buildings	Occupied Residences	Occupied Businesses	
Block 1	3.2	48	1	7	1	57
Block 2	3.0	25	0	4	2	31
Block 3	0.7	19	0	2	0	21
Total	6.9	92	1	13	3	109

Government provided several assurances that this was a sound plan. A live business was planning to take over one of the blocks they were acquiring, and several others had shown interest in the other blocks (Burgos 2001). A legally regulated relocation process which guaranteed communication and fair compensation (American Street Empowerment Zone Community Trust Board Minutes). These assurances helped forge a general agreement among community leaders and government representatives that the use of eminent domain might be justified (Becher 2010).

Government started serious movement on using eminent domain in late 2000. A team of administrators from various city departments worked out a plan they thought could get the property on block 1 in time for Reline Brakes. They began the official process in late 2001. There were delays, however, because of a process tied up with unrelated properties, and the takings were stalled for six more months by a lack of agreement between two government agencies over the contract guaranteeing payment for the acquisition. Before the land was in government hands, Reline Brakes pulled out and relocated outside of the city.

A first set of very cryptic letters informing owners of block 1 of the plans went out at the very end of 2001. In the spring and summer of 2002, government hosted a community meeting about the eminent domain process and sent out more letters to property owners. In late 2002, as owners started to acknowledge and fear the impending use of eminent domain, public conflict erupted. A community leader and nearby resident named Rosemary Cubas, led the anti-eminent domain activity under the banner of the Community Leadership Institute (CLI), a recently formed local organization dedicated to politically empowering organized residents. Rumors spread about plans to acquire a much larger part of the neighborhood, and competing community meetings in the fall of 2002 led by the CLI and by the Empowerment Zone drew hundreds of people. Despite the activism, the takings moved forward, though they took much longer than originally expected. Cubas' leadership around the American Street Takings birthed a citywide, grassroots effort to fight eminent domain that has continued, and has continued to use the American Street story as evidence of what should be stopped.

It was 2007 when the neighborhood saw a new building operating on block 1, the first of the three blocks to see new development. In 2009, block 2 had been cleared and made vacant, though there is a private owner of half of the block with plans to develop it. The other half of the block is still in government hands, as is the vacant block 3 parcel. Negative evaluations of these takings often reference disappointment with the development results.

Mobilizing Support

The Community, not the Courts

Few of the condemnees along American Street litigated. Most did not consult attorneys because of the cost or because they were convinced it would make no difference. The attorneys a few of them consulted said the law should not give the property owners much room for optimism. Property owners would have little chance of having a judge reverse the city's use of eminent domain on any individual property (Ackelsberg 2007, Interviews 2008). Filing a collective action, the possibility broached with a few attorneys, would not happen. One resident's lawyer suggested that the neighbors cooperate and do this, but they said that the most vocal of their neighbors/relatives refused, so none of them considered it (Interviews 2007 and 2008). When neighbor and activist Rosemary Cubas took the residents' cause to one local attorney with a sympathetic ear for struggles of the disenfranchised, he did not perceive a clear enough injustice to take on the case (Ackelsberg 2007). There was a general failure to envision a good match between the messy, real story of what happened and any possible litigation.

The outside parties from the libertarian movement building around *Kelo*, who might have assisted this local group, did not take on American Street as their own. Institute for Justice Senior Attorney Scott Bullock became involved with the Philadelphia anti-eminent domain group that organized in response to American Street but did not file any litigation. In a phone interview, he told me his perception of what was happening in Philadelphia at the time: some people who had real investments in their property were swept up with the taking of mostly abandoned properties, and there is not much opposition to the latter (Bullock 2006).[4] The

4 I would add that this case did not have as clear a moral story of government capture by private interests; there was never a big corporation asking government to take this property. The property owners in this case involved might have also been less picture-perfect than Susette Kelo. The outsides of their houses were not in perfect condition (though many were well kept on the inside). Many of the owners had taken to using abandoned lots beside their properties as yards, whether they owned them or not. Some of the owners had failed to pay taxes. All of the owners were Puerto Rican, and many did not speak English. Together, these facts do not seem to have formed material for the most convincing test case, either in court or a more public setting.

Institute for Justice did slowly help Rosemary Cubas and others design their approach by sharing materials, coming to Philadelphia occasionally, and hosting a few Philadelphians at their national activist training conferences. They did not, however, become any more directly involved in framing the Philadelphia struggles or acting on their behalf.

As previously mentioned, some condemnees did turn to lawyers, but most believed they could not afford them, and even if they could, the lawyers would do little for them. Only one condemnee filed a motion asking the court to stop the condemnation. He lost at both the Court of Common Pleas and on an appeal of their decision; he stopped there. His daughter explained, "We had a lawyer and everything, a really good lawyer that helped Chinatown when they were trying to build that stadium down Chinatown, and he won that case. But he said he can't change the law … I think he tried, I mean he knew what the law was, but the RDA [Redevelopment Authority of the City of Philadelphia] was really unfair." Another condemnee also used a lawyer but did not litigate. When her neighbors did not follow his suggestion to have him represent the group, he did little more than read over the settlement papers. Looking back years later, she said, "I understand it, the city does whatever it wants to do, and who is going to fight the city? We got a lawyer and we couldn´t do anything."

When asked whether they thought of talking with a lawyer, one resident-owner responded, "We are poor people what can we do? We cannot hire our lawyers. … We did not have the money. Like I said, we all were poor people, always good people. Nobody could have helped us even if we tried, and if we did hire a lawyer maybe what we are almost going to do is waste our money because who else is going to get our money back, regardless?" (Interview 2008). Another owner told me, "No, I tried to call, but they say I have to pay for it, that they don't have any free lawyers for that matter. Then I was introduced [to an employee of the RDA]; he came out to my property. And he started to work with me and explain to me that I have to move because it is eminent domain, and you can't really fight them off when it is the government that is taking away your property" (Interview 2008). One more owner said, "I thought of that but also I thought that they would charge me a lot of money. After I thought, leave it like it is, and I left it like that" (Interview 2008). The one homeowner-occupant who was happy that eminent domain came through, because she could get more money for her house, still had to persist to get what she thought she deserved. She did not consult a lawyer either. She told me, "I said to myself, 'No, it is not necessary.' I even said to my daughter and son, because they mentioned, 'Mom, if they tried to gag you and offer less than what you deserve, you can call a lawyer.' And I said, 'Yes I know my rights, but I do not think I need it.' So that is what I said, 'I do not think I need it because I know how these people work'" (Interview 2008).

In a sort of haphazard fashion, one condemnee and then others did turn to a community leader, Rosemary Cubas, for help, and fought outside the courts. Cubas says she was conducting a community meeting on predatory lending when an older woman came up to her, waving a letter in front of her, saying the city was going to take her house. When Cubas organized community meetings around the issue, several of the residents faced with condemnation came. But they stopped attending, they reported, when they realized this group wasn't going to be able to stop what the city was doing. The two residents who were the last to relocate stayed involved with the Community Leadership Institute as it developed an anti-eminent domain campaign. This campaign was in its early stages when the Philadelphia City Council held a hearing about the taking of one of the blocks of North American Street, and several residents registered their complaints. Those people opposed to the takings voiced their complaints at these legislative hearings, in media coverage and organizing materials, and in interviews with me. I use the rest of this chapter to understand the claims they made in these venues.

Fighting for Stability through Possession of Property

Some aspects of the American Street conflict focused on property rights as possession, like the national public debate over *Kelo*. To most Americans, the meaning of property provoked by the *Kelo* backlash was relatively simple: Property is ownership. What's mine is mine, unless I want to give it to you. Eminent domain opponents both in New London and Philadelphia spoke of what they were fighting for in this way. Condemnees and their supporters demanded that property rights allow owners to retain that to which they had legal title. In defense of their position, condemnees opposed to the acquisitions demonstrated that the homes were rightfully *theirs*. They talked about how they had paid for the properties; most of them did not even have a mortgage; they had paid for their houses in full. They had paid their property taxes, and they were the legal owners. In a 2008 interview, one American Street condemnee proudly but sadly told me that she still hangs on to her deed, several years after the taking. Making all the motions with her arms to demonstrate, she explained to me that during the upheaval, she mused about returning to her lot, knocking on the door of whatever new building had replaced her home, and waving the deed in the new occupant's face to prove she was the true owner of the property.

Already, fighting to keep possession of property does not seem to fit perfectly into a neoliberal agenda thriving on vibrant market activity. There is no obvious conflict, but strengthening owners' right to keep something, in and of itself, is somewhat neutral towards government. Nor does this demand give much support to a market as the organizing institution. First, keeping property, rather than selling it, is unlikely to promote market exchanges. Second, property owners talked about how their property had utility value to them much beyond what a market would recognize. Property owners talked about how their economic losses would not be compensated with a principle of "full market value" used for accounting, because their properties had value particularly for them. No one argued that fair market value was more than the $20,000 American Street owners were first offered, but people involved knew that this amount would not even replace the utility value of these properties in the hands of their current owners.

Residents spoke about how they had improved their kitchens, repaired their roofs, and even created handicapped accommodation for older family members; none of this would be reflected in the market price in a neighborhood with such a depressed market.

Fighting for the Possession of a Home

As in *Kelo*, only select properties became the focus of public attention: the privately owned, occupied houses. Activism and press coverage surrounding both New London and American Street focused primarily on the taking of houses rather than other kinds of property that were also condemned. Protests about American Street explicitly focused on 13 homeowner-occupied properties, but the same bills that sanctioned these takings approved condemnation for more privately owned properties of different kinds: 92 lots, a vacant building, and three occupied businesses. The intense focus on the fate of owner-occupants (and sometimes renters) suggests that the taking of an occupied house evokes considerable rancor. In Philadelphia protestors generally remain practically silent about the much more common condemnations of vacant lots and buildings, and even sometimes of rental homes and occupied businesses (Becher 2009). I would argue that the condemnation of small businesses is often successfully protested if and when they seem like part of home themselves, as in a family-owned business.

Even though protestors of the American Street Takings were only talking about occupied houses, they might have easily used the word "property" to make their points. But they were much more likely to use the word "home," even as they spoke about "rights." Resident leader Rosemary Cubas' initial call for mobilization started, "Your home may be in danger of expropriation." A condemnee's daughter said on an anti-eminent domain video, "It is like as if we do not have any rights, even though we get to vote." She recalls her father's astonishment at learning about the eminent domain plans: "This cannot happen, because this is not a communist place, we are free here, nobody can come and take my home" (Community Leadership Institute, Philadelphia Folklore Project, and Dornfeld 2004).

Protestors of the takings on American Street often used the word "home" in a way similar to how the dissenting opinions in *Kelo* did, to reference the emotional value that is sometimes, but not always, a part of property ownership. When they talked about home, eminent domain opponents associated with American Street often referred to the emotional or identity value in it, a value they argued could not be exchanged or recreated (for a description of property as identity value, see Goffman 1961, Radin 1982). Owners and their advocates associated with the Community Leadership Institute said that the decades residents had been there represented significant personal investments, which also would not be represented in a market price. Ten years was the shortest time any of the families had lived in the houses on the first block condemned (the median was greater than 20 years). The psychological attachment to a house is one reason people may argue for it having a privileged legal status, compared to other kinds of real property. In the midst of an effort to win public support, stories about particular dislocated residents can be a strong emotional appeal that helps people who may know nothing of this particular neighborhood identify with the experience of having an emotional attachment to home broken (Goodwin, Jasper, and Polletta 2001). The following section explains one more, and more surprising, meaning attached to the claims for home that even a stronger individual right that respects emotional attachment would do little to address.

Fighting for Security through Community

The final thread I noticed in anti-eminent domain claims used the word "home" and stories about it to make demands about the public-good side of the conflict between individual and community. Residents of the neighborhood made demands that look more like communal than individual property rights. This demand, for community control over land, involved wanting to balance community change with security about the future and wanting to preserve the connection of a certain group of people to each other and to the physical space that helped make them a community. All of these meanings of home seem almost irrelevant to a neoliberal ideology focused on shrinking governments and growing markets.

In the neighborhoods surrounding American Street, even before the conflict erupted, a sense of home pervaded a common effort to bring neighborhood improvement. In the 1980s and 1990s, there was a period of cooperation among residents, business owners, and government representatives to engage government in creating community change. A fuller history of the American Street Takings, summarized earlier in the chapter, reveals resident interest in neighborhood improvement rather than simply preservation. In my study of American Street, I witnessed that residents also repeatedly said that they wanted to see neighborhood change and, as explained earlier, some sought government assistance for that purpose.

Residents knew the neighborhood had problems, and leaders thought government action might spur development that would help solve those problems. The testimony at the legislative hearings – even by residents facing condemnation at the height of the conflict – reveals a surprising degree of shared interest in community improvement, to be achieved with help from government. One resident member of the Empowerment-Zone governing board explained to me, "I supported that [first acquisition] only because I saw the importance of bringing jobs because the neighborhood is dying. And it needs to be revived, and if we don't bring jobs we are going to die" (Interview 2008). People who live near but not in the areas that were acquired had similar attitudes. One woman, who lives directly across the street from a block that was cleared for a new warehouse, had knocked on some neighbors' doors at the time this plan was in the works; she found them to be generally happy about the prospect of new housing, and they were eager to hear plans for a local factory providing jobs.

As plans for eminent domain ensued, residents demanded attention to home, in the sense of wanting the security of knowing what the future would bring for them collectively. The problem was that, despite the efforts of many different people and organizations trying to spawn the area's development, no one seemed to know what would work. The elephant in the room was uncertainty. Residents, businesses, and government were not content to keep things as they were, nor were they committed to a certain path to progress. They were all engaged in a struggle over what you do when you do not know what is best to do (this is similar to a definition of uncertainty offered by Jens Beckert [1996: 804]). No one could assure that any plan would come to fruition, or at least which parts of it would be realized and which parts would not. The history of urban planning, full of failed experiments, supports this kind of skepticism.

It is important here to understand how this skepticism of the effects of future government policy affects negotiations and decisions in the present. No one explicitly discussed planning in the face of uncertainty even though that is exactly what everyone was doing. Instead, each side engaged in the conflict (once it erupted) painted a picture of either full certainty or complete uncertainty. In attempting to garner support for the plan, government bureaucrats painted as pretty and certain a picture as possible in public. They talked about the real business-owner who wanted to develop the land, how many jobs would be provided, and the government policy that would ensure fair treatment of property owners. Residents wanted more assurances. What would residents and owners get? When would they get it? What would be developed on the taken land? What kinds of new jobs would there be? Who would get them? How could they be sure all or any of this would actually happen? Those against the takings argued that they had no idea what would happen, as one woman testified:

> Now, I don't know how this works … In order for residents to be willing to move, we do want to know what we're going to get … We're not going to want to move if they're not going to tell us what we're going to get … We want to be involved. We want someone, anyone, to set up meetings with us … because we don't know anything, and we're like lost out in space (Council of the City of Philadelphia 2002: 208–9).

In making the case that condemnees be allowed to stay, activists demanded a collective right to keep a community of people – often understood as an extension of home – intact. Even if their individual houses were nothing special, people said they had a right to maintain their physical and social connection to the networks of people there. Especially in the first area condemned they had created a safe, quiet block within a more dangerous area by depending on each other. The residents were mostly related to one another and say that the group of seven households felt like family, whether related or not. When I asked one relocatee if she had looked for a replacement house in the same area, she responded negatively, and her daughter explained, "It was a good block, not a good neighborhood." Many residents also had several different relatives and long-time friends scattered through the neighborhood. Anti-eminent domain leader Cubas complained about the city "wiping out a neighborhood" by moving away some of its long-timers. (This idea of home as a network of people, or kin, is what urban ethnographers have found to be a primary economic resource of the urban poor (Stack 1974, Duneier and Carter 1999, Venkatesh 2006).)

Some of the value that condemnees knew would not be compensated derived from the informal forms of organization their community had developed. They had built informal arrangements that government workers had a hard time recognizing when they calculated compensation. One of the most dissatisfied condemnees was unable to get government to recognize the informal arrangement he had with his brother about ownership. Even though his brother did not live there, his name was on the title, and the brother told the authorities that he was the owner in name only. Still, government workers refused to treat the brother who lived there as an owner, and treating him as a tenant brought him fewer relocation benefits. This infuriated him because he and his brother knew he was the *real* owner. In addition, government would not compensate him for the lots he had been using, which government saw as illegal squatting, and he saw as caring for and using land others had abandoned and used as a dumping area. His next door neighbor was in a different position from the start because she wanted to move; she had not sold because she expected that eminent domain was coming her way and was convinced she would get more if she waited it out. Indeed, she feels she had few problems getting exactly what she deserved in terms of compensation, because she could show receipts for the work she had done on the house and had clear title. Her only complaint was in regards to a plot to which she did not have title, though she had possession; she thinks government should have paid her a couple of thousand dollars for an abandoned lot adjacent to her home and for which she had cared as if it belonged to her. She knew that she could have gotten title for that property from the City for one dollar but just had not gotten around to it. As far as she was concerned, it was hers. She could have argued adverse possession, but she had no lawyer, and the amount the property was worth would not have covered representation.

Conclusion

The American Street Takings involved legal mobilization against eminent domain, without the litigation. To protest takings along American Street, condemnees and their neighbors mobilized legal concepts. Philadelphia organizers, with little hope that they would make any progress in the courts, took their case to the streets – and asked the public and the politicians to support demands that their "rights" be respected. Taking legal terminology out of the courthouse, they could imagine a public audience, not a judge. In framing their arguments, they might have imagined their neighbors deciding what the rules were instead of the written law.

This chapter was dedicated to understanding what their demands entailed in these conditions. Philadelphia community leaders organized around the American Street Takings and hit the local news just before national organizers pushed eminent domain in New London, Connecticut through the courts and into the national news. American Street organizers eventually connected with the Institute for Justice, but there is little evidence that the national organization had any significant impact on local work when the American Street issue was at its hottest. What rights – what rules – did American Street condemnees and their allies appeal to their neighbors to uphold? What particular notions of property rights did these claims include? To what extent would these appeals support a neoliberal ideology, dedicated to shrinking government and growing markets?

The rights pushed for in the fight over American Street most directly involved a demand for respect for a right to property as a possession, an idea which seems to have little in common with a neoliberal ideology. Owners claiming that they should be able to keep what is already theirs may require smaller government in this particular policy arena (property expropriation), but it is not a demand for increasing market exchanges. In fact, it seems to be the opposite. As long as people hold on to their property, there is no market.

The condemnees and local activists opposed to the American Street Takings quite clearly claimed that houses should get enhanced protection. They did not really fight for rights to possession of any kind of property. In defense of this special protection, they cited the special nature of a house, especially the emotional value to an owner. Again, eminent domain opponents were not supporting a neoliberal agenda dedicated to market exchanges of property. They fought for government respect of idiosyncratic values that an idealized market involving arms-length exchanges cannot account for.

Finally, the opponents of the American Street Takings made clear and direct demands that the community had rights to control its own destiny. For decades before this conflict erupted, residents of American Street organized to increase care for the neighborhood. Many community leaders invited government in to help, and even sanctioned the very limited use of eminent domain, under conditions for development and relocations that they prescribed. When government continued with the eminent domain but failed to meet those conditions, some of these same leaders turned to oppose it. Thus, they pushed for community change, but they wanted a very strong say in its direction. In addition, descriptions of eminent domain as unjust – because it would destroy a community – suggested that the community had some right to exist, a right they expected government to observe. Because it seems so antithetical to a philosophy that privileges individual rights, this demand for a right to community sovereignty is the most orthogonal to both neoliberal and libertarian agendas.

The condemnees on American Street seem to have articulated parts of a moral philosophy concerning individual and communal rights in conflicts over land development such as the ones they faced. By grappling with the complex issues of governing a struggling neighborhood through the 1980s and 1990s, and facing a highly contentious government intervention, they developed three basic tenets. First, one's possession of property has more value than property that is for sale on a market. Second, a house deserves special protection as a possession, especially to the extent that the owner has invested emotionally in it. Third, a group of people who have built a home, a residential community, ought to have a strong voice in how the community changes. These three tenets may all be helpful additions to the American legal code as it relates to eminent domain and other land development issues. None of them seems to lend significant support to a neoliberal ideology; in fact, they probably do the opposite.

What about *Kelo*? Did the eruption of the local conflict and the national reaction to the Court decision reflect similar sentiments? I would predict that if we studied the struggles in *Kelo* that happened before, during, and after the conflict, we would also observe that people in New London wanted more from government. Their demands would likely have included such phrases as home security, demands that would be difficult to express and harder for government to demonstrate it had fulfilled. New London property owners likely wanted to ensure the success of their neighborhood's future, and to be a part of it. They likely wanted assurances about uncertainties along the way and respect for the informal community agreements they had developed, and that gave the area a sense of cohesiveness when business and government had little interest. (Plaintiffs' attorneys have repeatedly mentioned owners' ties to their homes and to their communities. See Wilkerson in this volume.)

Whether or not New London looked anything like Philadelphia, the American Street case is informative about what public demands might really lie beneath what appears to be wholehearted support for a property-rights agenda. It seems that when faced with the real problems of struggling neighborhood economies, Philadelphians may have stretched the idea of property-as-practiced away from property-as-litigated. Through a fight over property, they demanded special protection for possessions, for emotional investments, and for community self-determination. Liberal political theorists were aware of the latter issue, as democratic rule, but understood property rights as in conflict with group rule rather than as encompassing them. When another community faced what American Street did, the flight of industry and the abandonment of land, they litigated that property involved communal rights (Lynd 1988). Though that argument failed in a judicial court of law, what happened on American Street makes it seem alive and well in the American public psyche.

This case reveals Americans struggling with principles that are in tension, rather than adhering to any ideology about property, government, or markets. The tenets that emerged from an analysis of the American Street conflict do not answer the question of when and where government should use eminent domain or act in many other situations because they can, and do, come into conflict. Together, these basic statements often represent a clear tension between individual and communal rights. Questions in that conflict fundamentally return to understanding what the community voice is, and whether government represents it. Americans seem to expect their governments to protect their home security through times of dramatic change in land use. This means that government is expected to attempt a combination of activities: Government ought to support grassroots attempts for community change, and protect individual interests in maintaining attachments to home and community.

PART II
Neoliberalism Abroad and Propertization

Chapter 5

Breaking the Sound Barrier: The Propertization of Spectrum Resources and Implications for Non-Profit Community Radio in Guatemala

Victoria L. Henderson

> The broadcast spectrum holds a special, almost holy, place in the economic analysis of law and the economics of property rights.
>
> (Lueck 1995: 419)

In 1996, a new, "radically liberal" (Bull 2005: 14) telecommunications law introduced in Guatemala shifted allocation of radio spectrum from a centrally planned, public interest model to a market-based, property rights regime. Scholars, analysts, and industry lobbyists argue that Guatemala's propertization experiment created what is "probably the most liberal spectrum policy in the world", maximizing resource efficiency, institutionalizing justice, and offering rich and poor countries alike a practical model for spectrum reform (Hazlett, Ibárgüen, and Leighton 2007: 442; see also Galbi 2003; Ibárgüen 2002, 2003, 2004, 2008; Leighton 2008). According to Guatemala's community radio practitioners and international bodies including the Inter-American Commission on Human Rights (IACHR), however, spectrum liberalization discriminates against those who lack the financial resources to purchase spectrum title, (re)criminalizes poverty, and effectively bars non-profit community radio stations from legal access to the airwaves (AMARC 2007; Henderson 2008; IACHR 2001, 2003). Of particular concern is the effect of Guatemala's spectrum reform on indigenous Maya broadcasters, the majority of whom operate without legal title to frequencies and so face ongoing threats of station closure, fines, and incarceration. Accused by commercial radio operators, scholars, and the mainstream press of "pirating" the airwaves, Guatemala's community broadcasters have mobilized to demand secure spectrum access, citing national and international covenants on freedom of expression and, more centrally, indigenous media rights in defense of their claims.

In what follows, I draw on primary and secondary data to analyze spectrum reform in Guatemala and its implications for non-profit community radio.[1] In keeping with the focus of this volume, I concentrate on the ways in which neoliberal policy prescriptions are entwined with, and co-constituted by, property rights, conceptualized as a mechanism for "assign(ing) order to the world" (Blomley 2003: 122). Legal scholars define propertization as the "the process of allocating ever greater rights in relation to resources to private individuals and collectives, as opposed to governing the use of these resources through the political realm, or else leaving these resources as part of the commons and not regulating their use at all", a process considered integral to neoliberalism, understood broadly as "the global expansion of free market capitalism" (Lawson-Remer 2006: 481, 487–488). Situating spectrum mobilizations in terms of cultural demands and legal actions, I consider not only mobilization "from below", that is, how community radio practitioners articulate and position their demands for spectrum rights, but also mobilization "from above", that is, elite reproduction of self-serving social structures and institutions (Nilsen and Cox 2006), including – and, perhaps, foremost – the institution of private property. To that end, I frame neoliberal (dis)order as a juridico-political struggle between "conscious direction" and "spontaneous order" (Hayek 1945), concepts invoked in the spectrum reform literature (e.g., Huber 1998; Ibárgüen 2004) to characterize those aspects of civil and common law traditions, respectively, that have conceptual and discursive currency in political economy and debates over property rights. The point is not to belabor the obvious schism between two organizing principles with distinct ontological and epistemological premises, but rather to tease out the idea that neoliberalism is "an unfinished process riddled by internal contradictions", and by all means *not* "an accomplished and monolithic state of affairs" (Nilsen and Cox 2006: 1; see also Harvey 2007).

Properties of Dispute

Research on property rights and neoliberalism reveals that disputes over rights and obligations often generate larger interpretive struggles that shift attention from rights and obligations as such to the rules and processes from which rights and obligations obtain (see Clark and Harrington, this volume). At issue in Guatemala's spectrum wars are not simply interpretive differences in rights-based claims deriving from existing legislation but also, and more critically, overarching

1 This research is part of a two-year project funded by the Social Sciences and Humanities Research Council of Canada. Three periods of fieldwork totaling five-and-a-half months were carried out in Guatemala: an exploratory phase (July–August 2006); a formal and extensive research phase (June–September 2007); and a formal follow-up phase (July 2008). In total, 36 people from Guatemala and the United States were interviewed, including: policy analysts, public officials, scholars, and community radio practitioners and advocates.

crises of accountability with respect to how the 1996 telecommunications law – part of a broader set of neoliberal reforms introduced on the tail-end of a 36 year civil war (Benson, Fischer, and Thomas 2008) – came to pass, especially in light of prior commitments by the Guatemalan state "to promote the abolition of any provision in the national legislation that is an obstacle to the right of indigenous peoples to have their own communications media" (Acuerdos de Paz 2003: 41). Drafted in 1995, the *Acuerdo sobre identidad y derechos de los pueblos indígenas* (Agreement on the Identity and Rights of Indigenous Peoples) obligated the state to recognize media rights for Guatemala's indigenous peoples, who represent more than half of the population and speak more than twenty languages, many of which are threatened by extinction (Henderson 2008). The agreement was included in a comprehensive set of Peace Accords that brought an official, if largely symbolic, end to Guatemala's civil war (1960–1996), which claimed the lives of an estimated 200,000 people, the vast majority from Maya communities targeted by military and paramilitary units for allegedly harboring communist sympathies. The accords, which motivated rapid deployment of indigenous community radio as a means of breaking the country's longstanding "culture of silence" (Henderson 2008), were collectively signed into law on December 29, 1996, one month *after* Guatemala's new telecommunications law took effect.

In claims for spectrum access, community radio practitioners repeatedly refer to the state's Peace Accord promises. Similarly, the IACHR, which investigated Guatemala's spectrum allocation regime at the request of community radio practitioners and international non-governmental organizations, has argued that the "obligation of the state to maintain democratic criteria in the concession of television channels and radio waves is evident in the very fiber of Guatemala's democratic consolidation and in the implementation of the Peace Accords" (IACHR 2003, Art. 414: 192–193; see also IACHR 2001). But the Peace Accords are challenged in varying ways and to varying degrees by commercial radio lobbyists and other advocates of spectrum reform. In 2007, the president of Guatemala's commercial radio lobby, itself a vociferous opponent of unauthorized ("pirate") radio, called community radio practitioners to task for having denounced Guatemala before the IACHR. "[I]t is not the purpose of the Peace Accords," Juan Ortiz told the national press, "to allow people to claim ownership of something that *does not belong to them*" (quoted in Mérida 2007: npn, emphasis mine). Analysts and scholar-advocates of spectrum reform underscore that the Peace Accords were rejected in a 1999 referendum and are, therefore, non-binding (Ibárgüen 2008; Liu 2005). Further complicating debates over spectrum rights and obligations is the fact that the *Ley de Radiocomunicaciones* (Radio Communications Law, also known as Law Decree 433), which governed frequency allocation in Guatemala prior to reform and which placed certain demands on broadcasters "to help raise the living standards of the (local) people, safeguard their property and language, and promote the material and spiritual values of the nation" (*Ley de Radiocomunicaciones* 1980: npn; see also, AMARC 2005, 23–24), was never abrogated. All of which, it is argued, leaves community radio practitioners in legal limbo:

> … the communities of the country face a *vacío legal* (legal grey zone) provoked by the incapacity of its authorities to issue legal frameworks that are appropriate, just and progressive […] For that reason, we cannot speak under any concept of illegal radios, but rather – and in all cases – of "a-legal" radios (AMARC 2007: 32–37).

On recommendation by the IACHR, a National Roundtable on Community Media was struck in 2005 to bring together key players in Guatemala's spectrum wars, including community radio practitioners and advocates, representatives of the state, and members of the commercial radio lobby. Negotiations were short-lived. During initial sessions of the roundtable, representatives from Guatemala's telecommunications regulator, the *Superintendencia de Telecomunicaciones* (SIT), proposed to set aside two to three frequencies nation-wide for community broadcasters, meaning the same frequencies would effectively be divided among community radio stations geographically defined, with rigid limits on broadcast range. Practitioners rejected the proposal, arguing it was "totally insufficient to meet the needs of ethno-linguistic communities and other civil society groups", particularly those in remote areas of the country where the spatial distribution of listeners demands a more expansive broadcast range (AMARC 2007: 40). Representatives of the state and the commercial radio lobby soon withdrew from the roundtable, fuelling harsh criticism from practitioners and raising concerns about the legitimacy of state-sanctioned mechanisms for dispute resolution (AMARC 2007: 33).

The (D)Evolution of Spectrum Rights

Until a property rights regime was established by the 1996 *Ley General de Telecomunicaciones* (General Law of Telecommunications), Guatemala subscribed to an administrative system of spectrum allocation. All radio frequencies were assigned by license and administered by the military. Licenses were technically free[2] and available exclusively to Guatemalan nationals; but the allocation process was undermined by rampant corruption and chronic clientelism (Ibárgüen 2003). In the early 1990s, as privatization initiatives rolled through Latin America and other regions of the global South, policy analysts in Guatemala began publishing papers on spectrum reform, arguing that launching Guatemala into the information age was "[as] simple as eliminating a couple of laws, privatizing some services, and creating a single, new and revolutionary law of radiocommunications" (Ibárgüen 1992: npn).[3] In many ways, this was an accurate assessment. Guatemala's 1996

2 A nominal fee (200 *quetzales*, approximately US$27) was required to process the application.

3 In 1992, telecommunications was the world's fastest growing industry; by 1993, it ranked second only to banking in terms of market value (Petrazzini 1995: 2).

telecommunications law passed with a simple majority; it is by all accounts revolutionary (Galbi 2003; Bull 2005); and it puts the country front stage center in offering "proof of concept" for Ronald Coase's 1959 call to establish property rights in radio spectrum (Hazlett, Ibárgüen, and Leighton 2006), a proposition written off in its day by critics who claimed to "know of no country on the face of the globe – *except for a few corrupt Latin American dictatorships* – where the 'sale' of the spectrum could even be seriously proposed" (anonymous, cited in Coase 1998: 579, emphasis mine).

Yet, the process of propertizing Guatemala's radio spectrum, if ultimately successful, has been far from "simple". As other scholars have forcefully argued, spectrum liberalization in Guatemala cannot be understood without taking into account mobilization from above, most notably "the role played by local economic groups" (Bull 2005: 227). Mobilization from above includes "the organization of multiple forms of skilled activity around a *rationality* expressed and organized by dominant social groups" (Nilsen and Cox 2006: 1, emphasis mine). In the case under study, local elites circumscribed in the classical liberal tradition of the Austrian school of economics and networked in an academic-institutional-media complex (Peet 2002)[4] mobilized to reproduce the rationality of neoliberal reform, arguing that countries like the United States could stand to learn from Guatemala's success in capturing "dead capital" – i.e., "real estate" – in the radio spectrum (Ibárgüen 2002, 2004; see also De Soto 2000).

Of TUFs and Pirates: The What and Who of Spectrum Wars

The idea that broadcast spectrum "holds a special, almost holy, place in the economic analysis of law and the economics of property rights" (Lueck 1995: 419) forces a conceptual shift away from the "thing-ness" of property (see Hatcher, this volume) toward an understanding of property rights as a socio-spatial ordering principle, or, more definitively, as "the hidden architecture that organizes the market economy" (De Soto 1989: 25). Under Guatemala's new telecommunications law spectrum property rights are codified in the form of security certificates known as *títulos de usufructo de frecuencia*, or TUFs (usufruct titles to frequency). Defined, defensible and divisible (the three conditions for property as such), TUFs entitle the bearer to a 15-year renewable claim on spectrum resources and can be leased, sold, subdivided or consolidated at will, or used as equity or collateral (*Ley General de Telecomunicaciones* 1996; Ibárgüen 2003; Hazlett, Ibárgüen, and Leighton 2007).

4 This network included individuals associated with Universidad Francisco Marroquin, analysts associated with the think-tank Centro de Estudios Economico-Sociales (CEES), and local media in Guatemala, as well as universities, think-tanks and media in the United States.

As mandated by the Guatemalan constitution, the state retains legal ownership of the electromagnetic spectrum (Government of Guatemala 1985 [1993], Art. 121). But TUF holders benefit from a carefully worded section of Guatemala's Civil Code, which states that usufruct "carries the right to use and enjoy the property of another to the extent that such use and enjoyment does not destroy or diminish its essential substance" (*República de Guatemala, Código Civil, Libro II, De los Bienes, de la Propiedad y demás Derechos Reales, Título III, Usufructo, uso y habitación*, cited in Ibárgüen 2003: 546). Because radio waves are infinitely reusable, being neither diminished nor destroyed through use, a TUF is a *de facto* property right – one which "the government may not arbitrarily reclaim" (Ibárgüen 2003: 546; Ibárgüen 2008).

In the first three years after the 1996 telecommunications law was introduced, the SIT received more than 10,000 requests for spectrum use rights (Spiller and Cardilli 1999: 76, fn 144). Existing licensees were parented TUFs free of charge. All frequencies in regulated bands[5] not claimed by existing licensees were put on public offer with contested frequencies allocated by auction to the highest bidder. To date, spectrum auctions in Guatemala have generated more than US$130 million,[6] netting significantly higher average returns than in other jurisdictions undergoing spectrum reform.[7] Usufruct rights to broadcast frequencies in and around Guatemala City have sold at auction for US$750,000 and lease for as much as US$4,000 per month (Ibárgüen 2003). Outside of the capital, TUFs average US$27,000 at auction (López 2006b).

The TUF market is largely alien to Guatemala's unauthorized broadcasters. Local radio practitioners reject the accusation – circulating in academic (Hazlett, Ibárgüen and Leighton 2007) and government (Government of Guatemala 2007) literature, as well as the mainstream press (Contreras 2008; Herrera 2006; López 2006; Ramírez 2007) – that they are airwave "pirates", saying: "Our principle consists in neither rebellion nor anarchy. *We want to be regulated …*" (AMARC

5 Prior to the 1996 reform, spectrum zoning in Guatemala followed the spectrum zoning model of the United States Federal Communication Commission, wherein blocks of bandwidth are set aside for specific applications (e.g., broadcasting, mobile telephony) and license assignments are deployed from each block. Post-reform, spectrum resources in Guatemala are distilled into three broad, technology-neutral categories: *unlicensed frequencies* for amateur radio operators; *reserved frequencies* for state use; and *regulated frequencies*, which require a TUF and which, despite the taxonomy, "are some of the least regulated frequency bands in the world" (Hazlett, Ibárgüen. and Leighton 2006: 444).

6 This includes auctions for non-broadcast spectrum. Seventy percent of spectrum revenues, up to a cap of US$3.7 million per annum, has been allocated to develop rural telephone services (Ibárgüen 2004). For arguments concerning the consumer welfare gains in mobile telephony achieved through liberalization, see (Hazlett, Ibárgüen. and Leighton 2007).

7 Through the mid to late 1990s, for example, FM auctions in New Zealand (a country with a per capita income three times higher than Guatemala) netted an average of US$18,000; in Guatemala, US$60,000. Analysts attribute high returns in Guatemala to the "unique property rights that were for sale" (Spiller and Cardilli 1999, 77–80).

2007: 35, emphasis mine). As noted elsewhere, specific discursive strategies (see Clark and Harrington, this volume) and media representations (see Becher, this volume) deployed in disputes over property rights work not only to (over) simplify complex issues, but also to shape legal outcomes and social sanctions. In Guatemala, TUF-bearing broadcasters, as well as print media outlets with strong links to the broadcast sector, actively construct a "pirate radio" stereotype, leading to a common assumption in the general population (palpable in this research) that community radio practitioners are outlaws or, on some accounts, "guerrilla" holdouts from the civil war era.[8] "In truth, it's upsetting", says one indigenous Maya radio practitioner, "because it comes out on the television and in the newspaper that they are seizing the stations, that the Ministry of Justice is showing up to take away the equipment. ... It upsets us. It makes us feel bad, because we say to ourselves, what about the Peace Accords?" (Rodríguez Guaján 2007).

Community Radio: Cultural Demands

Estimates on the number of community radio stations in Guatemala vary: from 168 (Cultural Survival 2008), to between 400 and 640 (González Arrecis 2007; Ibárgüen 2003; Pérez 2006), to between 800 and 1,000 (Herrera 2006; López 2006; *NotiCen* 2006; Herrera 2007), to upwards of 2,500 (RWB 2006). Fieldwork interviews confirm that investigations are pending against 350 radio stations broadcasting without a TUF, although officials at Guatemala's Ministry of Justice caution that this number includes only those stations against which a *denuncia* (formal complaint) has been filed (Castañeda y Castañeda 2008).[9]

The difficulty in establishing the exact number of active stations stems not only from a lack of representation in national accounts, but also from discrepancies in defining community radio as such. The prevailing opinion among scholars, public officials, and members of the community radio movement who participated in this research is that the majority of unauthorized radio stations broadcasting in Guatemala are affiliated with religious institutions (principally evangelical Christian churches) and/or political parties, and/or are commercial (for-profit) stations (Castañeda y Castañeda 2008; Hazlett, Ibárgüen, and Leighton 2007; Liu 2005; López 2006b). Substantive data to prove or disprove these claims is unavailable; however, it bears underscoring that unauthorized community stations

8 Legal radio stations with an organizational structure and programming content similar to that of unauthorized community stations tend to define themselves as "alternative" radio rather than "community" radio precisely because the latter term has such a negative connotation in Guatemala. I thank Pati Galicia for this observation.

9 Fieldwork suggests Ministry of Justice figures on unauthorized community radio are low. In one municipality of the department of Sacatepéquez practitioners told me there are four unauthorized community radio stations while the Ministry of Justice lists only nine unauthorized broadcasters department-wide.

are not, theoretically, being targeted for generating revenue, but rather because they either do not hold usufruct title to a frequency band, or because they lack a valid license for broadcasting equipment.

In an attempt to formalize, and therein to reconstruct, the image of community radio, the National Roundtable offers the following definition:

> "Community Media Service" refers to the provision of public interest, non-state radio and television by organizations, associations and civil institutions, or any other form of organization customary to Maya, Ladino, Xinca and Garífuna communities[10] which is non-profit, holds educational, cultural and popular objectives, and which serves the development of different sectors of the community – whether geographically, ethno-linguistically or otherwise defined – with interests, shared aims and common concerns directed toward improving quality of life and wellbeing for its members (reprinted in AMARC 2007: 53).

Attempts to recover local voice and break Guatemala's culture of silence are at the center of the community radio movement and the Maya movement more broadly. Beginning in the 1970s, there emerged a growing awareness of indigenous languages as "a symbol and ongoing practice of indigenous identity" (Nelson 1996: 292). Maya intellectuals stress the importance of community media, especially radio, as "a means of ethnic expression and reproduction" (Cojtí Cuxil 1996: 42–42), a view consistent with the position of the *Academia de Lenguas Mayas de Guatemala* (ALMG, Maya Academy of Languages) that "decolonization of the Maya begins with knowing how to use technology and not being used by it" (ALMG 1990: 42; quoted in Nelson 1996: 292). The reference to decolonization is critical insomuch as "culture" conceived under colonial rule, radiated outward from the capital and its ruling class to the rest of Guatemala (Figure 5.1). Cultural demands for community broadcasting are premised on the idea that local media reverses, or at least unsettles, colonial information flows, facilitating the circulation of ideas within distinct, often peripheral, ethno-linguistic cultures (Molnar 1989: 8, quoted in Ginsburg 1991: 98).

Against the tendency of spectrum liberalization advocates to defer juridico-political questions having "implications far beyond telecommunications policy" for "future research" (Hazlett, Ibárgüen, and Leighton 2007: 443), community radio practitioners argue that disputes over spectrum property cannot be considered a purely "technical" matter (Government of Guatemala 2007). As has been argued elsewhere, such a technocratic-bias fails to "uncover interests *systematically* excluded from policy debates" (Dryzek 1999: 108, emphasis mine). In Guatemala, this observation takes on critical force given the conclusions of two truth commissions mobilized to investigate civil war crimes. The commissions

10 Ladino is a widely used term in Guatemala. It refers broadly to individuals of mixed racial lineage, although it may also refer to indigenous people who have adopted a "Western" lifestyle. Xinca and Garífuna are distinct ethno-linguistic groups.

Figure 5.1 (Post)Colonial culture

Note: The inscription reads: This is the site of the old University of San Carlos, founded in 1675. From here, culture radiated to the rest of the kingdom of Guatemala.

Source: Photo by V. Henderson 2007.

registered more than 600 massacres, including acts of genocide, and underscored "the undeniable existence of racism expressed repeatedly by the State as a doctrine of superiority" (CEH 1999, Conclusion Pt. I and II; see also REMHI 1998; cf. Sabino 2007).

Scholars have mapped the correlation between massacre sites and Maya linguistic communities (Steinberg, Height, Mosher et al. 2006), and it is largely in these same ethno-linguistic areas that the bulk of Guatemala's unauthorized community radio stations are located. The concentration of unauthorized broadcasters in the west and northwest of the country is well-understood by state officials, and arguably well-represented in a sample of radio stations publicly listed as "pirate" by Guatemala's Ministry of Justice (CERIGUA 2006). Statistical comparison between the number of pirate radios registered by the Ministry of Justice and the percentage of Maya speakers by department indicates a moderate correlation (Figure 5.2). Widespread poverty, monolingualism, and illiteracy problematize the use of national, Spanish-language media in these communities, making community radio a critical source of information, in addition to a means of cultural and linguistic preservation.

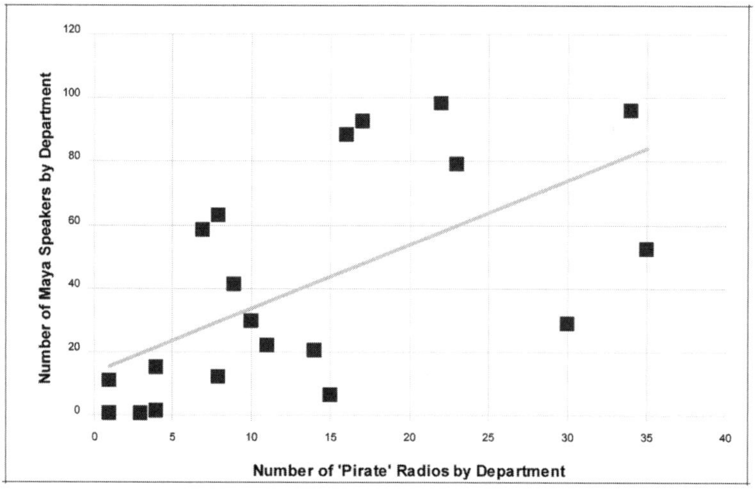

Figure 5.2 Correlation number of "pirate" radios vs. Maya speakers by department. Pearson's correlation index: 0.6047

Source: Data compiled by V. Henderson from figures released by the Ministry of Justice (CERIGUA 2006) and Prensa Libre (2008). Statistical analysis and graph by E. Sanmarti.

Community Radio: Legal Actions

The 1996 *Ley General de Telecomunicaciones* conferred authority on Guatemala's telecommunications regulator to sanction spectrum property transgressions. In accordance with the law, blocking access to spectrum resources or broadcasting without a TUF in regulated or reserved bands carries a fine of between US$10,001 and US$100,000. Repeat offences in these bands automatically incur the maximum fine (*Ley General de Telecomunicaciones* 1996, Art. 80, 81). In addition, parties may sue for damages. Between 1997 and 2005, the SIT registered 217 interference complaints, 73 percent of which originated in the FM band, which is the preferred band for community radio (Escalante 2005). Since 2000, the SIT has levied 104 fines. Of these, 25 were before the courts for non-payment in 2007, and another 22 cases of non-payment were being processed (Government of Guatemala 2007). Additionally, criminal charges, including *hurto de frecuencia*, or theft of frequency, have been levied against broadcasters transmitting on a frequency for which they do not hold title. The charge of theft in Guatemala carries a one- to six-year prison term (Government of Guatemala 2007, *Penal Code*, Art. 246). All cases of *hurto de frecuencia* are tried before the court for Drug Trafficking and Environmental Crimes, a practice community broadcasters say further stigmatizes local radio practitioners, as it implicitly lends support to allegations from the commercial radio lobby and mainstream press that unauthorized broadcasters maintain close ties with drug traffickers (Contreras 2008; Palencia 2008; Xunic 2008).

In the main, court rulings on spectrum property in Guatemala support the closure of stations operating without a TUF and the confiscation of broadcasting equipment. In 2006, the first case of *hurto de frecuencia* was tried and successfully prosecuted; seven additional convictions were subsequently registered. All of the accused pleaded guilty. In two cases, charges filed by community radio practitioners *against* the state were tried by Guatemala's Constitutional Court. In both cases the plaintiffs challenged the state's right to force station closure and confiscate "private property" (radio equipment and other items belonging to the station). The court found in favor of the state in both cases (Government of Guatemala 2007), illustrating what practitioners charge is the very selective way in which private property claims are enforced. A defense of the state position was made public in 2007 with the release of a government policy paper to "resolve the problem of the 'illegal radios'". The policy paper itemizes criminal cases decided in the state's favor and makes clear the state will continue to prosecute unauthorized broadcasters – a threat highly criticized by members of the National Roundtable, who issued a public statement arguing that "(a)ny public policy that seeks to resolve conflict through sanctions and penalization is counter-productive when it is applied to situations *provoked* by a violation of human rights" (cited in AMARC 2007: 32–37, emphasis mine).

Only months after the heated exchange incited by the government's policy paper, the community radio movement scored its first court victory. Blanca Estela Toxcón Alvarado, a Maya K'aqchikel lawyer, successfully defended Anselmo Xunic of *Radio Ixchel* against the charge of *hurto de frecuencia* on the grounds that it is impossible to "steal" radio waves because they are not *bienes muebles*, or "moveable goods" (for an expansion of this argument, see Loretti 2007). The judge ruled lack of merit in the case and all charges were dropped (AMARC 2007: 46; Xunic 2008). While community radio practitioners hold fast to the belief that the case is precedent-setting, the doctrine of precedent is less established in civil law (the law tradition in Guatemala) than it is in common law (Summers 2000).

Great Expectations

In 2006, Guatemala's radio spectrum was declared "saturated" by Óscar Chinchilla, head of the SIT. Referring specifically to broadcast bands, Chinchilla reported to the national press that a 2005 technical study determined zero frequencies were available in the AM band and only 18 frequencies for departmental coverage and 11 frequencies for municipal coverage remained unassigned in the FM band (Pérez 2006). With 95 percent of the broadcast spectrum legally titled and hundreds of unauthorized community radio practitioners continuing to press for legal access, Guatemala's spectrum wars are unlikely to be resolved any time soon. Without fanfare – although ostensibly in reaction to reports from the Inter-American Commission on Human Rights (IACHR) declaring spectrum auctions "incompatible with democracy" (IACHR 2001; CIDH 2003) – the SIT has ended auctions for broadcast spectrum and put a hold on all unassigned frequencies in the FM band.

A *Community Media Law* drafted in 2007 by members of the National Roundtable for presentation to Congress demands that at least one-third of the broadcast spectrum be reserved for community radio, to be administered by a new regulatory body, the *Consejo Nacional de Medios de Comunicación Comunitaria* (National Council of Community Media). On the basis of "open and public" competitions, spectrum licenses known as *títulos de derecho de uso de la frecuencia* (titles to the right of use of frequencies) would be created. Distinct from a TUF, the licenses issued by the National Council would be defined but not divisible and would not carry the option to lease or otherwise alienate rights derived from the assignment (*Proyecto de ley de medios de comunicación comunitaria*, reprinted in AMARC 2007: 56).

Given that the bulk of spectrum titles in the SIT registry are valid until 2011 and renewable for an additional 15 years upon request, the demands of the National Roundtable cannot be met in the short term without recalling titled spectrum, a move that would undoubtedly meet with protest from those holding title to spectrum property. Property is, above all, a set of "stable expectations", then any action altering or unsettling those expectations can serve as a basis for a takings claim, as much in land (see Hatcher, this volume) as in radio spectrum (Winer 2003).

Great expectations were at the center of the "high power dog fights" (Spiller 2006: 45) that ensued over Guatemala's spectrum reform. Pablo Spiller, one of the US-based scholars hired to consult on spectrum liberalization in Guatemala, explains that parenting property rights to incumbent broadcasters was necessary, "*otherwise the broadcast wars would have killed the government*, so they were given that windfall" (Spiller 2006, 45, emphasis mine). Ironically, Thomas Hazlett, who consulted with Spiller on the Guatemalan reform, has long argued *against* such windfalls insomuch as they uphold politically motivated "marriages of convenience" between incumbent broadcasters and government (Hazlett 2001) and are, therefore, antithetical to "free market" principles.

The decision to gift spectrum to industry incumbents in Guatemala raises questions about the feasibility of vetting politics from policy in the transition from an administrative to a property rights regime, an arguably problematic issue for advocates of neoliberalism given propertization is advanced as a *cure* for the pathology of clientelism. While industry analysts and international financial institutions have labeled Guatemala's spectrum liberalization an overall success for having achieved significant consumer gains in mobile telephony, there is recognition that the liberalization process "failed to remove the political elements from just one portion of the communications market: the broadcasting side, and, in particular, FM radio. So that actually remained highly political" (Leighton 2008). Even The World Bank, which provided $5.2 million in financing for Guatemala's spectrum liberalization as part of a 1998 "technical assistance" loan, has now acknowledged that "(t)he distribution of licenses for television channels and radio frequencies solely through auction to the highest bidder is unlikely to produce a range and diversity of services that meet the needs of all sections of society" (World Bank 2008: 232).

Common Law and Civil (Dis)Order

Warnings that interference deadlock could cause Guatemala's radio broadcast system to collapse (Liu 2005) invoke images of a tragedy of the commons and lead to debates over the role and nature of property in assigning order to the world. That Guatemala's broadcast spectrum is in a state of "disorder" (Castañeda y Castañeda 2008; AMARC 2007) is not under dispute. The cause of that disorder, however, is. Pro-reform scholars and industry insiders, including the commercial radio lobbyists, say the problem is not that spectrum liberalization has failed the broadcast sector, but that there is a lack of regulatory will to enforce the rule of law. Analysts charge the SIT "has been reluctant to enforce FM band TUFs from interference", arguing further that TUF holders with FM frequencies are increasingly opting not to report cases of interference as a result of "their lack of faith in the government's commitment to rights enforcement" (Hazlett, Ibárgüen, and Leighton 2007: 467; see also Palencia 2008). The implication is that Guatemala faces a classic case of regulatory capture, wherein the SIT has been co-opted by one or more well-connected special interest groups with a stake in maintaining the status quo.

At issue, according to Guatemala's pro-reform scholars, are not simply different interpretations of the law but fundamentally distinct legal philosophies. The extent to which advocates of spectrum propertization in Guatemala – as elsewhere – argue for the principles of common law cannot be understated. Key theorists on spectrum reform state flatly that "nothing grander than common law is even practical anymore" (Huber 1998: 36), a sentiment shared by Giancarlo Ibárgüen, the intellectual force behind Guatemala's *Ley General de Telecomunicaciones*:

> [T]he working principle behind the spectrum reform was the idea of general rules of just conduct. … The generality principle is familiar in application to the common law tradition. However, it is unlike the civil law of Guatemala, which in many cases is the law of special groups or interests (2004: 4).

The scholarship of Friedrich Hayek and Richard Posner is central to the arguments of scholars keen to emphasize a link between common law, political liberty and economic growth.[11] Hayek sees legal traditions as reflections of "different philosophies of government" and laws themselves as deriving from specific understandings of liberty: common law establishing "the individual's freedom to pursue individual ends", and civil law establishing "the government's freedom to pursue collective ends" (Mahoney 2001: 511, 523). Posner argues that common law's adversarial system "tends to result in the survival of efficient, and the demise of inefficient, rules" (Mahoney 2001: 506; see also, Posner 1973) and secures "just" distribution based on a principle of wealth maximization that "pays homage to the 'productive'" (Posner 1979: 119–123; paraphrased in Hackney 2003: 377). As other

11 This is not to say that Hayek and Posner share the same views on law and economics (see Zywicki 2008).

scholars have noted (see Clark and Harrington, this volume), such "adversarial legalism" is arguably unfolding apace with neoliberal restructuring.

Critics of this view underscore its central biases: (1) that the claimant of the right whose use is productive is favored over the claimant whose use is consumptive; and (2) that the rich claimant whose use is consumptive is favored over the poor claimant whose use is consumptive (Baker 1975: 9). There is much more to this debate, but my purpose here is to illustrate how these biases map onto spectrum policy. First, and as a general rule, the "analog (broadcast) monopoly" is considered unnecessarily "consumptive" in a digital age (Ryan 2005). A liberalized spectrum policy that is technology- and application-neutral assumes spectrum will be deployed to the most productive (least consumptive) use. Second, and as is evidenced in the Guatemalan case, among competing consumptive uses of broadcast spectrum, resource rich claimants (predominantly large, commercial broadcasters) are favored over resource poor claimants (predominantly non-profit community broadcasters).

Pro-reform advocates suggest two options for Guatemala's non-profit community broadcasters: broadcast in the UHF (rather than FM band); or negotiate with individual TUF holders to allow community broadcasts on selected (titled) frequencies as a demonstration of "corporate social responsibility" (Ibárgüen 2008). Community radio practitioners reject these suggestions, saying they are not prepared to accept spectrum "scraps" and will not "fall into the trap of buying what belongs to us" (Xunic 2008). Practitioners argue that individually negotiating the use of frequencies does nothing to protect the rights of community broadcasters *as a group* – rights, they reiterate, which are guaranteed under the Peace Accords and other national and international covenants. In at least two communities with predominantly indigenous populations, Santa María de Jesús and Patzún, residents have taken the law into their own hands, mobilizing in local uprisings that successfully blocked public officials from closing unauthorized community stations (Henderson 2008).

In the final assessment, criticism of Guatemala's revamped spectrum policy does not deter pro-reform scholars, who argue that of the "many lessons" to be drawn from liberalization, "[t]he one lesson that stands above all others is the importance of applying politics by principle, instead of being guided exclusively by special interests or expediency" (Ibárgüen 2004: 4). If other countries are to seriously evaluate Guatemala's experiment in spectrum property rights, however, a full(er) picture of cultural demands and legal actions is needed. To the extent that property law determines who can (and cannot) claim rights to a given resource (Waldron 1990), propertization is always already a barrier – one Guatemala's community radio practitioners remain determined to break.

Chapter 6

Transnational Perspective on Human Genetics and Property Rights Mobilizations of Indigenous Peoples

Andrea Boggio

> The present invention relates to a human T-cell line (PNG-1) persistently infected with a Papua New Guinea (PNG) HTLV-I variant and to the infecting virus (PNG-1 variant). Cells of the present invention express viral antigens, type C particles and have a low level of reverse transcriptase activity. The establishment of this cell line, the first of its kind from an individual from Papua New Guinea, makes possible the screening of Melanesian populations using a local virus strain. The present invention also relates to vaccines for use in humans against infection with and diseases caused by HTLV-I and related viruses. The invention further relates to a variety of bioassays and kits for the detection and diagnosis of infection with and diseases caused by HTLV-I and related viruses.
>
> (US Patent 5397696—Papua New Guinea human T-lymphotropic virus, issued on March 14, 1995)

While the rather arcane scientific jargon of Patent 5397696 describes the properties of the patent, it fails to account for the political, economic, and cultural tensions associated with patenting biological material. This chapter will bring them to the surface by discussing indigenous opposition to various biotech and genetics research initiatives. What form of resistance did indigenous people use to mobilize against neoliberal intellectual property rights (IPRs) regimes? In what ways did the colonial context shape these mobilizations, particularly with regard to DNA sampling?

Indigenous peoples' mobilization and resistance against assignment of IPRs offers a remarkable opportunity to uncover some of the contradictions in neoliberalism, particularly of the way patent law rubs against communal understandings of ownership. In the aftermath of the public announcement of Patent 5397696, Pat Mooney, an indigenous advocate, called the patent "another step down the road to the commodification of life" (Rigden 1997, para. 5). Resistance to this use of IPRs was launched to oppose a new form of colonialism, its unmistakable neoliberalist imprint, and the risk of disappearance of indigenous culture.

After discussing the encounter between science and neoliberalism under the flag of IPRs, the chapter looks at indigenous mobilization, its strategies and its reasons, and assesses its significance for the power struggle of indigenous peoples in an era of biocolonialism and neoliberal commodification.

The Biotech Revolution and Indigenous Opposition

While the study of genetics dates back to 1865 (Barry 2005: 424), genetic research on a large scale became possible only after major advancements in genetic engineering technology during the late 1960s and early 1970s. Especially after polymerase chain reaction (PCR) was invented in 1985, scientists became able to analyze and manipulate DNA from the smallest samples. PCR changed the way things were done in science so dramatically that it is often referred to as the "genetic equivalent of a printing press" (Lee and Tirnady 2003: 62).

Nowadays, large genomics research projects and biotech initiatives involving disparate populations are building blocks of current and future genome initiatives (Guttmacher and Collins 2005: 1400). Furthermore, PCR reinvigorated comparative studies of genetic traits of diverse populations. Populations that had lived in peaceful isolation for centuries, suddenly found themselves projected in the midst of the biotech revolution, as Francis Fukuyama labeled these extraordinary progresses in science (Fukuyama 2002: 19). Since the early 1990s, participants in biomedical research have been recruited among indigenous communities. Some of these projects have led to securing IPRs on inventions triggered by the study of indigenous genes.

Intellectual Property Rights and the Encounter of Neoliberalism and Science

The rise of genomics and biotech initiatives took place—more by coincidence than by design—at the same time the world social and economic history underwent a parallel revolution: the shift towards neoliberalism. The neoliberalism paradigm embeds certain political and economic practices, which, according to theorists such as David Harvey (2007: 64–65), include championing private property rights, free markets, and free trade by creating institutional frameworks and legal structures that will secure the function of markets (p. 2).

In the past three decades, science and neoliberalism have intersected. Their encounter was due, in great part, to law, and in particular to IPRs. Indeed, data on patent filings provide evidence that the simultaneous surge of neoliberalism and of biotech operated jointly and successfully.[1] In fact, IPRs have been used as instruments

1 In 1987, 139,455 patent applications were filed. A sharp increase followed in the past two decades: 232,424 were filed in 1997 and 484,955 in 2007 (US Patent and Trademark Office).

to advance neoliberalist policies. They have expanded the domain of private property to the human intellect and its products, and also to various forms of human life (DNA, cells, proteins). Furthermore, they have facilitated commodification and market exchanges of human life through licensing arrangements. The holder of a patent has the right to limit or exclude others from using an invention. *De facto*, IPRs privatize certain forms of knowledge and human life.

Indigenous Mobilization against Biotech and Genetic Research Initiatives

Not all of these populations warmly welcomed their participation in the biotech revolution. Indigenous peoples in particular were reluctant to embrace their inclusion in genomics and biotech initiatives. The first instance of indigenous peoples' opposition to genetic research relates to the Human Genome Diversity Project (HGDP). By collecting DNA samples from various populations around the world, the HGDP aimed to create an inventory of genetic variations and explain human evolution through genetic connectiveness of various populations around the world. Partly motivated by the historical opportunity presented by the availability of technology that enabled documentation of human diversity on a large scale, the HGDP was urged by the desire to study populations that were on the verge of extinction.

Although the inclusion of indigenous populations in the Project was a key feature, the HGDP generated vigorous indigenous resistance. It was the first opportunity for indigenous peoples to mobilize in the context of genetic research and to organize a transnational movement to oppose genetic research. Several indigenous coalitions, including the World Council of Indigenous Peoples, Survival International, the Third World Network, raised the voice against the Project at the First International Conference on the Intellectual and Cultural Property Rights of Indigenous Peoples held in New Zealand in 1993.

Two assumptions of the study were particularly problematic. First, the idea that all humans are genetically connected and share a genetic code that spread out over the course of generations from the same ancestors, was problematic. Although scientifically sound, this assumption implicated a sense of horizontal equality among populations around the world that, at least in the eyes of indigenous peoples' advocates, trumped social justice. Common ancestry could have led to believe that after all we are all equally positioned in this planet, thus obscuring centuries of colonial domination and the resulting unequal distribution of power among groups. Genetic equality could not cast out man-made differences.

Second, the HGDP proposed the primacy of genetic knowledge over other forms of knowledge. The Project pushed the idea that only genomic information could definitively tell the story of human history, and the migration that shaped the world as we know it. A genetic narrative would have trumped oral history accounts of the origins of various indigenous groups. To indigenous movements, genetics became just another instrument of Western imperialism.

Indigenous peoples' advocates were also concerned with issues of commercialization and patenting rights. In 1993, these issues were formalized for the first time in *The Mataatua Declaration on Cultural and Intellectual Property Rights of Indigenous Peoples*, adopted at the end of the First International Conference on the Intellectual and Cultural Property Rights of Indigenous Peoples. In 1997, the indigenous peoples' organizations gathered again in Ukupseni, Kuna Yala, and issued a resolution condemning "all attempts to commercialize genetic material, or genetic cell lines of human beings, and in particular those of indigenous peoples" and "the use of existing mechanisms in the legalization of intellectual property and patent systems, use of existing mechanisms including intellectual property rights and patents to legalize the appropriation of knowledge and genetic material, whatever their source, and especially that which comes from our communities" (Ukupseni Declaration, Kuna Yala on the Human Genome Diversity Project, sub 2). A representative of an indigenous group commented that "You've taken our land, our language, our culture, and even our children. Are you now saying you want to take part of our bodies as well?" (Andrews 2001: 94). Debra Harry, a vocal opponent of the Project, stressed that the HGDP raised "inevitable questions regarding both ownership of the genetic samples themselves and who stands to profit from the commercialization of products derived from the samples. The Project puts indigenous peoples' most fundamental property—their own genes—in the hands of anyone who wants to experiment with them" (Harry 1994, para. 7).

The HGDP was not the only initiative that provoked indigenous opposition. In the 1970s, Canadian researchers collected samples among the residents of the remote South Atlantic island of Tristan da Cunha, a population suffering from the highest incidents of asthma in the world. In the hope of locating the gene that predisposes people to asthma, the researchers shipped DNA samples to a California-based genomic company, Sequana, which partnered with the German firm Boehringer in the effort to develop and commercialize therapeutics from asthma genes. The indigenous group tried to prevent the companies from acquiring IPRs on discoveries flowing from the DNA collection on the island, but they failed. However, they were able to negotiate free equipment to diagnose asthma and drugs for treating the disease (Rigden 1997, para. 8). In the 1980s, a similar controversy surrounded DNA collection among the Hagahai People in Papua New Guinea. DNA collection led to US Patent 5397696 on the Papua New Guinea human T-lymphotropic virus. The patent was eventually issued in 1995 (Resnik 1999: 16). Yet, this and other patent filings were challenged by indigenous group advocates. In 1996, the advocate Pat Mooney commented that "with Panamanian indigenous people from the Guaymi General Congress, we successfully pressured the US to withdraw its first patent application for an indigenous person's cells. Later, in collaboration with the Solomon Islands Government, [we] suppressed another US government patent application for the cells of a citizen of that country" (Action Group on Erosion 1996, para. 3).

Resistance to biotech exploitation has become even more robust over time. Biotech initiatives, often inspired by neoliberal ideals favoring private ownership and commodification of genetic resources, clash with the collective nature and anticapitalist sentiments of indigenous life (Hall and Fenelon 2009: 26). A compelling example is offered by the opposition to the establishment of a genetic database of the inhabitants of the Kingdom of Tonga, an archipelago in the South Pacific Ocean. The interest of scientists was driven by the fact that Tongans are highly affected by diabetes and obesity. An Australian biotechnology company, Autogen, thus approached local communities in an effort to set up the database in the archipelago (Rouse 2001: 8; Weber 2000: 1910). In November 2000, Autogen announced that it had reached an agreement with the Tongan Ministry of Health in exchange for researchers' access to the island to collect DNA samples from its inhabitants. The agreement provided for a package of benefits to the advantage of the indigenous group, which included annual research funding for the Tongan Ministry of Health, royalties to the Tonga government for any commercially successful discoveries, and provision of drugs from such discoveries free of charge to the people of Tonga (Dickenson 2007: 166–167). The agreement between the government and the biotech company had been reached without public consultation—Tonga is, after all, a kingdom consisting of an archipelago of 169 islands, making public consultation very difficult. The lack of involvement by the public proved to be a mistake that cost Autogen the deal. In fact, after the agreement was made public, Tongans expressed their opposition to it.

Mobilization was organized by the Tonga Human Rights and Democracy Movement. The Movement's spokesman, Lopeti Senituli, argued that "Existing intellectual property rights laws favor those with the technology, the expertise, and the capital. All we have is the raw material—our blood. We should not sell our children's blood so cheaply" (Dickenson 2007: 167). Mr. Senituli talked precisely about "selling," thus implying ownership of blood and the related right to trade it. For the first time, a clear assertion of property rights of DNA in the context of an indigenous population was made. History probably played a role: opposition to this biotech-capitalist venture came from the only island nation in the region to have avoided formal colonization. The historical sentiments of opposition in Tonga to Western domination mobilized local resistance in unprecedented ways, despite the fact that the Tonga government had reached a reasonably attractive deal for its citizens.

Over time, indigenous advocacy groups have increasingly stressed the need for both control of their own resources, and recognition and respect from the international community for past, present, and potential contributions of indigenous peoples' own resources. These concerns have been primarily voiced through political opposition to the recognition of IPRs to researchers and research institutions. This culminated with the call for the establishment of a Life-Form Patent-Free Zone in the Pacific at the third workshop in Suva, Fiji. Since then, entitlement claims to human genetic resources have become part of the political, legal, and ethical discourse of advocates opposing forms of biocolonialism.

Sometimes large genetic studies were able to address concerns of indigenous advocates. For instance, since its establishment in 2002, the HapMap Project (a project aiming to determine common patterns of DNA sequence variation in the human genome to facilitate the discovery of sequence variants that affect common diseases) was able to overcome the resistance of indigenous peoples' advocates by building upon the lessons of previous projects. Public consultation sessions were organized to foster involvement of the communities included in the study. Patenting concerns were addressed:

> Initially, because of concern that third parties might seek patents on HapMap data, users were required to agree to a web-based "click-wrap license", assenting that they would not prevent others from using the data ... In December 2004 this license was dropped, and all data were released without restriction into the public domain (The International HapMap Consortium 2005: 1317).

Indeed, the HapMap investigators were very conscious of the implications associated with participation of indigenous groups, and wanted to communicate clearly that past mistakes would not be repeated. The project's website insists on pointing out how this project was different from the HGDP:

> The purpose of the HapMap and its sampling strategy make this project very different from the [HGDP], an anthropologically oriented effort proposed more than a decade ago that was designed to learn about human population history and the biological relationships among human populations. The HGDP would have studied genetic variation "to see if, for example, the Irish are more closely related to the Spaniards or to the Swedes," according to the project's material. A number of groups representing indigenous peoples were concerned that the project would exploit vulnerable individuals and populations. They also objected to the HGDP's potential intrusion into cultural beliefs about population origins. Ultimately, and in large measure because of the criticisms, the HGDP was never carried out (National Human Genome Research Institute, para. 9).

On the other hand, indigenous peoples' property claims did not disappear from the international debate. Large genetic projects are for the most part international, cross-national endeavors. The increased awareness of indigenous opposition forced investigators to foster stakeholder participation, thus giving a forum and a (well deserved) audience to indigenous peoples' advocates. Over time, this plurality of voices participating in the debate from different corners of the world gave rise to a transnational network of indigenous advocates, engaged in voicing its opposition to various projects. Property rights are still often raised by indigenous peoples' advocates.

A recent example of how framing resistance in terms of ownership rights is relevant, a full decade after the initial skirmishes, is offered by the Genographic Project. The study's aim is to analyze, in five years, "historical patterns in DNA from participants around the world to better understand our human genetic roots" (The National Geographic Society, website). Since DNA from up to 100,000 indigenous people is gathered worldwide, the study's Ethical Framework addresses in a detailed manner some of the issues surrounding indigenous peoples' participation. Community participation and the "proper degree of flexibility needed to respect the views of diverse indigenous communities around the world" are part of this framework. The history of exploitation is also acknowledged as well as the fact that "indigenous people operate on the basis of relationships rather than 'contracts'" (The National Geographic Society, *Ethical Framework*, 3). Finally, the study's Ethical Framework reassures participants that no patents will be sought as a result of the research, that participants can withdraw at any time, and that the findings will be held for the public's benefit.

Moreover, a study based on the early work completed by the HGDP on the complex evolutionary history of Africans and African Americans was published in 2009 (Tishkoff et al. 2009: 1035). Finding more extensive genetic diversity in Africa than expected, the paper calls for more DNA collection and further large-scale genotyping of African populations. As published, the paper does not address tensions that were raised in conjunction to opposition to the HGDP—biology-based accounts of history versus indigenous traditions and the idea of genetic equality versus inequalities created by colonization—culture is only mentioned in passing ("Of interest for future anthropological studies are the cases in which populations have maintained their culture in the face of extensive genetic introgression … and populations that have maintained both cultural and genetic distinction …" p. 1043). On a more positive note, the researchers "thank the thousands of people who donated DNA samples used in this study" (p. 1043).

Indigenous Mobilization and International Policymaking Efforts

Property rights mobilization was also organized along a second track: international policymaking, particularly at the United Nations level. In fact, since 1982, indigenous peoples have formalized their presence through selected representatives at the United Nations and its bodies. It began with the establishment of the Working Group on Indigenous Populations of the Sub-Commission on the Promotion and Protection of Human Rights. In the following years, the UN Permanent Forum on Indigenous Issues (UNPFII), an advisory body to the Economic and Social Council, was also created.

The United Nations was certainly instrumental to the creation of transnational, indigenous networks. After a series of international conferences in the 1990s, which brought together indigenous advocates from all over the world, UN meetings proved to be the most effective networking opportunity for indigenous peoples. The databases set up by the Civil Society Organizations System, developed by the Department of Economic and Social Affairs, offered an easy tool for transnational interconnectivity, to the point that in 2009, 132 indigenous NGOs are listed in the database as organizations having consultative status.

Participation of various indigenous entities and groups in the UN process as well as coordinated opposition to various genomics and biotech initiatives led to the creation of transnational advocacy networks that "address a broad range of issues, such as collective and individual rights, self-determination, globalization, colonization, and education" (Corntassel 2007: 139). These networks include all "relevant actors working internationally on the issue, who are bound together by shared values, a common discourse, and dense exchanges of information and services" (Keck and Sikkink 1998: 46).

The networks' efforts led to the adoption of several important international legal instruments. In 2006, the United Nations Human Rights Council adopted the UN Declaration on the Rights of Indigenous Peoples, and the General Assembly adopted the Declaration the following year. Some ownership rights are recognized in the 2007 Declaration, making it a great success for advocates struggling to advance indigenous peoples' interests. Article 26.2 provides that "[i]ndigenous peoples have the right to own, use, develop and control the lands, territories and resources that they possess by reason of traditional ownership or other traditional occupation or use, as well as those which they have otherwise acquired." This success was clearly part of the wave of political steps towards achieving the broad political platform of indigenous peoples. While indigenous groups have won rights to traditional land holdings in a number of countries, including Australia and Canada (Russell 2005: 207–213; Williams 2007: 155–163), the Declaration is willing to recognize just a limited number of those rights that constitute "property" when it comes to human genetics—and other resources: "[i]ndigenous peoples have the right to maintain, control, protect, and develop their cultural heritage, traditional knowledge and traditional cultural expressions, as well as the manifestations of their sciences, technologies and cultures, *including human and genetic resources*, seeds, medicines, knowledge of the properties of fauna and flora, oral traditions, literatures, designs, sports and traditional games, and visual and performing arts" (Article 31.1, emphasis added). During the same year, the UNPFII adopted The Declaration on Indigenous Peoples' Rights to Genetic Resources and Indigenous Knowledge, which reiterates the principles stated in previous declarations.

International instruments recognize and protect indigenous peoples' interest, making it appear that these mobilizations have been effective. Yet the success of indigenous peoples' mobilization is less effective in at least two regards. First, full ownership claims are circumscribed to "lands, territories and resources that they possess by reason of traditional ownership or other traditional occupation or use." Human DNA is excluded from this more intense protection. Ownership claims to human DNA are second class claims. In fairness, establishing a right of ownership was not the goal of advocates in relation to human genetics. The primary concerns included making certain that studies on indigenous DNA would not lead to the assignment of IPRs to public and private institutions in a way that would somehow diminish indigenous peoples' control over the resources from which useful data were generated. Clearly, the 2007 Declaration does not guarantee that: applications generated from research conducted in collaboration with indigenous populations are still patentable. The UN declarations do not change the rules of the game.

Second, the indigenous peoples' involvement by international organizations can be seen as a cooptation strategy. Cooptation "occurs if, in a system of power, the power holder intentionally extends some form of political participation to actors who oppose a threat" (Lacy 1992: 83). The key cooptation processes, blunting and channeling, create an illusion of inclusion for indigenous peoples participating in global forums. Blunting entails altering the indigenous peoples' mobilization agenda to fit the norms set by the very same institution that mobilization intended to challenge. Channeling occurs when indigenous peoples accept limitations of their mobilization efforts to the global fora set up officially by the United Nations, which aim to institutionalize forms of mobilization otherwise politically more threatening to Western points of view. Corntassel (2007) shows empirically that, by accepting the channeling of mobilization into the UNPFII—ordinarily in the form of a "three-minute speech"—"Indigenous communities are dissuaded from engaging in grassroots mobilization and/or directly confronting corporate/state practices," as in the case of the movements that stopped the HGDP and biotech initiatives in the Pacific Islands (p. 140). Because of the "illusion of inclusion" that comes with participation in global fora, "Indigenous peoples are unable to effectively pursue basic strategies of surveillance and shame within this global forum in order to maximize influence on state behavior" (Corntassel 2007: 162).

Understanding Indigenous Mobilization

Thus far, the analysis has highlighted the mechanisms of and paths to indigenous mobilization. Some of the reasons for indigenous opposition and resistance to biotech and genetic research initiatives have also emerged from the discussion. However, it is now time to explore in depth the reasons for indigenous mobilization, and to connect them to the broader agenda of indigenous movements.

The reasons for indigenous opposition greatly overlap to broader agenda of the indigenous social movements. Their aims are primarily threefold: avoiding appropriation of land and natural resources by non-indigenous hands; fighting capitalism; and protecting indigenous culture (Hall and Fenelon 2009: 5). Each of these aims is reflected in indigenous mobilization against biotech and genetic initiatives. In particular, three aims of mobilization emerge that are very much attuned to the broader agenda of the indigenous social movements: struggle to protect indigenous culture; assertion of property rights to resist biocolonialism; and quest for recognition of indigenous autonomy.

Protecting Indigenous Culture

Indigenous mobilization against biotech and genetics initiatives aimed to protect indigenous culture. The central critique to capitalism that is dear to indigenous peoples is that private property, free trade, and free market run against the traditional view that indigenous peoples have espoused around the world: the idea that ownership of resources is communal. Indigenous culture denies the overarching dominance of private property rights. The patenting on inventions based on indigenous culture has resulted in the invasion and commodification of public and private spheres that previously remained outside the reach of capitalist interests (Robinson 2004: 7). Accepting such regime would have forced indigenous peoples to accept a framework that is inconsistent with indigenous culture—with communal ownership, which is so central to indigenous identity.

An individual's right to own is a cultural construct. Although Westerners have a hard time envisioning a society in which private property rights are not recognized, other cultures modeled their communities around other conceptual frameworks. In indigenous cultures, "knowledge and property (including body elements such as hair, blood, semen, etc.) can be viewed as a sacred and inalienable aspect of the existence of individuals and kin-related groups" (Gillett and McKergow 2007: 2098). For instance, Maori construe genes as genealogy:

> A physical gene is imbued with a life spirit handed down from the ancestors, contributed to by each successive generation, and passed on to future generations. Maori have two terms to describe a human gene, both of which are interlaced with a broader reality than western scientific definitions. The first is *ira tangata*, which is the actual word for a gene and translates as "life spirit of mortals". The second term is *whakapapa*, which means to set layer upon layer. It also means genealogy and is the word most commonly used by Maori to conceptualize genes and DNA (Mead 1997, para. 10).

Within this cultural context, indigenous mobilization against IPRs was very much needed: IPRs were to privatize what was not to be privatized, and indigenous peoples could not accept it.

Biocolonialism

Indigenous movements saw IPRs as agents of biocolonialism. IPRs were seen as new forms of colonial exploitation as they could have resulted in indigenous peoples losing the right to control and use genetic resources that were located within regions inhabited by indigenous communities. Natives' loss of control of biological resources evoked well known patterns of colonialism, which are in many cases at the root of underdevelopment of many indigenous peoples' communities.

Consequently, accusations of biocolonialism followed biotech and genetic initiatives. Just as colonizers did in the past, biocolonizers aimed to acquire privileged, and often cheap, access to natural resources. During this colonization era, high volumes of natural resources were transported from colonies to the other side of the world to serve the need of the rulers: coffee beans, tea, spices, fruits, artifacts, but also timber, minerals, and oil. In many cases, colonial exploitation of national resources has left behind depleted lands, impoverished communities, and discontent. The sense of injustice associated with domination and exploitation is still vivid and politically compelling to communities once under foreign rule. Colonialism is very much alive in the minds of formerly colonized nations, and early signs of this new form of colonialism, often referred to as "biocolonialism", were captured by indigenous movements when Western researchers and companies started collecting genetic information from indigenous peoples and securing IPRs on inventions originating from those investigations. As Loeppky (1998: 245) points out, "[t]he deployment of new forms of neocolonial exploitation reinforces the power/knowledge base harnessed by capitalist production." Privatization through patenting of natural resources creates a monopoly power for the patent owner that sets up an asymmetrical power relation between the owner and non-owners (Harvey 2005: 68). Reviving negative feeling towards colonization, these efforts have therefore been resisted by indigenous peoples.

Indigenous Autonomy

Close to biocolonialism and the associated fear of losing control of natural resources, the third aim of indigenous mobilization is the quest for recognition of indigenous autonomy. Colonizers created nation-states that were not based upon the territories of indigenous peoples, but instead grouped indigenous peoples together into artificial boundaries. As a consequence, indigenous peoples found themselves sharing governance of territories that once were theirs, or more likely losing control of those territories to whatever group of thugs was given power by the colonizers. As a result, indigenous peoples lost their autonomy. They never acquired (or acquired a rather minimal) sovereignty. Sovereignty, which can be defined as "supreme authority within a territory" (Philpott 2001: 16), is a fundamental legal concept that allows for the recognition of the ability of a community to be self-ruling, i.e., for autonomy. At least initially, biotech and genetic ventures disregarded indigenous norms of communal ownership of genetic material and collective decision making with regard to matters that affect an indigenous community. Indigenous norms are not formal laws of a nation-state. To the eyes of the promoters of the first biotech and genetics initiatives, these norms mattered very little, and they often acted as if indigenous norms did not exist. Mobilization against this way of conducting business aimed to assert indigenous right to autonomy by establishing the idea that rules set by indigenous communities ought to be respected, even if indigenous polities had not formal standing as sovereignties. In this regard, property claims are still the bedrock of the indigenous political platform as they aim to "carve out social space where [indigenous peoples] can continue to exist" (Hall and Fenelon 2009: 122).

Furthermore, sovereignty allows for a community's legal standing as a subject under international law. Indigenous peoples had no standing in international law as a collectivity, because they were not organized as nation-states, but rather sub-national groups. The lack of standing under international law constituted a substantial obstacle to the realization of indigenous peoples' rights. Indeed, traditionally "many international legal theorists—especially those who are Europeans—have tended to underemphasize the importance of indigenous peoples' rights" (Buchanan 2003: 408). Consequently, indigenous movements were drawn to a political strategy that gave them a seat at the table in international forums as discussed earlier as a form of cooptation.

Indigenous Peoples' Mobilization: From Opposition to Cooptation

Studying property rights mobilization of indigenous peoples reveals important lessons for understanding political claims in a globalized world. But was indigenous mobilization ultimately able to achieve the intended results? The answer lies somewhere between "yes" and "no."

Indigenous peoples were clearly successful to the extent that they were able to overcome the limited opportunities offered by legal and political processes to seek protection of their rights, both in the domestic and international arena. Through grassroots movements and later by having a voice in international policymaking venues, indigenous peoples' advocates were able to have their critiques heard by the international community. To indigenous groups, the neoliberal policy agenda is the old spectrum of colonialism that appears again in new clothes. Property rights were therefore mobilized not to secure ownership of resources that were already under the stewardship of indigenous communities, but to affirm two important political goals: sovereignty rights over natural resources and political and legal standing, with the related right to participate in the global governance of natural resources. In this regard, mobilization in part achieved these goals. Successes are clear. Through mobilization, indigenous peoples' advocates were able to stop some initiatives, force the withdrawal of some patent applications, and secure a number of concessions. For example, current research ethics frameworks consistently include a discussion of how a project may take into consideration indigenous peoples' interests, through group consent provisions, limitations on IPRs, and/or benefit sharing arrangements. International declarations recognize indigenous peoples' right to control and manage human genetic resources. Mobilization through creativity and transnational cooperation was, indeed, effective.

However, the progressive cooptation of indigenous peoples' networks at the international level shifted the focus of mobilization efforts from opposition and resistance to generating declarations that recognize the interests and rights of indigenous peoples. Researchers are still engaged in mapping genetic diversity and thus perpetuating the superiority of Western science over traditional, indigenous accounts of the history of humanity. For instance, the 2003 National Geographic documentary *Journey of Man: The Story of the Human Species* "continually recasts indigenous and Western knowledge as a distinction between story and science, and genomic knowledge emerges at the top of the hierarchy, as a corrective to the current wisdom of both indigenous tradition and archaeological evidence" (Wald 2006: 325).

Furthermore, a paradox followed indigenous resistance to this new form of colonialism: Not long after resistance efforts started, indigenous peoples' advocates adopted the same language and conceptual tools used by the proponents of international genomic studies and biotech ventures—the key tool being the concept of property. The fact that the indigenous movement adopted the same language and constructs that it aimed to fight might have weakened the fight against biocolonialism. Yet, the legal battle was not fought in court, but in the political arena. Ultimately, indigenous mobilization proved to be an effective, significant page in the history of the power struggle against biocolonialism. Although not all political goals of the indigenous movement were achieved, indigenous mobilization against biotech and genetics initiatives led to significant changes in the way in which these ventures are now conducted.

Chapter 7

Juridical Takings in NAFTA: Disputing Investors in the World of "Free Trade"[1]

Gabrielle E. Clark and Christine B. Harrington

It is commonly assumed that private property rights have been empowered with the creation of transnational trade tribunals, such as the one authorized by the North American Free Trade Agreement's (NAFTA) Chapter 11. This treaty creates an arbitration process for protecting private property rights akin to what is generically known as "regulatory takings" in the US context (Fischel 1995, Been and Beauvais 2003). Unprecedented in international law, the NAFTA Tribunal (hereafter the Tribunal) enables private foreign investors to challenge state regulations they perceive as harmful to their property interests and investments (Howse 1999).

Undergirding this type of neoliberal market-based transnational trade regime is an economic policy that assumes the way to attract foreign capital, generate domestic growth, and stimulate innovation, is dependent, in part, on protecting investors' property from regulatory takings, particularly in the global south. Like property, foreign investments came to be seen as a "bundle of rights" to be protected from government actions, such as nationalization and expropriation. Free trade protection regimes for foreign investments also incorporate general principles of justice that go well beyond the scope of US regulatory takings law. For example, the principle of justice embodied in NAFTA's Chapter 11 standards of treatment hold that investors are not to be discriminated against and should receive "fair and equitable treatment". These standards aim to place foreign investors on an equal playing field with local market actors operating within their own domestic regulatory contexts (Been and Beauvais 2003).

Empirically, however, we know very little about whether the mobilization of private property protections under Chapter 11 has altered the power relations between states and private transnational foreign investors. We also have little empirical evidence to help understand the full implications of property rights

1 We would like to thank members of the Law and Society Association's Collaborative Research Network on Transnational Transformations of the State for comments on earlier versions of this work. Chris Arup, Tom Ginsburg, Terry Halliday, Heinz Klug, Bronwen Morgan, Sol Picciotto, Nancy Reichman and Gregory Shaffer provided particularly helpful suggestions and comments. Our NYU research assistants, Sarah Lensing and Alexander Panayotov, were invaluable and we thank them too.

claiming practices on the relationship between foreign investors and their host states. How, and in reaction to what state regulatory practices, do investors mobilize property rights protections? In what sense are foreign investors treated as equivalent to domestic private capital in the eyes of the state? And to what extent does the relationship between foreign investors and their host states get reconfigured through property rights disputes?

Contrary to scholarly assumptions that property rights protections destabilize domestic regulation in the current era of neoliberal reforms, we find empirical support for suggesting that *over time* transnational tribunals, like NAFTA, may curb the reach of investors' property rights claims. For example, initially foreign investors mobilized NAFTA's dispute process under Chapter 11, and made extremely aggressive claims that endeavoured to redefine the political and social relationship between foreign investment and host administrative and regulatory states. The Tribunal initially accepted these arguments and responded with what we call a "jurisprudence of access" (1996–2001). However, limits on the scope of investors' rights emerged when international law standards were asserted by states to protect their sovereignty and then adopted by the Tribunal to form what we call a "jurisprudence of state regulatory sovereignty" (2002–2007). Thus we take exception to the scholarly focus upon the Tribunal's rulings in favor of investors' material claims in a couple of high profile cases, such as *Metalclad v. United Mexican States* (2000), and the conclusion that NAFTA is an "'investors' rights" tribunal. Our findings suggest a more complicated story about state sovereignty defenses to investor property claims grounded in international law that lead to curbing the scope of investor property protections in transnational tribunals, such as NAFTA's. In addition, we argue that it is also important to analyze the claims that failed, were struggled over, and were not vindicated by the Tribunal. Here, we see that the Tribunal delimits investors' rights. Despite initial decisions favorable to investors, there has been a narrowing of investors' rights over time (1994–2007).

Interestingly, given state participation in the neoliberal market project, state actors objected to investors' mobilization of new interpretations of property rights meanings tied to their assertion of a new balance of power relations between foreign investors and host states. This precipitated a legal-ideological struggle over the reach of neoliberal market-based protections, the scope of international investment law, and, ultimately, the parameters of state sovereignty. This chapter documents: 1) investors' mobilization of property meanings in a transnational tribunal; 2) the impact of legal-ideological struggles on a transnational regime; and 3) the paradoxical recreation of non-market state regulatory authority through property rights disputing. As such, our analysis considers the legal indeterminacy of transnational legal rules (Berman 2007) by looking at property disputing practices – how investors mobilize particular treaty provisions, how states respond to them, and how tribunals rule – over time. We observe that the investment disputes became "larger" interpretive struggles encompassing legal issues that were bigger than the property disputes themselves. The disputes are not just about rights and obligations in property in a particular case, but about the *rules* that define investors' ability to shape how states will regulate investors' property rights and obligations. Given state power in international relations and law, we find that they are well-placed to define the rules (Galanter 1974).

Like other contributors to this volume, we find empirical support for the theory that mobilizations of particular legal meanings in property create concomitant sites of "meaning-making". New legal protections open up spaces for new types of claims, which, in turn, change the configuration of a particular legal regime anew (see Becher this volume and Hatcher this volume). Similarly, akin to Henderson (this volume), we suggest that the neoliberal propertization of assets does not merely engender ideological struggles over the rights to objectified things, such as radio spectrums and investments, but over the balance of power in particular social relationships constituted through things. Ultimately, like in regulatory takings cases and libertarian property mobilizations, we suggest that what is at stake in the micro-political dynamics of foreign investment disputes is the shaping of not only law but new structures of sovereignty The case of NAFTA is one wherein the state has been successful in maintaining regulatory authority vis-à-vis private investors. This suggests that neoliberal state transformations do not merely elevate property interests at the expense of state power, but occur and maintain state power through and despite the politics of property legal disputing.

In this chapter we question the extent to which state sovereignty is disciplined by a rule-based transnational legal regime, such as NAFTA Chapter 11. The legal disciplining of states in an era of globalization is a common conclusion in scholarship on international and transnational legal regimes as well as NAFTA scholarship (Raustiala 2003, Cutler 2001, McBride 2006). As others have argued, however, state sovereignties and their transformation need to be studied through a framework that considers the new ways in which the state manages and performs "sovereignty" (Gill 1989, Schneiderman 2008, Sinha 2006, Mitchell 1991). Building on this perspective, our theoretical argument suggests that investor property rights mobilizations challenging state regulation in transnational tribunals – "law-in-action" – perform and produce the meaning of sovereignty associated with neoliberal globalism. In other words, NAFTA is not simply a terrain where sovereignty is necessarily won or lost. Rather we suggest, based on our empirical data, that NAFTA's Chapter 11 Tribunal is a juridical institutional site where new regulatory parameters and cultures are forged through disputes between states and private investors.

Part I of this chapter discusses how NAFTA's Chapter 11 legality was designed to create an ostensibly transnational legal framework privileging foreign investment by giving foreign investors unprecedented rights of standing at the international level (Gantz 2006). We then turn, in Part II, to an interpretative account of the legal and political controversies investors bring to arbitration, as well as the transnational institution's decisions about the meaning of this juridical regime. Our analysis considers the population of disputes that have generated a Tribunal decision – 15 cases out of a total of 45 as of December 2007. Other filed cases were either dropped (a little over 25 percent of the cases) or are still pending. In the cases we analyze, investors targeted all three countries who are party to the treaty type of claims. We trace the contours of these disputes to understand and explain the jurisprudential development of investors' access to regulatory processes and state regulatory sovereignty over time.

The NAFTA Dispute System

Unlike the World Trade Organization (WTO) where disputing is state-state, the NAFTA Chapter 11 disputing framework is an investor-state arbitral forum.[2] NAFTA's Chapter 11 framework was pulled directly from the US bilateral investment regime (BITs). These treaties between developed and developing countries proliferated since the 1980s and provide standing for investors to bring claims against states through investor-state arbitration. Like BITs, NAFTA Chapter 11 protects foreign investment interests from state expropriation by a developing country, such as Mexico, with a history of contentious nationalizations (Been and Beauvais 2003).

However, NAFTA is a multi-lateral, rather than a bilateral treaty, and it was the first to incorporate investor-state arbitration. It was also the first treaty signed between two developed countries that gives foreign investors standing in a transnational arbitral tribunal (Been and Beauvais 2003). For example, under Chapter 11, US and Canadian investors can bring suits against their US and Canadian host states. In this way, cross-border FDI investors can challenge regulations enacted by developed host states just as northern capital can make claims against developing states.[3] As such, the rules for the protection of foreign investment apply to all three countries. All states have been targets for cross-border foreign investors.

Procedurally, NAFTA Chapter 11's adjudicatory framework employs existing institutional structures of arbitration, i.e., the International Center for the Settlement of Investment Disputes (ICSID) and the United Nations Convention on Trade Law (UNCITRAL). Under NAFTA, arbitration is compulsory, meaning that states do not have to consent to the arbitration. Similarly, the awards arc binding under the 1958 New York Convention on the Recognition and Enforcement of Foreign Arbitral Awards (McBride 2006).

After signing NAFTA, each state established a "NAFTA secretariat" in their home country. Investors submit their intent to file a claim against a state to a

2 Chapter 20 of NAFTA provides for state-state disputes.

3 In 1996, US total FDI investment in Canada was $85.4 billion while Canadian investment was $54.6 billion. In 2006, US investment had reached $250 billion, and while Canadian FDI had reached $160 billion (Bureau of Economic Analysis, http://www.bea.gov/international/di1fdibal.htm). Thus, in the 10 year period US FDI increased 2.93 times, while Canadian investments increased at the same rate.

country's secretariat under Article 1119. However, these offices maintain very loose control over Chapter 11 disputes because the actual procedures are controlled by the World Bank ICSID "Additional Facility"[4] rules, and/or the arbitration rules of the UNCITRAL.

Each state has a designated office that handles NAFTA Chapter 11 disputes. The Canadian office is in the Department of Foreign Affairs and International Trade. In the US, the Office of International Claims and Investment Disputes in the Office of the Legal Advisor at the US Department of State is responsible for managing NAFTA challenges. In Mexico, the Department of International Negotiations in the Ministry of Commerce and Development controls the Mexican defense [5]

When a claim goes to arbitration, states maintain two procedural mechanisms for shaping adjudication, to defend themselves against claims brought by market actors. The first is found in Article 1128 of Chapter 11, which says that states can make submissions to the Tribunal on questions of legal interpretation. The second is found in Article 1131, which says that the Free Trade Commission can promulgate binding interpretations of NAFTA law to the Tribunal. The Free Trade Commission is established by NAFTA, comprises the trade minister of Canada, the US Trade Representative, and the Secretary for Trade and Industrial Development from Mexico, and meets once a year. Essentially this Article incorporated into NAFTA what the Vienna Convention of the Law of Treaties already specified, namely that subsequent "agreements" among parties becomes a part of the treaty law its enforcers must apply (McBride 2006).

We will suggest below that state use of adjudicative procedures in Article 1131 and 1128, enables state participation in crafting NAFTA, and thus defending themselves against regulatory takings claims. The legal-ideological struggles between investors and states, which are using Article 1131 and 1128 procedures, reshape the meaning of property and sovereignty in NAFTA.

Jurisprudential Struggles and Development

Our analysis of NAFTA Chapter 11 analyzes investors' adversarial claims and strategies of states' defense over time. It approaches and unpacks what other scholars have seen as an aggressive, investor-driven process by assessing not only the material, but the relational aspects of the regulatory takings claims that investors have brought to the tribunal (Been and Beauvais 2003, Schneiderman 2000 63–7) over time.

In contrast to other authors' views of NAFTA that have focused upon the broad definition of property in Chapter 11, we view the expansiveness of claims as part

4 Neither Canada nor Mexico is party to the ICSID Convention; thus the arbitration occurs according to the ICSID "Additional Facility" Rules, where only one disputant need be a party.

5 See www.nafta-sec-alena.org/DefaultSite/index.html.

of the "adversarial legalism" NAFTA investor-state arbitration established. By adversarial legalism we refer to what Kagan (2001) has described as the "formal legal contestation, litigant activism" characteristic of de-centered "common law" type litigation (Kagan 2001: 12). In this sense, we argue that NAFTA did not merely establish investors' rights, it exported to the transnational level a particular litigation style apt to constitute new kinds of justice claims. The aggressive litigation surrounding regulatory takings we now see taking place in NAFTA is related to the adversarial legalism that permeates many aspects of American law and lawyering. Similar to the US environment where litigation within the administrative state is constituted by "complex legal rules concerning public notice and comment, restrictions on ex parte and other informal contacts with decisionmakers" (Kagan 2001: 12), NAFTA claimants are now bringing such procedural claims to the transnational level. The structural features of US administrative law are helping foreign investors make particular types of procedural claims upon the state, such as rights to participate in local regulatory processes. While successful at first, such claims are increasingly foreclosed through state struggles to narrow the NAFTA Tribunal's interpretations over time.

The failure of many investors' claims is occurring because adversarialism is relational. Thus, it is not a foregone conclusion that new treaty protections will result in greater investors' "rights." How states respond to such claims, and how they manage them through legal ideological strategies is central. This form of activity is not necessarily a new one for states, as agencies charged with defending the government interest, such as the Office of International Claims and Investment Disputes at the US State Department have long participated in international arbitrations. Nonetheless, what is perhaps new is that such agencies are now participating in activity that bears not only upon affording investors compensation when they are affected by state action, but in defending the procedural practices of the administrative and regulatory state from investors' adversarial claims. Such activity, when successful as it has been in NAFTA, enables the reconsolidation of sovereignty's meaning in the transnational plane (Harrington and Turem 2006).

Corporate investors have pushed for judicial review of administrative regulations and procedures in all three countries that affect their property rights claims. In many of the cases investors have found the protection of their investment interests to be consistent with and contingent upon making procedural participatory legal arguments. They seek greater access to the particular domestic regulation regimes as a way to ensure that their assets will not be unduly affected by such sovereign measures, often times legitimating regulation for noncommercial purposes that affect foreign investors' access to the domestic market (Howse 1999). Clearly from the investors' claims, access to regulatory processes is one of the ways in which they understand what having economic citizenship in foreign territory entails (Schneiderman 2008: 74). Access to the regulatory process is valued as a means to influence domestic regulatory standards in much the same way as domestic parties assert their interests. Investors thus push for the most expansive interpretation of the provisions, attempting to penetrate domestic administrative procedure itself (Vasciannie 1999).

After investors began to make procedural arguments in an attempt to penetrate administrative state processes, states changed their form of participation in the adjudications. States have come to use Article 1128 of Chapter 11 vigorously and utilized Article 1131 once. In Article 1128, the government parties submitting these briefs are the *same* parties as "respondents" in other cases (when they are filed against their own governments). All three departments who normally defend their governments' claims participate in this written practice, using the submissions to lay out their subjective position on the law. This has produced a running conversation among state parties that is mutually supportive and aimed to limit the reach of investors' claims. It has also shown to the Tribunal that the governments are united when they are the "audience" in the disputes, ultimately allowing them to shape legal outcomes (Mather and Yngvesson 1980). These arguments were eventually echoed in a Free Trade Commission interpretation of NAFTA treaty standards, which did not stop investors from making procedural participatory arguments, but did alter the legal struggles somewhat.

Through both Articles 1128 and 1131, states have endeavored to *narrow* the applicability of the NAFTA investment protections and expand their own administrative and regulatory power. This can be most clearly seen in the conflict that has emerged over Articles 1105 and 1102. Article 1105 NAFTA has been termed NAFTA's "due process" article by Been and Beauvais (2003). Article 1105 reads: "Each Party shall accord to investments of investors of another Party treatment in accordance with international law, including fair and equitable treatment and full protection and security" (NAFTA Article 1105(1)). This particular legal construction brings together international law norms regulating state treatment of foreign property, historically embedded in the law of nations, with newer legal norms originating in bilateral investment treaties. Article 1102 ensures that foreign investors will be treated akin to domestic parties. As investors have used both to make processual and procedural claims against states, states have argued that neither affords participation rights in the regulatory process to foreign investors.

We now consider the adversarial style of investor litigation as it emerged over time. Significantly, the Article 1128 practice was only used by the US after the *Metalclad* case in 2000, and became more frequent as investors and tribunals challenged Canadian and US regulations. Thus, a powerful "audience" to the ensuing disputes only emerged when developed countries, presumed to have "rule of law" investment protections, were confronted with claims that their administrative and regulatory procedures had violated NAFTA standards. As such, we label the following two sections "the jurisprudence of access" and "the jurisprudence of state regulatory sovereignty" to capture the initial adjudications, when states (Mexico and Canada) were unsuccessful in defending the claims against them, and to capture the new normative framework produced after states redefined the parameters of property rights disputing.

The Jurisprudence of Access: Investors' Right to Participate in State Regulatory Proceedings, 1996–2001

It was in the *Metalclad* case, filed in 1996 and decided in 2000, that claimants first sought compensation for perceived material losses arising from public regulations in a tribunal constituted under NAFTA Chapter 11. Like cases that would later ensue, the regulations they challenged were ostensibly based upon legitimate public interest grounds; however, claimants developed specific procedural arguments to make their case to the Tribunal that Mexico had violated its NAFTA obligations. At the core of the waste company's claim was the fact that they had not been given access to the administrative process, and that the process itself was colored by corruption and collusion between the local government and domestic waste companies. In regards to the former, they articulated two arguments. First, "the absence of any established practice or procedure as to the manner of handling applications for a municipal construction permit" was a violation of their due process expectations under Article 1105 of NAFTA. Second, they argued that they were denied notice and hearing in two processes: 1) the town council meeting where the municipal permit was discussed; and 2) when the governor and coordinator of environment in San Luis Potosí passed an ordinance designating Metalclad's waste disposal site an ecological preserve (Investor's Memorial, *Metalclad* 135). In regards to their argument that an aura of corruption shrouded the entire process, they asserted that the governor conferred with local domestic waste managers without consulting the foreign waste company. That they had been denied compensation, they contended, constituted expropriation under Article 1110. In order to prove that the regulations were indeed expropriatory, however, they argued that decisions were made in the absence of due process. Here, they relied on Article 1105 of NAFTA: "the absence of due process and fair and equitable treatment join an equally harmful denial of rights in the failure of any fair market value compensation" (Investor's Memorial, *Metalclad* 163).

The three arbitrators in the Tribunal awarded the US company almost $17 million as compensation to the company for the economic losses they incurred at the hands of Mexican administration and officials.[6] The *Metalclad* tribunal found that Mexico had violated several of the provisions of NAFTA Chapter 11, including the international law protection of foreign investment in Article 1105, and the expropriation provision in Article 1110. The decision intimated that the investors' rights under Article 1105 had been violated because investors had rights to a transparent process, rights that had not been afforded in this case. The Tribunal stipulated that "Metalclad was not notified of the town council meeting where the permit application was discussed and rejected, nor was Metalclad given any opportunity to participate in that process (*Metalclad v. United Mexican States* 17). Furthermore, according to the Tribunal, the municipality that had issued the

6 Although, when Mexico appealed the decision in a British Columbian Court, the award was reduced.

challenged regulations had not given any consideration to the construction permit as "there was no evidence that there was an established process with respect to municipal construction" (*Metalclad v. United Mexican States*, 22).

Interestingly, in this adjudication both the US and Canada exercised their Article 1128 right to participate in the process; yet, unlike future submissions, their arguments at this time were silent regarding the investors' efforts to claim rights to notice and hearing. Furthermore, unlike subsequent adjudications where both the US and Canada would submit several briefs apiece, in *Metalclad* each country only submitted one document to the Tribunal (US and Canada Article 1128 submissions, *Metalclad v. United Mexican States*).

At the time of the decision, US investors had also filed three cases against Canada, and Canadian investors had filed four against the United States. One case, *SD Myers v. Government of Canada* (2001) was decided shortly thereafter against Canada and in favor of the investor. Like in the *Metalclad* case, the US investor, a hazardous waste disposal company, argued that Canadian regulations had been developed without adequate procedures. For example, they contended that in making waste disposal regulations Canada did not "provide fair administrative hearings, administrative due process, and independent review of these hearings." The investor argued that the regulations had included "covert" meetings between the Minister of the Environment and lobbyists from Canadian processors of hazardous waste (Investor's Memorial, *SD Myers* 58). The corporation argued that Canada had willfully not consulted its representatives when making the regulations, giving domestic investors greater entrée while denying them fair access to the regulatory process, violating Article 1102 (national treatment) and Article 1105 (due process) (Investor's Memorial, *SD Myers* 53).

Unlike in *Metaclad,* the Tribunal did not go so far as to find that Canadian regulations had constituted expropriation. Instead, they concluded that Canada had violated Articles 1105 and 1102, or its obligation to accord foreign investors the "minimum standard of treatment" under international law and to treat foreign investors in a nondiscriminatory fashion. They reasoned (akin to *Metalclad*) that international law included certain procedural and participatory protections throughout the regulatory process. Moreover, the Tribunal found that the regulatory issuances had been promulgated in a manner that contravened Canada's treaty obligations under NAFTA because they privileged domestic investors to the disadvantage of foreign investment in the rule-making process. The *SD Myers* tribunal reasoned that Article 1105 enabled them to judge discriminatory administrative action on due process grounds, which included the investor's expectation to be included in the regulatory process (Partial Award, *SD Myers* 58–67).

Throughout this litigation, Mexico made three Article 1128 submissions while the US wrote one. Again, the US was silent on the participatory arguments of the investors, although one Mexico submission did address the investors' participatory claims. Mexico stated that it agreed with Canada's interpretation and defense in the case, which strongly argued that there was no state obligation to consult with investors throughout the regulatory processes.

Following the *Metalclad* and *SD Myers* cases, states, particularly the US, began to engage more vigorously in defining the meaning of NAFTA standards. States were attempting to stop investors from making participatory arguments and to regain sovereign discretionary powers in regulation. An interpretive struggle thus occurred over the meaning of Articles 1105 and 1102, strategically mobilized by states in response to investors' claims. However, this conflict was not only waged at the level of language and doctrine, it also utilized an increased and different mode of participation. The states' role shifted from merely that of respondent to include that of "audience." Here, the US and Canada began to demonstrate that they had interests in the legal definitions and outcomes of particular cases beyond the immediate dispute. We first observe a stepped up level of state participation in the *Pope & Talbot v. Canada* (2000) case, where US investors again argued that Canada breached its treaty obligations in the regulatory process. Here, the investors asserted that such a breach occurred as Canada developed quotas for the fee-free export of lumber to the US and allotted *Pope & Talbot* a decreasing share in comparison to Canadian companies. Like the two previous cases, *Pope & Talbot* made procedural and participatory claims to challenge the state regulations. They argued that they had not been a) permitted to have a fair hearing in respect to their quota allocation; b) informed of the process governing the allocation of quotas; c) given reasons for their declining share of the quota; and d) given a chance to participate in a review procedure (Statement of Claim of Investor, *Pope & Talbot* 26–28 and Memorial of Investor, *Pope & Talbot* 73-90). *Pope & Talbot* and counsel claimed that they had been left out of the regulatory process in violation of Articles 1102 and 1105 of NAFTA, as the meaning of national treatment and fair and equitable treatment gave them equal access to regulatory procedure as domestic parties.

Before the *Pope & Talbot* tribunal issued its decision, Mexico submitted six Article 1128 briefs, while the US submitted eight. Three of the US submissions directly related to the legal standard in Article 1105 governing Pope & Talbot's procedural claims. The US wrote, "Article 1105's provision for 'treatment in accordance with international law, *including* fair and equitable treatment' clearly states the primacy of customary international law" (Fourth Submission of the United States of America, *Pope & Talbot, Inc. v. Government of Canada* 2). They further stipulated that this entails a complete separation of Article 1105 from other provisions in NAFTA (such as Article 1102) and that it is a standard on its own, not a category to be applied to judge state behavior in the regulatory process. At the heart of this doctrinal argument was their effort to stymie the investor's claims. For customary international law was the baseline minimum standard of protection a state needed to afford investors, and did not historically include participatory standards in the regulatory process. Mexico's submissions took similar positions, contending, in particular, that states do not have an international responsibility to give foreign investors rights in the regulatory process (Submissions of Mexico, *Pope & Talbot, Inc. v. Government of Canada*).

The *Pope & Talbot* tribunal did not find that Canada had violated the administrative fairness "rights" of the investor, as the corporation charged. They did, however, find that Canada had breached fairness notions more broadly – namely, it had treated the investors with overall "bellicosity" and had caused the investors great trouble in time and money by making it difficult for them to participate in the regulatory process. The Tribunal based its decision on a legal interpretation of "fair and equitable" treatment as additive to the international minimum. They reasoned, "investors under NAFTA are entitled to the international law minimum, *plus* the fairness elements" (Award on the Merits, *Pope & Talbot v. Canada* 48). They came to this decision by accepting the investors' arguments that fairness included certain procedural expectations in regulatory processes such as notice and participation (ibid. 49).

The Jurisprudence of State Regulatory Sovereignty, 2002–2007

During July 2001, and in response to tribunal rulings disfavoring states and giving investors procedural claims to the regulatory process through property disputes, the Free Trade Commission (FTC) issued a formal statement to all the tribunals regarding the "fair and equitable treatment" standard and the "minimum standard of treatment in international law." FTC defined the minimum standard of treatment as "the customary law standard," a term not in the original NAFTA text. They further specified that the "fair and equitable treatment" standard is subsumed within the "minimum standard of treatment in international law". "Fair and equitable", the FTC wrote, refers only to the customary international law standard for the treatment of aliens "as the minimum standard of treatment to be afforded to investments of investors of another party" (Letter from Principal Counsel, Trade Law Division to Chapter 11 Tribunals, August 10, 2001, http://www.dfait-maeci.gc.ca/tna-nac/phases-en.asp#comm). The FTC's argument thus implied that access to the regulatory process was not included in a state's NAFTA obligations as the historical customary standard did not include such participatory rights.

Investors did not curtail their aggressive claims vis-à-vis Article 1105, as a result of the FTC issuance, however. In two subsequent cases private investors brought against the US, they continued to push for regulatory participation rights (*ADF Group v. United States*). Despite the fact that the tribunal accepted the FTC interpretation[7] which effectively narrowed the scope of Article 1105, investors' claims attempted to bypass this understanding. Thus, states had to continue to argue NAFTA did not include foreign investor participation in the regulatory process.

7 In *Mondev*, the first case to be decided following the official statement, the Tribunal reasoned that they could not simply impose their own standard of "fair and equitable" treatment; thus they reasoned that Article 1105 refers to the "customary international law standard".

In *ADF Group v. United States* (2003), a Canadian-based company argued that the US Federal Trade Commission's rule-making procedures had been, in the area of federal procurement guidelines, discretionary and contrary to NAFTA. ADF Group argued that the US regulatory process had not been transparent or accessible to them (Investor's Memorial, *ADF Group*, 59–60). In order to make this processual and participatory claim, ADF Group argued that the fair and equitable standard in Article 1105 included the right to participate in the regulatory process. Even if the FTC, states, and the Tribunal conceptualized the fair and equitable as emanating from but not additive to the customary international law standard, they reasoned, states' claims to the contrary, the customary international law standard did in fact include regulatory participation rights. They justified this claim by arguing that at the time NAFTA was signed, the customary standard included several thousand bilateral investment treaties which include a high level of protection for foreign investment, especially vis-à-vis administrative and executive organs. They challenged states' arguments that the customary international law standard is a longstanding set of norms that pre-dates the BITs associated with global investment protections (Post-Hearing Submission of the Claimant ADF Group on NAFTA Article 1105: 8). Thus, investors offered the Tribunal a set of legal arguments in support of regulatory participation, despite the FTC rulings that had attempted to foreclose such claims.

In response to this aggressive claim made against the US government by a Canadian corporation, the Canadian and Mexican governments separately submitted Article 1128 briefs explaining their position on the matter. Each submitted twice on the subject of Article 1105. Both Canada and Mexico agreed "with the submissions of the US to this Tribunal" that an investor cannot argue successfully that fair and equitable treatment standard requires a state to treat it above the minimum treatment in international law. Thus, there are no rights to participate in domestic regulatory processes.

Ultimately, the Tribunal was persuaded by the US arguments and the other two state submissions. The Tribunal ruled that fair and equitable treating is subsumed to customary international law, which does not include investor access to regulatory processes. ADF Group's claim that the US breached NAFTA treaty standards faltered. The Tribunal further stated that the US measures were not to be considered arbitrary or unjust in international law because "something more" than discretionary rule-making procedures was necessary to prove a breach of customary international law under NAFTA (ibid. 94). What this "something more" was, the Tribunal left unspecified. Importantly, their decision departed from past NAFTA Tribunal rulings. They no longer used "fair and equitable treatment" broadly as a means to review states' regulatory procedures based upon investors' participatory claims. State interpretations of the NAFTA standards were shaping the Tribunal's reasoning.

The next case was slightly different in scope than the *ADF Group* case, as it challenged local state law and policy-making processes rather than federal agency procedures. *Methanex v. United States* (2006), like its predecessor, challenged state regulations on participation grounds. The regulations in question were a 1999 California Executive Order and a subsequent Senate bill 521, which the Canadian company (Methanex) argued were protectionist in nature. Methanex manufactured MBTE, a methanol-based gasoline additive. The Senate Bill banned MBTE, favoring another gasoline additive, ethanol. Methanex consequently argued that the Bill was designed to favor their domestic competitors in the ethanol business. Methanex argued that they were being pushed out of the gasoline additive market. They asserted "the ethanol lobby instigated the California ban" on methanol on a pretext of environmentalism, since the ethanol lobby had "undue influence" in California politics (quoted in *Methanex v. Government of United States* 223). In making their claim, they characterized the procedures leading to the regulations as "arbitrary, grossly unfair, unjust, and idiosyncratic." Further, Methanex argued that they had experienced discrimination in the law-making process because they were a foreign investor (Second Amendment of Claim 205). Methanex maintained that they should have had greater access to state law-making processes akin to domestic parties, and that these processes also needed to be transparent.

Both Canada and Mexico filed four Article 1128 submissions each in this case. Two Canadian and two Mexican briefs made arguments pertaining to Article 1105. They asserted that, as long as regulatory measures were in accordance with international legal norms, they did not include expectations or rights to access in the local law-making processes (Article 1128 Submissions of Canada and Mexico, *Methanex v. United States*).

The Tribunal agreed with the states. The Tribunal found that "the plain and natural meaning of the text of Article 1105 does not support the contention that the minimum standard of treatment precludes governmental differentiations as between nationals and aliens" (*Methanex v. Government of United States* 269). They reasoned that the "customary" international law standard makes clear that "in the absence of a contrary rule of international law binding on state parties, whether of conventional or customary origin, a state may differentiate in its treatment of nationals and aliens" (ibid.) in regulatory processes.

While both *ADF Group and Methanex* cases included the US as respondent, other cases filed, such as one against Mexico, also applied the narrowed standards and resulted in state wins. In *Waste Management II v. United Mexican States* (2004), the Tribunal did not rule in favor of a US investor's claim that the City of Acapulco did not follow proper procedures when it cancelled Waste Management Corporation's Mexican subsidiary, Acaverde's concession agreement with the city (*Investor's Memorial, Waste Management II v. United Mexican States*, 16). While the company argued that the government's failure to provide notice in writing prior to rescinding the concession constituted a lack of due process of law under Article 1105, and led to measures that were "tantamount to expropriation," the Tribunal applied the narrowed interpretation of Article 1105 and ruled that the Mexican action was not arbitrary and unjust under the customary international legal standard.

Conclusion

Ultimately our interpretive analysis has demonstrated the paradoxical legal dynamics in property disputing within neoliberal globalism and transnational investment law. States manage the process of transnational disputing and their treaty obligations by engaging in forms of dispute participation that narrow the meaning of property claims. In this sense, they can impose new normative frameworks (Mather and Yngvesson, 1980 1: 775) upon investment friendly regimes and circumvent the property claims investors seek to impose upon them.

The story of NAFTA's jurisprudential development demonstrates that non-market sovereign regulatory discretion can be re-legitimated and reconsolidated through property rights disputing. Mobilization of property norms and values does not *a priori* result in the vindication of the meanings property owners attribute to the "bundle of rights" associated with their investments. In fact, new meanings emerge producing the relational framework between public and private parties in global neoliberalism.

PART III
Bureaucratic Legality, Conflict, and the Meaning of Property

Chapter 8
The Limits of *Kelo*: Bureaucratic Legality and Adversarial Conflict in Land Use Regulation[1]

Richard A. Brisbin, Jr., Susan Hunter, and Kevin M. Leyden

Fed by media and interest group hyperbole, the Supreme Court decision on the scope of state and local eminent domain powers in *Kelo v. City of New London* (2005) aroused a fear of big government kicking people out of their homes (Wolf 2008). As with policies such as affirmative action, people sense that government is stripping them of possessions and power and redistributing their hard earned benefits to others. What this frenzied public behavior ignores is that appellate court takings rulings about regulatory takings are but the visible tip of the iceberg of American land use and real property policy. In this chapter we posit that interest group ideological activism and appellate adjudication of governmental land use takings since the 1980s, such as the *Kelo* case, and subsequent changes in state eminent domain law have had limited influence on how political institutions commonly regulate American real property. Instead, political institutions seldom face neoliberal group litigation about the broad range of decisions that affect the use of private property.

To an extent the relative absence of neoliberal arguments is a function of the legal and institutional context of common place property regulation. Neoliberal interest group challenges to takings use the discourse of property "rights" to assert government regulation and regulatory taking of land is a transgression of moral principles of justice, an interference with the natural freedom of persons, and a subversion of the natural operations of markets.[2] However, much more commonly government and private parties frame or constitute property as a private legal "interest" or a preference for land that lacks moral connotations.[3] With property

1 The authors thank the Office of the Dean, Eberly College of Arts and Sciences, West Virginia University, for support of this project and David Sikes for research assistance.

2 The definition of neoliberalism used here relies on Rose (1996).

3 Property as interest thus recognizes it is an *entitlement to a possession* originally acquired under statutory law from the government by purchase of a portion of the public domain (or colonial royal domain), occupied under the provisions of a preemption statute, or devised to a private party by a government grant. American governments also have supported the acquisition of an interest in property by statutory and common law

framed as an interest, people assume a duty not just to protect their interest in property, but they expect other persons to treat their property interest in a socially responsible manner. To prevent disorderly uses of property, such as the creation of nuisances and dangers to the health, safety, and morality of other property owners and the broader public, governments can police its use (Alexander 1997, Novak 1996). Especially politically appointed local government officials on planning commissions and boards of zoning appeals can pragmatically regulate land use to either protect a vested interest in property or decide which interests of competing private property owners should prevail. Their choices frequently address a conflict between property owners. On one side are property owners who fear a diminishment of their interest in the value of their property and whose attitude toward land use change is "not in my backyard." On the other side are those owners who would put land or buildings to new uses in the interest of profits or personal pleasure (Hunter and Leyden 1995). On occasion persons or groups with an interest in civic improvement, historical preservation, or community aesthetics also might enter into conflicts with some property owners or developers. Unlike the situation presented in Supreme Court litigation on takings, this situation creates a role for government officials as a broker rather than as an adversary of property owners.

In serving as brokers, local policymakers design land use plans, consider claims for adjustments in their plans, make choices on the claims at administrative hearings, or consider appeals about the choices made by other officials who participate in land use policy making. Legality or the texts of law, the history of their institutional interpretation and enforcement, and widespread popular understandings of law and legal practices, control the range of these regulatory choices (Ewick and Silbey 1998: 22). Although the conduct of routine land use policy decisions may be constituted more as a question of interest than rights, the presence of regulatory legality opens the door to litigation. Robert Kagan (2000: 9–11, 2001: 9–14) has argued that regulatory policy making and implementation, such as the design and management of the legal landscape, is adversarial and subject to *legal contestation*—of legal rules, procedures, and rights—and *litigant activism*—the assertion of legal claims and the presentation of evidence to courts and other adjudicatory institutions—to advantage their economic, political, or social interests. If Kagan is correct, we should expect that persons frequently mobilize the law by engaging in litigation to contest the decisions of regulatory bodies. Also there should be litigant activism and legal pressure on the regulatory bodies. This pressure might come from organized interests, such as the property rights interest groups described in the chapters of this book written by Laura Hatcher, David Wilkerson, and David Schultz. Finally, there should be evidence that the pressure affects the land use regulators. Therefore going beyond appellate

provisions that protect property titles and transactions, tax subsidies, exemptions, and deductions for home and farm owners, loan programs for the purchase of property, support of the private mortgage market, and the construction of infrastructure that provides access and value to land.

eminent domain litigation, we explore the question: How and to what extent does adversarial legal action, employing either the discourse of rights or interest, affect the broad range of regulatory policies that configure the American landscape?

Hypotheses

The literature on American land use regulation commonly emphasizes that it is a conflict-ridden process that features adversarial legal battles (Babcock 1966, Babcock and Simeon 1985). However, it might be that the truth is nearer to Rutherford Platt's (1996: 41) observation that, "Very few land use disputes actually reach the courts and even fewer are appealed by the losing party to a higher ('appellate') court." As described in the chapter by Debbie Becher in this volume, people mobilize and challenge local land use policies without entering into adversarial litigation. Therefore, we first hypothesize that—in land use policy making—goal-seeking individuals and interests infrequently employ adversarial litigation or mobilize to file lawsuits. Instead, the process might better fit what Kagan (2001: 10–11) defined as *bureaucratic legalism* or "uniform implementation of centrally devised rules, vertical accountability, and official responsibility for fact-finding," often with a "restricted role for legal representation and influence by affected citizens or contending interests." Our second hypothesis asserts that there is little evidence that land use decision makers fear adversarial legal action as a threat to their regulations and practices. They do not experience neoliberal ideological interest group pressure on their decision making. Our third hypothesis is that legality nonetheless constrains the range of choices made by land use decision makers. It provides behavioral norms, defines who can participate in land use decisions, and bounds the range of choices that participants consider. Together these hypotheses contend that Americans see land use issues through a legal lens, but they infrequently enter into ideologically grounded adversarial legal actions about land use policies.

Data Collection

To examine our hypotheses we combine observation, interview, and survey data. Observations of planning commission and zoning board decision making and interviews with planners took place in the cities of Hagerstown, Maryland, Washington, Pennsylvania, and Morgantown, West Virginia and the counties of Washington, Maryland and Harrison, Jefferson, and Marion, West Virginia. Maryland has a "smart growth" statute that is designed to control urban sprawl by the imposition of state standards on local planning and infrastructure development and state agency intervention in certain local land use actions (Cohen 2002). The other states leave land use policy principally under local governmental auspices. Harrison and Marion counties and Washington, Pennsylvania are economically depressed communities that have experienced a decline in industrial economies based on steel, chemical, and glass production and coal mining. Hagerstown and Morgantown are older commercial and industrial cities rapidly adjusting to an expanding services-based and light industrial economy. Jefferson and Washington counties are at the western fringe of the Baltimore-Washington, DC metropolitan region. Developers have undertaken or proposed large subdivisions in these counties, which are experiencing rapid population growth.

We also sent a brief questionnaire with questions about land use law and litigation to a random sample of 390 municipal and county chief planners or persons with similar duties across the United States. Respondents returned 125 questionnaires for a response rate of 32.1 percent. Although we rely on a small number of responses, we believe that the initial pattern of responses provides support for the reliability of the conclusions we draw from the observations. Respondents represented communities ranging in population from 3,000 to 1,500,000 residents (mean=149,645). Of the respondents, 72.0 percent worked for a municipality, 18.4 percent for a county, 8.8 percent for a joint city-county agency, and 0.8 percent for a regional agency. The wording of all questions used in this analysis can be found in Appendix 1.

Mobilization

Our first hypothesis is that in land use policy making individuals and interests employ a bureaucratic legalism that allows the avoidance of adversarial litigation. In large measure the infrequent mobilization of litigation to challenge officials' decisions is a result of institutional procedures and practice. Local officials consider public views and concerns when making policy, and they employ an administrative process that provides procedures to address claims and resolve grievances and disputes. Property owners have to utilize the administrative process before they can litigate. They must petition for administrative legal action about proposed changes in the use of real property prior to challenges in court.

Procedures that Dissuade Litigation

American land use policy making is largely a responsibility of municipal and county governments. The role of federal and state governments, although increasing since the 1970s, remains restricted. Local governments cannot regulate federal land holdings, and local land use law must comport with several federal laws aimed at protecting public goods.[4] A few states have legislated restrictions and oversight

4 These laws include the Coastal Barrier Resources Act, Coastal Zone Management Act, Clean Air Act, as amended, Clean Water Act, Endangered Species Act, Energy Independence and Security Act, Fair Housing Act, Food Security Act, Housing and Urban Development Act, Marine Protection, Research and Sanctuaries Act, National Environmental

of aspects of local land use planning and land policy implementation in an effort to control urbanization and the environmental consequences of development of forests, mountain heights, and seacoasts. Related legislation designed to manage growth exists in several states (Cullingworth 1993: 133–55, Cullingworth 1997: 136–51, Gale 1992, Knaap and Nelson 1992, Landis 2006). Also, states govern aspects of law through construction codes, fair housing laws, farmland protection acts, environmental protection laws, and development management acts, and they have established state or regional authorities to conserve land, provide parks and conservation areas, and manage coastal and riverfront lands (Platt 1996: 345–66). Some local governments have enacted architectural and historic preservation codes. Finally, local land use policymakers often find that federal and state grants for infrastructure can significantly affect their ability to plan and to respond to demands for changes in land use.

Because they are based on the model Standard Zoning Enabling Act and State Planning Enabling Act developed by the United States Department of Commerce's Advisory Commission on Zoning in 1926 and 1927, most local land use decisions today feature a similar institutional process (Cullingworth 1997: 56–63, Platt 1996: 234–35). The first is a local planning commission, which is frequently a part time politically appointed or volunteer body composed of citizens without special training in land use law or professional planning. Its task is to propose or amend legislation that defines how land can be used in its locality. The members of the commission rely on public input at hearings, other contacts with the public and developers, and, often, the expertise of its professional planner, its planning office, or private consultants to devise a comprehensive land use plan. With the plan as a guide they then will propose a zoning ordinance describing land use in areas or zones and a map with zones or geographical areas dedicated to a specific form of land use. Proposals for zoning must be enacted as law by a local legislature such as a city council or county commission. This legislative body can also amend planning commission proposals. Our observations and interviews indicate that, for political reasons such as electoral support, goals of civic improvement, or responsiveness to community organizations such as neighborhood or landlord associations or chambers of commerce, the local legislators will sporadically address very specific concerns about how the law will influence economic development or neighborhood stability in selected areas of their jurisdiction. The public can appear and comment on the proposed ordinance at public hearings or through informal communications to the councilors. Rarely the council will adopt an ordinance to phase out nonconforming uses, a policy called "amortization." The local legislative body usually entrusts the implementation of the zoning

---

Policy Act, National Flood Insurance Act, Flood Disaster Protection Act, National Trails System Act, Resource, Conservation, and Recovery Act, Comprehensive Environmental and Response, Compensation, and Recovery Act, Surface Mining Control and Reclamation Act, and Wild and Scenic Rivers Act. The federal government also requires the creation of metropolitan planning commissions to establish transportation plans for urban areas.

or land use ordinance to a building or code enforcement bureau or officer. The planning commission approves petitioners' proposals for new construction, including construction of structures on land taken for economic development. Remodeling plans must receive permits from this office. If the office determines that a proposal does not comply with the zoning or land use ordinance and cannot receive a permit, the person or corporation sponsoring the proposal has the option to seek a "variance." To obtain a variance the sponsor files a request with the local board of zoning appeals or adjustment (BZA). The BZA often has the authority to permit "conditional uses" also. Conditional use allows a lawful land use to be subject—possibly—to later review to ensure it has not had an adverse effect. Under the law of most states, general public notice and specific written notice to adjoining property owners about the variance or conditional use request must be given. Acting as an administrative adjudicatory forum, BZA members consider the written proposal, comments about it from the planner or planning office staff, and oral and written testimony from the sponsor and other interested or opposing parties at an administrative hearing. It may then grant or deny the variance request, which effectively adjusts the policy and rules contained in the zoning or land use ordinance. In theory and design this process is both representative and democratic. The institutional setting allows for direct public input, commentary, and criticism. However, persons or businesses dissatisfied with the policy product can litigate their discontent through appeal of BZA decisions to a court.[5]

Participation

The first hypothesis contends that decisions on land use are not adversarial, but exhibit bureaucratic legalism, including restricted participation by legal representatives and limited influence by affected citizens or contending interests. Our observations indicate that most land use decisions by planning commissions or zoning boards followed a pattern marked by both low conflict and limited participation. For example, only the authors attended when the Hagerstown planning commission pored over the details of the zoning ordinance with the potential to have major effects on the city's regulation of property. In Washington, Pennsylvania a proposal from the County Redevelopment Authority to acquire and tear down 44 properties and construct 25 new single-family houses passed with only officials and the authors in attendance.

Even when planning commissions attempted to encourage participation, few persons attended meetings. As part of a process to involve the public in the drafting of a new zoning ordinance, Morgantown's planning commission held community forums. However, fewer than 30 persons attended and a small

5 Some new uses of land will also require approval or assistance from state and local public agencies that construct and manage road, water, and sewage infrastructure, protect historical structures, and oversee environmentally harmful discharges or disturbances of the land.

number of citizen activists from neighborhood associations who attended more than one meeting often dominated the discussions. Likewise, community outreach meetings conducted by the Marion County planning commission featured limited attendance and few comprehensive proposals about the future of land use in the county. Instead, the issues raised were often beyond the authority of land use bodies, such as the provision of water and sewer service, highway construction and repair, and assistance to volunteer fire departments. The only proposals that could be linked to zoning or land use law addressed problems with dilapidated structures and dumps.

Additionally, the residents who attended meetings appeared ill-informed about the authority of land use policy making bodies and the impact of their decisions on residents' property, wealth, and quality of life. Organized interests did not exist to stimulate participation or to influence policy making. The policy making was nonpartisan, and political parties did not arouse attention to policy making by the boards and commissions. In this environment of low visibility policy making the adversarial controversy that is the fountainhead of litigation did not occur. Indeed, with one exception, petitioners presented their own case without the assistance of a lawyer.

Decision Making: Consensus Solutions and Deference to Expertise

Respondents to our survey most frequently indicated that either consensus in policy making or a lack of conflict was the norm in their community (see Appendix 1, Q15). Indeed, 72.8 percent indicated that "overall the process was consensual." For example, a respondent from Little Rock, Arkansas reported that consensus is "reached or almost reached" on most planning issues. A respondent in Pullman, Washington noted that "compromises can be (and usually are) reached," despite a "myriad of competing interests." The Little Rock respondent reported that often the government had to function as a broker and build consensus, especially when conflict between two property owners, "with the City in the middle," occurred on rezoning issues. As in the observed meetings reported above, in Galesburg, Illinois there is an attempt to work with developers to "come to an agreement" or, as in Apple Valley, Minnesota, to "ensure smooth development." A Cedar Falls, Iowa respondent reported official efforts to "encourage extensive dialogue ultimately often resulting in "'acceptable' outcomes." In Hammond, Indiana there was an effort "to interpret the regulations to the benefit of obtaining the best possible development." Respondents from Florida, Georgia, Indiana, Michigan, Minnesota, New Jersey, Ohio, Pennsylvania, Oregon, and South Carolina described procedures or actions undertaken to accommodate developer ideas with city objectives in new developments. In other cities and counties planners used what the Rock Island, Illinois respondent called "concerted efforts to notify, involve, and consult with citizens and neighborhood/business organizations." As a Manitowoc, Wisconsin respondent summarized the initiative for consensus, "avoiding political fallout is important."

At the observed planning commission and zoning board meetings the paradigm was the presentation of a request for a variance, conditional use permit, permit for subdivision of property for residential or industrial development, or other action by homeowners, businesses, or developers. Because procedure normally required petitioners to discuss the proposed construction and land use with the professional planner or planning office, the interaction of petitioner and professional staff usually produced requests that did not raise flags or signal potential controversy to the commission of board members. Petitioners learned about zoning and land use law through the consultation and usually adjusted their proposal in light of planning staff recommendations. Although procedure varied by jurisdiction, the planner discussed both the details of the law, the need for a plan and map of requested changes, and the need for a "community impact statement" or, alternatively, "findings of fact" such as answers to a series of questions about the proposed changes in land use, especially new construction, driveways, and parking lots, and the notification of nearby property owners of requests for conditional use or zoning changes. Commissioners or board members might also offer detailed suggestions for the improvement of the project, such as how to space aisles in a parking lot, fencing, landscaping, and location of dumpsters. Often the planner would note cooperative consultation during his presentation of the proposal to the commission.

Although individuals and small developers have their proposal shaped by consultation with planners, larger corporations and experienced developers can exert more influence over decisions. For example, we observed that experienced developers in Morgantown, called by their first names by planning commission and zoning board members, had not only consulted with planning staff, but had designed detailed projects before going into discussions with the planners. Also in Morgantown the Kroger's grocery chain brought in an expert from a regional office to explain its redesign and landscaping of a parking lot. Here, as well in Jefferson County, West Virginia and Washington County, Maryland, experts and experienced petitioners offered detailed presentations with diagrams and designs of housing and parking to the boards and commissions. They also were prepared for questions and were ready to deflect any objections to their proposal.

The influence of a prepared petitioner especially surfaced in one observed proposal. In Harrison County the DuPont Corporation asserted affirmative control over the rehabilitation of a site suffering severe environmental degradation from zinc and other chemical pollution into parcels for lease to light industry. At the combined planning commission, landmarks commission, and Economic Development Authority hearing on its proposal, DuPont presented a very detailed plan for the remediation of the site that it had negotiated with the state's Department of Environmental Protection. The plan also included a park, bike path, and groundwater monitoring plan. DuPont had so well-prepared its proposal that *it* asked for public comments about the preservation of any historical structures or objects at the site, and proposed a website for the release of more information about the site. Commissioners then briefly discussed the DuPont proposal rather than offering independent assessments about the future of the site.

The deference board members and local legislators exhibited toward prepared petitioners often extended to their professional staff. During the revision of the zoning ordinance in Hagerstown, the senior planner went through the text of the proposed ordinance. She indicated to planning commissioners the changes that the planning office staff recommended and had placed in the text. She often justified the changes with references to ordinances adopted elsewhere and the professional literature on planning. In one instance her supervisor interrupted to support her citation of the reasons for a change with additional reference to new legal standards. The commissioners deferred to all but one of the recommendations. Thus the law underwent modification because of deference to the planner's professional knowledge and knowledge of the law, not through reference to a lawyer's advice.

In almost all meetings when the municipal or county planner or planning staff had concerns about a petitioner's proposal, they signaled the concern in the introduction or presentation of the request to the commission or board. After the planner's presentation, the party would then speak to the concern, and a polite colloquy with commissioners or board members might ensue. During this discussion the commissioners or board members would refer to past requests, their understanding of the zoning ordinance, and their personal norms about appropriate land use. Such norms often included their concerns about aesthetics, traffic, and parking. For example, commissioners questioned a petitioner seeking to establish a storage yard for construction supplies in Jefferson County about whether the yard could be seen from a highway. Morgantown zoning board members routinely asked about the location, size, landscaping, and surface of parking lots when considering retail and apartment proposals. At observed meetings there were no direct references to the comprehensive plan. Instead, at their request, the planner would answer specific questions about the zoning ordinance. A few legal references, almost always directed to the planner, were for clarification of ordinance standards and commission or board procedures. The commissioners and board members wanted to be sure they acted legally, but legal references were still a rare feature of most meetings. However, the pattern in decision making remained deference to expertise, a desire to allow community improvements, and concern for the quality of community life by having any objectionable features in a proposal adjusted prior to decision making.

Controversy and Adversary Conflict

Only 27.2 percent of survey respondents reported that adversary conflict characterized land use policy making in their community. Yet, in any jurisdiction adversary conflict cannot be completely avoided. There appear to be three sources of conflict. First, as a respondent in Fort Walton Beach, Florida stated, "lawyers usually make issues adversarial and difficult to compromise or find creative solutions." Indeed, a respondent in Washington County, Pennsylvania reported that lawyers "try to intimidate municipalities" by threatening lawsuits. Also, a respondent in Bristol, Virginia commented that many lawyers are "poorly versed in land use and zoning law" and confuse the process, but "plow ahead [with litigation] anyway!" A respondent in Lexington-Fayette County, Kentucky echoed this assessment. However, as indicated by a respondent in Olympia, Washington, "introducing attorneys into the development process slows the process, but does not generally change the result."

Second, as indicated by respondents in Oneida, New York and Huber Heights, Ohio and as echoed by a respondent in Green Bay Wisconsin, "the process becomes adversarial when politics start to take a role," especially when local elected officials try to influence planning and zoning decisions. In the City of Billings, Yellowstone County, Montana officials identified the source of litigation as a failure to "heed staff recommendations or base decisions on findings of fact."

Finally, some issues generate adversary conflict. Usually the conflict is between homeowners and property developers. A respondent in Jackson, Wyoming related adversary conflict to decisions affecting property values, a respondent in Naples, Florida cited "major" zoning and land use matters as the source of conflict, a respondent in Concord, New Hampshire saw conflict arising from "people trying to get what they want regardless of the zoning ordinance," and a respondent in Pittsburgh, Pennsylvania associated adversarial conflict with developers attempting to "cut corners" and running into objections from the city. A Columbia, Tennessee respondent noted that proposals for mobile home parks and multi-family zoning "bring out the worst in folks through fear and uncertainty." An Alice, Florida respondent reported the source of adversary conflict was a population with "little to no understanding [of] land use planning and zoning" who were "*very* shortsighted about the cost of development," and not "investing in the long-term, creating community development that would earn them more in the long run." A respondent in Iowa City, Iowa echoed this assessment.

Yet, we witnessed only limited adversary conflict. In observed meetings we witnessed public comment on only three proposals. A comment sent in writing to a zoning board from a senior center adjacent to a building that a developer sought to divide into apartments, suggested that the proposed apartments would cause litter in an alley next to the senior center. The board postponed the award of a conditional use permit so the developer could address the litter issue. At the next meeting he returned with a proposal and supporting letters from the local trash hauler and another neighbor on whose property he would lease space for a dumpster. The board then approved the conditional use permit.

A petitioner in Washington, Pennsylvania sought to have a former nunnery and personal care home converted into a group home for juvenile offenders. When the petitioner first went to the planning commission to propose the home and seek a variance to operate it, the commissioners had serious reservations, and about 50 citizens appeared to oppose the juvenile facility. Once aware of commission and neighborhood opposition, the firm reworked the proposal so that the facility would serve as a short-term residence for unmarried teenagers and their children. At the meeting on the revised proposal the petitioner had an attorney present his modified request and a representative of the national corporation take questions from the commissioners. When the session was opened to public comments, only one man spoke. He opened a three-ring binder with information on the proposal, but then only posed questions about the details of the proposal, the provisions in the proposal for parking, and commission procedures.

Despite lengthy agendas in Jefferson County, public comment appeared only on one proposal. It was a plan to subdivide a parcel into 10 "estate lots" of approximately 10 acres each with natural area buffers surrounding the subdivision. One man briefly commented that the subdivision would negatively affect the local viewshed, and a second man alleged that the development would cause wells in the area to dry up, and would cause overcrowding of schools. Then a property holder spoke strongly in support of the project as the kind of development he wanted to see in the county. The developer rebutted the charge about wells, stating that the County Heath Department had not informed him of any problems. The planner noted his staff's approval of the project had come after consultation and partial redesign of the subdivision. After a few brief procedural questions, the commissioners unanimously approved the subdivision plan.

Only one party had a proposal rejected at the observed meetings. In Washington County, Maryland, the planning commission rejected a proposal from a developer whose petition for a three-tier stack of lots with a "panhandle" to allow access to a road upset some commissioners' desire for well-planned new housing developments. When it rejected the petition, the commission chair informed the developer of a right to appeal to the zoning board or a court. She did not directly respond to a mildly voiced criticism of the decision by the petitioner.

We witnessed only one citation of a property owner for violation of land use law. The citation, issued by the Jefferson County planner through county legal staff, involved the operation of an illegal salvage yard. When the planning commission approved the citation, members commented that the process took too long. The planner replied that the property owner had not replied to a series of legal notices required by state law, and had not responded to the planner's efforts to negotiate a resolution of the violation. This behavior by property owners was less an overt adversarial contestation of land use regulation than a subversion of official power.

Despite the limited contestation and references to law or threats of litigation at observed meetings, there were outliers. For example, Jefferson County employed a consultant to develop new land use and zoning plans. The consultant's report became the object of controversy. When the planning commission held public hearings on the consultant's proposed comprehensive plan, divisions among the public appeared. At one hearing, attended by more than 100 persons, 32 residents or their representatives each made five minute statements to the planning commission and presented additional remarks in writing on a draft comprehensive plan for the county. With few exceptions, speakers lined up as pro- or anti-development. Their comments focused on the effect of specific details of the plan on property values, groundwater, the size of residential lots, jobs, traffic and infrastructure costs, and agriculture. The participants did not voice rights claims or articulate a political ideology. Rather, the distinction among the speakers was between those who feared a change in property regulation might diminish the value of their property and those who sought changes that they thought would provide for economic growth beneficial to their interests. The conflict thus reflected different views of how government might enrich people. The controversy about comprehensive planning in Jefferson County also generated litigation to enjoin land use decision making. County counsel described the suit as an effort by a family to enjoin the future authorization of subdivisions, because they feared the pollution of groundwater by faulty septic systems. The suit did not feature interest group participation or ideological argumentation.

Summary

Our data and observations support the first hypothesis. Land use policy consensus, not adversary litigation, is the norm. Three factors shape this result. First, to satisfy petitioner requests, construction and land use requests win approval if they meet commissioners' interpretation of a plan, and zoning board members issue variances and conditional use permits that adjust the plan, zoning ordinance, and initial petitioner proposals to satisfy petitioner requests and their own conceptions of an acceptable landscape. This satisficing and adaptation of policy also occurs because decision making around specific issues is related to one or a small number of parcels of land. Second, land use policymakers rarely tackle issues that affect multiple interests such as the consideration of the new comprehensive plan in Jefferson County. Most petitioners simply seek official authorization of changes in property use with minimal effect on adjacent real estate. Third, controversy is avoided because of decision making officials' deference to planners and petitioners, and barriers to participation faced by citizens such as the lack of information about cases, limited knowledge of the land use law, and the cost of employing an attorney. Normally the result is the gradual adaptation over time of land uses in a community.

Additionally, from the observed and reported controversies it is possible to identify situations associated with adversarial conflict about land use policy. One situation occurs when a policy or policy proposal has disproportionate effects on the wealth of organized or articulate parties in the community, such as developers. A second situation, identifiable from the city of Washington group home conflict, occurs when a proposed policy change creates a perception of danger or risk to persons, especially children, or to existing property values. Third, as indicated in some survey responses, the interests of some elected officials and their intervention in the activities of planning commissions and BZAs introduces adversary conflict. Yet, adversarial controversy is not likely because land use policy making institutions and personnel in many jurisdictions encourage informal mediation and consensus.

The Threat of Litigation and Neoliberal Activism

Recent research by Charles Epp (2008, 2009) finds that perceptions of the *fear* of civil litigation coming from localized legal pressure and resources is an incentive that influences the choices of local government officials and employees. Yet, as with adversarial controversy, cognition of the threat of litigation barely existed in the communities we observed. Therefore our second hypothesis is that there is minimal evidence that land use decision makers *fear* adversarial legal action. Also, they do not confront neoliberal organizational intervention or ideological-focused litigation.

Data from the survey, presented in Table 8.1, suggests that the planning officials did not report that the threat or fear of lawsuits affected either effective land use planning or zoning decisions (see Appendix 1, Q9 and Q10). Of respondents, 71.5 percent reported that the threat or fear of lawsuits rarely or never affected decision making about effective land use planning. Also, 72.1 percent reported that the threat or fear of lawsuits rarely or never affected zoning decision making. Although 74.8 percent of the respondents reported their jurisdiction received letters from lawyers about land use actions and accusing wrongdoing or threatening suit, the reported mean was only 9.0 letters for the previous five years or less than two letters a year. As indicated in Table 8.2, the filing of law suits, trials, and out-of court settlements were also very infrequent (see Appendix 1, Q11–Q14). Since respondents reported that their jurisdictions issued a median of 1,595 permits for new construction the previous year, the low number of letters and legal actions seems especially astonishing (less than one legal action for every 1,000 permit decisions). The respondents' limited fear of lawsuits thus seems grounded in empirical reality. Their decisions will infrequently generate adversarial litigation.

Table 8.1 Fear of lawsuits

Frequency	About Land Use Planning (percentages, n=122)	About Zoning Matters (percentages, n=122)
Never	19.5	22.1
Rarely	52.0	50.0
Sometimes	26.0	24.6
Often	1.6	2.5
Almost Always	0.8	0.8

The absence of a threat of litigation is further evidenced by the nonparticipation of governmental counsel in policy making. As noted above, Hagerstown revised its zoning ordinance in the absence of an attorney. With one exception, observed meetings proceeded without the presence of governmental legal counsel, and in that meeting counsel left a third of the way through the meeting. Of survey

Table 8.2 Legal action in land use policy in last five years

Legal Action	Jurisdictions Reporting Action (Percentages, n=123)	Number of Actions	
		Median	Mean
Letters from Lawyers	74.8	3	9.0
Lawsuits Filed	73.1	2	4.3
Trials	60.2	1	2.2
Settled Out of Court	38.7	0	0.7

respondents 78.5 percent reported that they consult with counsel "occasionally, but not in a majority of decisions". Only 6.5 percent responded that they "almost always" consult with counsel (see Appendix 1, Q7). Also, we observed that few petitioning parties brought counsel to planning and zoning meetings. The only lawyer who spoke for his client appeared in the Washington, Pennsylvania group home dispute. Observations suggest that counsel appears to be involved in advising *some* parties before a petition is submitted and, more commonly, after a planning commission or BZA has made a decision.

The lack of a fear of lawsuits, however, might mask what Epp has styled as "legal pressure" from organized interests that employ lawyers. A Lantana, Florida respondent reported that "lawyers drive the system" and threats of legal action "create fear in local officials" and "accommodation" in laws. Survey data indicate that 36.3 percent of respondents believe that lawyers have "far too much" or "quite a bit" of power in the planning and zoning process, and another 45.2 percent attribute "some" power to lawyers in the process (see Appendix 1, Q5). Also, the more powerful lawyers are perceived to be, the more they perceive the land use policy making to be adversarial (r=0.19, significant at the 0.05 two-tailed level). Also, we found that when planners perceive that lawyers have "quite a bit" of power, they feel that the threat of lawsuits affects land use planning (r=-0.27, significant at the 0.01 two-tailed level) and feel that the threat of lawsuits affects decisions on zoning matters (r=-0.22, significant at the 0.05 two-tailed level). Additionally, we found significant associations of the fear of lawsuits affecting zoning decisions with the number of letters received from petitioners' lawyers (r=0.21, significant at the 0.05 two-tailed level) and the number of lawsuits settled (r=0.28, significant at the 0.01 two-tailed level). Also, the more letters the planners received from lawyers, the more they were likely to see the process as adversarial (r=-0.28, significant at the 0.01 two-tailed level) (see Appendix 1, Q11, 12, 13, 14). Thus, although we find very infrequent adversarial actions about land use policy making and little fear of adversarial legal action among respondent planners, evidence of the power of lawyers, especially as interventions challenging decisions, changes land use policy making. "Legal pressure" in the form of the appearance of lawyers at hearings and letters from them to officials makes the policy process more adversarial, and is an important qualification of our second hypothesis. Adversary conflict is also associated with larger communities (r=-0.23, significant at the 0.05 two-tailed level), perhaps because greater socioeconomic diversity or a greater population increases the possibility of litigation or perhaps because of the greater availability of lawyers who can bring pressure in urban settings.

Also, the planners' fears and knowledge may affect their assessment of the consequences of legal pressure. The more the planner respondents fear lawsuits about both planning (r=-0.25, significant at the 0.01 two-tailed level) and zoning decisions (r=-0.26, significant at the 0.01 two-tailed level), the more adversarial they are likely to view the process (see Appendix 1, Q9, 10). The less confident they are about their knowledge of the law, the more they fear lawsuits about planning decisions (r=0.19, significant at the 0.05 two-tailed level) (see Appendix 1, Q6, 9). This evidence suggests that planners' lack of information about the infrequency of litigation and the meaning of the law skew their assessment of the process toward the perception of adversary conflict and the expectation of legal pressure.

Finally, more than fearful of adversarial litigation, it appears that land use policymakers might be afraid of a broader political conflict and controversy arising from land use decisions. This fear of political controversy can appear in extreme form. In Marion County, West Virginia the planning commission was so afraid of conflict about land use policy and zoning—the "z-word" one commissioner refused to voice—that it had no mission statement, no comprehensive plan, and proposed no land use law in 11 years. Although the commission seemed somewhat concerned about the quality of life in the county, its members sought out no information and offered no land use proposals related to dilapidated property, economic development, new construction, or the environment. They simply did not want to create political controversy.

The evidence on legal participation and perceptions of the threat and avoidance of litigation suggests that, in part, hypothesis two is not supported. Despite few experiences with their decisions producing litigation, some land use policymakers with less knowledge of the law do fear litigation, and act to avoid suits and general political controversies about property regulation. Consequently, in the limited number of instances of public participation we observed, to avoid litigation and conflict local officials accommodated the claims voiced with little reference to a discourse of rights. In large measure, the lack of rights discourse in the accommodation process stemmed from its neglect by the participants. Developers and their lawyers presented their cases with discussions of the economic and social benefits of their investments for the community. They regarded property as an interest or a commodity. They were also supportive of governmental subsidization of infrastructure and other policies that would enhance the value of their interest in profiting from the commodity. Homeowners sought zoning and other land use policies for the protection of their interest in their "home" or "property values," code words that implied support for the status quo and opposition to changes that might induce racial, environmental, or economic change in nearby properties. They often treated property as an interest containing an emotional worth and as a locale for private life. However, they also expressed a freedom to make some changes in their property to enhance its market and personal value free of what they regarded as government interference—the "my home is my castle" argument (e.g., Blomley 2005, Claeys 2008, Perin 1977, 32–80). Planners often employed professional language and concepts derived from their profession, referencing the communitarian ideological themes present in the profession's contemporary interest in the control of urban sprawl, smart growth (e.g., DeGrove 2005, Downs 2001), the new urbanism (e.g., Fulton 1996, Talen 2005), sustainable development (e.g., Wheeler and Beatley 2009), growth management (e.g., Landis 2006), and climate change policy (e.g., Wheeler 2008). Added to this mix were BZA officials who usually employed a loose use of legal terminology and land use history in the community to appease petitioners or guide their decisions. Consequently, as these authors noted in a study of property regulation in Canada (Brisbin and Hunter 2006), the policy product of local land use regulation contained a tangled mélange of various interests. The neoliberal organizations and arguments present in recent appellate eminent domain litigation did not figure in local affairs. Even among the many critics of the Jefferson County plan, the legitimacy of land use regulation was not criticized by neoliberal assertions that it was an inefficient interference with the market, politically authoritarian, and an interference with rights, or a scheme of governance that inhibited economically sound private choices. Instead, people *pragmatically* used legality simply to seek decisions that protected or bettered their status or wealth.

The Effect of Adversarial Legality on Land Use Policy Making

Despite the lack of adversarial conflicts and litigation, we found evidence that the planning commissioners, planners, and zoning board members think legally, especially about the legal boundaries of governmental power, due process and legalized procedures, substantive rules of law, and the range of their policy making powers. Therefore there is support for the third hypothesis that holds legality constrains the sphere of choices made by land use decision makers. Their perspective on legality was that they should follow the black letter law that treated real estate as an interest.

Although not legally trained, planning commissioners and zoning board members consistently offered statements that indicate they thought their authority had to function with the law. Indeed, we observed that they often struggled through complex problems raised by provisions in the zoning code that appeared to limit creative construction and land use improvements. Although the zoning boards in particular could effectively amend the ordinance by granting conditional use permits and variances, they often adjusted the ordinance for specific cases only after some discussion of the precedent they might create, and the longer-term legal implications of their actions. Often in observed jurisdictions they delayed action on proposals requiring a variance or conditional use permit until they acquired more information, or had time to consider fully the meaning of their action.

The planners responding to the survey also indicated that they were very confident (63.7 percent) or somewhat confident (34.7 percent) that their knowledge of land use law and the local zoning ordinance helped them make decisions that avoided lawsuits and court challenges. Indeed, again and again we observed commissioners and board members deferring to the planner's interpretation of ordinances. As a respondent in Cedar Falls, Iowa remarked, because they and the commissioners knew and followed the codes, "attorneys do not normally 'sway'" the planning and zoning commissioners. The implication is that nonprofessional legal expertise offsets threats of litigation or other assertions made to the planners and commissioners by attorneys. However, there might be limits to their expertise in some jurisdictions.

Due process and procedural rules mattered. For example, in Jefferson County planning commissioners devoted a half-hour of one meeting to a draft of by-laws and a discussion of procedures. The discussion indicated that all members took procedural rules seriously. However, the discussion was not centered on whether their procedures meet any state statutory guidelines. Rather, the commissioners divided between those who wanted expeditious consideration of proposals, in part, because state law granted four months for the consideration of proposals, and those who wanted committees and, apparently, more public involvement in decisions. The discussion was civil, but the commitment of commissioners to their position was apparent to the observer. However, given both time considerations and a perceived need for more public participation, they agreed to postpone the decision on procedures to a special session at which counsel could be present and advise them on any legal requirements of due process.

Substantive legal rules also mattered. Planners, commissioners, and board members recognized they could not exceed the authority granted them by law. For example, when revising the zoning ordinance, Hagerstown planning commission members questioned their legal authority to specify certain property uses. They posed questions for the group or the two planners present about their authority to control empty big boxes. These were large retail buildings closed by their owner when the owner built an even larger store but which the owner refused to sell or lease to keep potential competitors out of the market. Although the discussion focused on the blight caused by the buildings and economic issues, it floundered because no one could offer a legal way to address the big box problem without professional legal advice.

Despite their apparent concern with legality, survey respondents recognized the vagaries of the boundaries on choices imposed by substantive law. In response to a question about legal ambiguity or the lack of a precise legal standard to guide their choices, 55.7 percent responded that legal ambiguity "sometimes allows me to take risks and design creative policies", and 30.4 percent said legal ambiguity had no effect on their decisions. Only 10.6 percent responded that laws and ordinances discouraged them from going forward with what they regarded as good policies and good decisions.

The implication of these responses and those about their fear of lawsuits and use of lawyers is that local planning officers recognize that they must function within a policy making sphere constituted by legality. Nevertheless, they believe that they have enough legal knowledge to navigate around the legal terrain of property and satisfy their policy objectives. Legality thus precludes them from some policy choices, but often they can move toward their goals by using the malleable rules of land use law.

However, by framing land use policy as the legal regulation of interests in specific petitions for permits or cases about specific land parcels or neighborhoods, officials often ignored the potentially distributive and redistributive consequences of their choices. They did not always consider how their choices could affect construction and manufacturing employment, patterns of social and racial interaction, access to schools, parks, and healthcare facilities, resource exploitation, environmental health, or the survival of the natural world (Delaney, Ford, and Blomley 2001, Fishman 2000, Ford 1999, Platt 1996, Warner and Moltoch 2000). They also avoided the discourse of property rights and neoliberal objections to regulatory takings. Instead, they simply thought and acted with the framework provided by statutory law.

Conclusion

Our data and observations indicate that adversarial legal action is not a central feature of the land use policy making process in the United States. However, local land use regulators sometimes fear litigation and employ law and their understanding of what the law means. The result is a decision making context that is less adversarial legalism and often similar to what Kagan (2001: 10–11) called bureaucratic legalism. Policy makers try to avoid conflicts and litigation and act with a concern for legal procedures and the substantive law. With limited public participation, most property regulation remains a process in the hands of local officials and, in larger jurisdictions, professional planners. Only in rare instances when attorneys intervene, does the process turn into adversarial litigation. The adversarial conflicts that appear also are commonly not tinged by neoliberal ideology. Instead the conflicts often pit two economic interests: property owners fearful of legal changes that would allow other private parties to diminish the value of their home or business, and property owners who desire legal changes that would allow them to develop property and increase the value of their holdings. Land use conflicts therefore often call on government to broker between the interests of two sets of capitalists. Less commonly, the conflicts considered the interests of community groups that government should regulate the nuisances created by some property owners or developers, such as threats to historical structures, the safety of children, and natural spaces and water.

These findings also suggest the need for further study of law and the political-legal construction of the landscape. More knowledge of widely varying local institutional procedures, the expertise of local decision makers, the influence of planners, and the role of attorneys would enrich our understanding of how land use law and politics affects the potential for conflict and litigation. Little is known about the conduct of land use litigation, especially when neoliberal lawyers or interest groups decide to transform it from a claim of economic or community interest into an ideological contest about property rights. Finally, although adversarial litigation can shape governmental authority over land use policy making and encourage legislative action, we issue a caution to persons who might conclude that interest group litigation of eminent domain cases will radically change American land use policy. Adversarial contestation and interest group ideological activism about land use takings occurs in a few atypical conflicts. The common place of the law is the creation of order and security in the possession of property and the management of risks or externalities that might result from investments in the development of real estate. It is not the expulsion of Ms. Kelo from her home.

Appendix 1—Survey Questions Used in Analysis

Q5. In your view, how much power do lawyers (for government and for petitioning parties) have in the land use planning process in your jurisdiction? [1, Virtually none to 5, Far too much]

Q6. How confident are you that your knowledge of land use law and the local zoning ordinance helps you to make decisions that avoid lawsuits and court challenges? [1, very confident, to 4, not at all confident]

Q7. How often do you rely on the advice of a lawyer (or legal counsel or solicitor) when making land use, planning, or zoning decisions? [1, almost always, to 4, almost never]

Q8. Often land use laws or zoning ordinances are legally ambiguous. In general, does the ambiguity of legal language: 1, Inspire you to design creative policies or to take risks? 2, Allow you to go forward with what you think is good policy or decisions? 3, Discourage you from going forward with what you think is good policy and good decisions? 4, Has no effect on my policy and planning choices?

Q9. Does the fear or threat of lawsuits affect what you regard as creative *land use planning*? [1, never, to 5, almost always]

Q10. Does the fear or threat of lawsuits affect your decision making on *zoning* matters? [1, never, to 5, almost always]

Q11. During the past five years, have lawyers *sent letters* to you or your municipality/county stating their client's concerns about a proposed land-use action, alleging wrongdoing or threatening suit? [1, No, 2, Yes—How many times?]

Q12. During the past five years, have lawyers *filed lawsuits* about land use decisions by you or your municipality/county? [1, No, 2, Yes—How many times?]

Q13. During the past five years, have you or your municipality/county had to *defend at trial* any official actions concerning land use? [1, No, 2, Yes—How many times?]

Q14. During the past five years have you or your municipality/county had to *settle out of court* any suits regarding any official actions concerning land use? [1, No, 2, Yes—How many times?]

Q15. Overall, do you feel the land use decision making process is adversarial or consensual?

Chapter 9
The Regulatory Response to the Legal Mobilization of Property Rights: An Institutional Analysis of Regulatory Decision-Making

Darren Botello-Samson

Neoliberal efforts to reform regulatory regimes in the United States have called for a reconfiguration of state authority from a coercive model to a market model based on cooperative principal-agent relationships (Harrington and Turem 2006: 202), or what some call a "customer service concept" (Sparrow 2000: 45). On the one hand, the advance of neoliberal political values has diminished the oversight role of the judiciary over executive agencies and marked "the end of active engagement by the courts to define and formalize the boundaries of rulemaking" (Harrington and Turem 2006: 204). On the other hand, courts have been called upon by advocates of neoliberal policies to make regulation of property more reliant upon market forces and free exchange than governmental control of property use.

Interest groups that advocate for strong protection of private property rights have used the courts to mobilize political support in their favor. The Thorpe, et al. chapter in this book indicates that property rights interest groups have served the role of informing the courts of issues and interests surrounding regulatory takings cases. Additionally, in his chapter, Schultz explains that the interest group who backed litigation in *Kelo* was one part of a larger political effort to shape eminent domain law. These observations indicate that litigious interactions between property owners and the state are more than efforts to solve specific conflicts; they are also components of the legal mobilization of neoliberal property values and, as such, each case can be seen "as just one potential dimension or phase of a larger, complex, dynamic, multistage process of disputing among various parties" (McCann 2008: 524).

A key tenet of the social mobilization of neoliberal property rights through litigation is the concept of a chilling effect, or a reduction in outputs by a regulatory agency caused by the perceived threat of property rights litigation. A zoning board, for example, that has been sued for a regulatory taking in the past, would likely reduce the number of restrictions it places on private property use, with the aim of securing some public environmental benefit, in the future, and/or rely on more cooperative, market driven techniques to achieve those ends. Property rights interest groups that seek a reduction in property use restrictions use litigation under the assumption that "greater compensation does deter government action" (Fischel 1995: 96). Interest groups seeking environmental or other public ends would fear that "local governments will have to do more individualized analysis of the expected impacts of land use changes and the conditions they impose on them. Not only will this be more costly, but it will likely have a chilling effect of regulatory activity at that level" (O'Leary 2006: 162).

In this chapter I question the assumption of a chilling effect resulting from such actions, in particular, regulatory takings litigation. I argue that the assumption that regulatory takings litigation will cause a chilling effect in regulatory outputs is based on a set of assumptions rooted in the jurisprudence of law and economics. While these assumptions have contributions to make to the analysis of regulatory behavior, they ignore significant institutional features that also affect the likelihood of a chilling effect. To identify these features, I conducted elite interviews with key regulatory personnel in state and federal offices charged with implementing the Surface Mining Control and Reclamation Act (SMCRA) (30 U.S.C. § 1201). These interviews were conducted with the intent of discovering how key regulatory decision makers act in the face of potential regulatory takings litigation. Through these interviews, I conclude that, while economic and budgetary factors do affect regulatory behavior, institutional obstacles to a chilling effect do exist, including bureaucratized decision-making, agency culture, and hermeneutic context.

Judicial Impact and Regulatory Takings

The assumption of a chilling effect caused by regulatory takings litigation is based on a set of assumptions made about regulatory behavior: an inborn desire on the part of governmental agencies to maximize the amount of regulatory activity in which they can engage, a natural fact of finite budgetary resources which those agencies can access, and a strategic response by those agencies which is characterized by the achievement of public goods through private cost, when possible. As property owners find the enjoyment and use of their property hampered by regulatory restriction, i.e., as public good is provided through private loss, they may choose to react litigiously, seeking compensation, not for property physically confiscated by the state, but for restrictions which are perceived to have the same effect. Through successful, or potentially even numerous unsuccessful lawsuits, the governmental regulatory regime learns that accomplishing their regulatory mission may entail compensating property owners, and, therefore, they may decide to curtail their regulatory behavior.

Despite the warnings issued by organizations concerned with the potential weakening of environmental land-use regulations, as well as the premature celebration of organizations long aiming at such declinations, some have questioned the existence of such chilling impacts. Most recently, Cornell Law Professor Gregory Alexander, in an excellent comparative assessment of takings jurisprudence, declared "the takings clause dead as a tool for conservative judges to end the expansion of the regulatory state" (2006: 63). While Alexander notes that continued property rights conflicts with and challenges against regulation will occur, and future confrontations will likely occur in legislative arenas, he portrays the Supreme Court as an institution that, although occasionally deferential to property owners' takings claims, has substantially upheld land use regulation against constitutional challenges (95).

Regardless of the perceived direction of regulatory takings jurisprudence, the above mentioned assumptions could still predict a chilling effect. First, even losing litigation imposes costs upon regulatory agencies and, second, property rights victories in regulatory takings lawsuits are not uncommon, and a single victory could impose significant costs upon an agency. But these concerns are still rooted in a set of assumptions about law and regulatory behavior that are worth questioning. Prevalent in these assumptions are economic models of political behavior and law. The influence of law and economics jurisprudence is central to the analysis of this chapter. This jurisprudence holds "that the law has a greater intelligibility than it appears to, and that the historical accidents to which it seems to owe its shape, are in reality the product of actions that conform to certain timeless laws of human behavior" (Kronman 1993: 226–27), namely the naturally economic mind of humanity, which, when pursuing efficiency, establishes the moral purpose of the law (ibid. 233).

Epstein, for example, generally distrusts public ownership and control of property, since such actions result in a situation in which "[i]ll-defined rights replace well-defined ones, and transaction cost barriers are likely to exceed the gains that otherwise are obtainable from any shift in land use or ownership. Another negative-sum game" (1985: 265). When governments must control private property, Epstein argues that the "ideal solution is to leave the individual owner in a position of indifference between the taking by the government and the retention of the property" (182). Likewise, Michelman views the questions of regulatory takings law as balancing the costs and benefits of a regulation (efficiency gains) with the costs of compensating those affected (settlement costs) and those similarly situated (demoralizing costs) (1967: 1171, 1214). The result of such calculations provides the legal answer as to whether compensation is due for a property restriction, and adds that the "decision not to compensate is not unfair as long as the disappointed claimant ought to be able to appreciate how such decisions might … [present] a lesser long-run risk to people like him" (1223). Finally, Fischel, whose analysis of regulatory takings law is more political than either Epstein's or Michelman's, would ultimately restrict the reach of the courts over such cases to situations in which natural market forces were inhibited and prevented from producing a natural, economic outcome (1995: 120). What these diverse theories of regulatory takings law share in common is an understanding of takings law in purely economic terms. The concern raised by this approach is that, if regulatory takings are understood in purely economical terms, the analysis of the impact of such cases will likely focus solely on economic factors.

Framing the question of takings impact within an economic actor context is understandable. Operating at the analytical level of the rational individual strategically working to maximize his or her own benefits, economic disciplines seem well positioned to answer the distributive questions of regulatory takings. Not only might the economic analysis of takings cases highlight moments when public benefits can be provided with less financial impact on individual citizens, but it may also demonstrate the unwillingness of government actors to pursue regulation when facing such compensation claims. Questions surrounding individuals' propensities to pursue takings litigation against the regulatory state are also pared down, with more attention paid to the costs and benefits attributed to all choices of action; a population's desire to avoid pollution and/or secure jobs, the pressure of economic competition from other jurisdictions, and the mobility of the regulated interest may all affect the willingness to sue and/or regulate (Butler and Macey 1996: 31–33).

Economic analyses of regulatory takings certainly add a dimension of understanding beyond the letter of the law and into the realm of observable human behavior. However, in the attempt to clarify and simplify takings jurisprudence, an oversimplification has been forged. In the process of narrowing the level of analysis down to the rational individual, institutional factors have been omitted, factors which greatly shape the practices of litigation and regulation, altering both the strategies of participants and the social contexts of meaning in which such actions occur.

Past research has already demonstrated that institutional analysis is an important step in developing an understanding of the management and regulation of private actors that access and use common-pool resources, a situation analogous to a private property owner whose property use arguably extends into a publicly held interest. Early approaches which dominated the commons literature had as their primary focus the efficient distribution of commonly held resources. This focus came from an early reliance upon Gordon-Schaefer economic models, which aimed at defining levels of resource extraction indicative of open access, maximum sustainable yield, and maximum economic yield (e.g., Dietz 2002: 9–10, Townsend and Wilson 1987: 317). The question then posed by Gordon-Schaefer models is as follows: What sort of "rules regulating access and harvesting practices limit effort to the economically optimal strategy?" (Dietz 2002: 9). While the logic of the model is cohesive, "that logic depends on a set of assumptions about human motivation, about the rules governing the use of the commons, and about the character of the common resource" (3). To address such assumptions, researchers within the commons literature have directed their attention away from the rational individual level of analysis to institutions which confine and affect the individuals acting within commons dilemmas. This development within the commons literature is worth applying to an inquiry into the impact of takings litigation.

First, by analyzing the impact of takings litigation at the level of the individual economic actor, one risks ignoring the special political circumstances in which regulatory takings litigation finds itself. "In a world of private bads, external costs that affect, and are confined to, easily defined economic agents are seen as a private matter by the common law. Economic theory sees the problem as a matter that may be resolved by bargaining" (Boudreaux and Yandle 2002: 58). The problem for economic analysis occurs when the subject being studied moves beyond the more predictable individual situations, and finds itself wrapped in a complex set of social institutions which would force each actor to adopt coping strategies:

> The economic analysis of public bads calls for a different theoretical approach than that required for private bads. Indeed, the economic theory of public goods and bads inevitably includes such things as collective decisionmaking, free-rider problems, government coercion, and strategic behavior. Because of the level of decision-making costs, the world of public bads is not as neat as the world of private bads. In the private world, the small numbers of agents and clearly defined property rights enable bargaining to emerge as a low-cost way to eliminate relevant private bads. The problem is more costly to resolve in the world of public goods and bads (60).

Since regulatory takings claims arise in the face of regulation aimed at the control of private property for the purpose of prevention of a public harm or the securing of a public good, an understanding of such litigation must incorporate political and social institutions and avoid the hegemonic role that economic factors have played in such studies.

Furthermore, studies of common-pool resource management have relied upon institutions beyond their strategic, rules-of-the-game components. "Accordingly, the emergence of institutions for the commons should include not only rules and governance systems but also new and changed patterns of behavior and norms and values" (McCay 2002: 362). Such an interpretivist approach to institutions can "reconstruct intentional states of mind and cultural or political contexts in the hope that [they] can induce with some confidence the reasons that led a particular person to adopt a particular course of conduct" (Gillman 1999: 78). Such hermeneutic factors can significantly affect the legal and political control of resource usage, as factors as varied as problem perception, trust in government intervention, scientific uncertainty, and the discounting of resource losses (Thompson 2000: 244) can affect the public desire to support regulation.

Likewise, the decision to take or not to take, to compensate or not to compensate is frequently about much more than distributing costs and benefits in an efficient manner. Regulatory takings are inherently political, touching upon issues of right and obligation, and any analysis of takings must consider that political dimension as well as how institutions shape and affect the values at stake in such litigation. One such institution may be the law itself, as it not only situates the strategic economic behavior of actors through the creation of rules of exchange and behavior, but it also acts as a source of norms and values that mold perceptions (361–63).

As the law is about values, and values can change, an understanding of the potential for a chilling effect brought about by litigation in a field of law, namely regulatory takings law, must address the dynamic complexity of values as expressed within the law. Operating from a constitutive legal perspective, from which "legal conventions routinely prefigure, delimit, and express the expectations, aspirations, and practical world-views of subjects" (McCann 2008: 526), regulatory takings law is as much about defining property and the reasonability of the expectations of its use, as it is about measuring some object cost of property value gained and lost. In her chapter in this book, Hatcher has also demonstrated that legal concepts (like "coast") are flexible in the face of changing physical, conceptual, and political environments. At the heart of regulatory takings jurisprudence is a conflict of law; at one level, this is a conflict between divergent ideas present at the writing of the Fifth Amendment, "free market-private property" conceptualizations of property and "the legal concept of 'just price'" rooted in the Christian tradition (Sax 1964: 55). The law, then, becomes a site of conflict over the definition of the law, an inevitable conflict between parochial "ideals of justice, liberty, and democracy" (Nedelsky 1990: 14), and the government's reliance on public rights and responsibilities over and against total private appropriation of property (Schorr 2005: 4–5). These conflicts are part of the context which defines property value, rights, and responsibilities through the social needs which give property its value in the first place (Sax 2005: 518–519).

This approach highlights the multiple avenues of action available to key regulatory decision-makers confronting potential regulatory takings challenges. The assumption that heightened compensatory rulings and property rights victories in regulatory takings cases produce a chilling effect in enforcement, presents a possible reaction of key regulatory decision-makers to litigious activity, but it ignores other possibilities. While budgetary concerns are likely to be high among key regulatory decision-makers, one cannot automatically assume that takings cases and compensation-threats are going to overpower every other variable affecting those concerns. For example, regulatory agencies are, after all, enforcement agencies (Sparrow 2000: 2) and are likely animated by a corresponding organizational culture, sometimes referred to as the "gotcha syndrome" (Scheberle 2004: 25), in which regulatory agencies are concerned with getting caught by federal overseers violating statutory requirements, which provides motivations counter to those central to the idea of a takings chilling effect.

The Surface Mining Control and Reclamation Act

The focus of the rest of this chapter will be on those multiple decision-making avenues available to regulatory agencies that confront regulatory takings litigation, and are potentially susceptible to a chilling effect. In particular, this chapter will look at enforcement of the Surface Mining Control and Reclamation Act (SMCRA) (30 U.S.C. § 1201). This environmental statute was chosen because of its expansive scope, which places significant restrictions upon coal mining operators in a manner that can quash their property use expectations. Furthermore, the history of SMCRA implementation is full of regulatory takings conflicts fought in state and federal courts.

Enacted in 1977, SMCRA was created, among other reasons, to fix the lack of uniformity among state efforts to regulate surface coal mining (Scheberle 2004: 166). The end result was a law that requires all surface mining of coal in the United States be conducted under a permit to guarantee that the end effects of the mining do not cause irreparable damage to the environment, agriculture, or the public. "Like many environmental laws, congressional architects chose a partial-preemption regulatory approach for implementing SMCRA. … [T]his approach returns regulatory control to the states, but only after the states adopt enforcement programs that meet national standards" (155). Having assumed the power to regulate surface coal mining from the states, SMCRA only allows the states to reassume regulatory authority upon approval of the Secretary of the Interior, which requires that the state establish a surface mining regulatory program "provid[ing] for the regulation of surface coal mining and reclamation operations in accordance with the requirements of" the federal law (30 U.S.C. § 1253(a)(1)). Even after primacy has been achieved by a state, SMCRA includes significant federal oversight powers to ensure compliance with federal standards. The Secretary is empowered to "make those investigations and inspections necessary to insure compliance with" (§ 1211(c)(1)), and is further empowered to provide for federal enforcement if the state program is determined not to be effectively enforcing the law in a manner consistent with the requirements of SMCRA (§ 1254(b)).

Central to the Title V regulatory provisions of SMCRA, and central to potential regulatory takings challenges, are the permitting practices used to implement the law. To insure that surface coal mining is conducted in a manner that balances environmental, agricultural, and energy interests (§ 1202(f)) requires that any surface coal mining operation, or underground coal mining operation with surface effects, be conducted with an approved permit, granted by either the federal Office of Surface Mining (OSM) or the state regulatory authority. Issuance of such a permit is conditional upon the ability of the surface mining operator to conduct such operations in a manner which insures the ability of the operator to reclaim the land, i.e., "to restore the approximate original contour of the land" (§ 1265(b)(3)), "minimize the disturbances to the prevailing hydrologic balance" (§ 1265(b)(10)), "control or prevent erosion and siltation, pollution of water, damage to fish or wildlife or their habitat, or public or private property" (§ 1265(b)(17)), "assume the responsibility for successful revegetation" (§ 1265(b)(20)(A)), "restore the land affected to a condition capable of supporting the uses which it was capable of supporting prior to any mining or higher or better uses" (§ 1265(b)(2)), and "conduct surface coal mining operations so as to maximize the utilization and conservation of the solid fuel resource being recovered, so that reaffecting the land in the future through surface coal mining can be minimized" (§ 1265(b)(1)). To guarantee post-operations reclamation will occur, operators must post a reclamation bond which will be forfeited if reclamation efforts are abandoned (§ 1259).

In addition to establishing a number of requirements which must be met by any surface coal mine operator, SMCRA also places upon regulatory personnel a strict set of inspection and enforcement requirements. Regulatory authorities are required to conduct, on average, monthly partial inspections and annual full inspections of all surface coal mining operations, and are further required to conduct such inspections irregularly and without prior notice (§ 1265(c)). In the event that the regulatory authority observes a violation of the permit which "can reasonably be expected to cause significant, imminent environmental harm to land, air, or water resources," or "creates an imminent danger to the health or safety of the public," the agent is required to immediately issue a cessation order (CO), which halts all relevant mining or reclamation practices until the violation is rectified (§ 1271(a)(2)). If the violation does not present an imminent risk, the issuance of a notice of violation (NOV) is required, which, if the violation is not corrected within the time-frame established by the NOV, will result in the issuance of a CO (§ 1271(a)(3)).

Surface coal mining operators, facing the broad requirements of SMCRA placed upon their planned mining activity, have occasionally brought regulatory takings challenges against the actions of either OSM or state regulatory authorities. Such challenged actions generally restrict the areas from which operators may legally attempt to extract coal, areas which can be considered the property of the operators, who have acquired either mineral rights or property rights in fee simple. These access restrictions are either the product of a determination by regulatory decision-makers that particular practices, which result in leaving some coal behind, must be a condition of a permit to protect environmental or other interests, or the area has been declared as land unsuitable for mining (UFM). Under the UFM designation provisions of SMCRA, individuals may petition the regulatory agency to designate a particular area as unsuitable for surface mining if mining activities in the area would result in significant damage to natural, historic, aesthetic, cultural, scientific, or resource values, or result in an unacceptable risk to public safety due to increased flooding or geological instability (§ 1272(a)(3)). Furthermore, Congress declared certain areas to be unsuitable for surface mining, including lands in the National Parks System and other federal lands programs and lands within specified buffer zones of public roads, occupied dwellings, public buildings, schools, churches, community or institutional buildings, public parks, and cemeteries (§ 1272(e)). These unsuitability designations, however, are subject to valid existing rights (VERs). These rights are defined by OSM regulations as "a set of circumstances under which a person may, *subject to regulatory authority approval*, conduct surface mining operations on lands" on which Congressional designations "prohibit such operations" (30 C.F.R. § 761.5, emphasis added). The existence of a VER is determined through OSM's "Good Faith/All Permits" standard, which allows for the possibility of surface mining operations when "all permits and other authorizations required to conduct surface coal mining operations had been obtained, or a good faith effort to obtain all necessary permits and authorizations had been made, before the land came under the protection of" SMCRA (§ 761.5(b)(1)).

Given the complexity of coal mining practices and the expansive regulatory scope of SMCRA, the doctrinal history of regulatory takings cases against SMCRA implementation could not be exhaustively summarized in this chapter. However, despite the proclaimed efforts of the Supreme Court to avoid the application of some "set formula" (*Penn Central* 1978: 123) to regulatory takings cases, federal SMCRA cases have been marked by the development of a doctrine which generally rules "that the goals of regulations embedded within SMCRA are of such a protective public nature that non-compensated restrictions on the property rights of coal mining operations are justified" (Botello-Samson 2008: 36). Some components of this doctrine merit further discussion.

When confronted with a regulatory takings challenge to SMCRA, the federal courts have consistently utilized what would eventually be referred to as the two-tiered *Chancellor Manor* (2003) test, which determines "whether a compensable property interest exists" (901), and subsequently, if that inquiry is satisfied, engages in a *Penn Central* analysis to determine if that property interest has been taken into account (902). "First, a court should inquire into the nature of the land owner's estate to determine whether the use interest proscribed by the governmental action was part of the owner's title to begin with" (*M&J Coal* 1995: 1154). This inquiry asks whether such uses were already limited by "the restrictions that background principles of the State's law of property and nuisance already place upon land ownership" (*Lucas* 1992: 1029). In this inquiry, the courts have determined that, if the regulated activity "constituted a nuisance in the state's common law, it can avoid paying compensation because the right to engage in the activity was excluded from the owner's title" (e.g., *Rith Energy* 1999: 115, *Apollo Fuels* 2002: 735). This inquiry does not always result in the finding of a nuisance, especially when the activity evaluated is the mining itself and not the production of externalities (*Eastern Minerals* 1996: 551).

When the federal courts do not find a nuisance in the regulated mining activity, or choose not to make such an inquiry, the second prong of *Chancellor Manor* is used, and "the court must then determine whether the governmental action at issue constituted a compensable taking" (*M&J Coal* 1995: 1154). This generally involves determining whether there was a categorical *per se* taking, involving a loss of "all economically beneficial uses in the name of the common good" (*Lucas* 1992: 1019), or engaging in a *Penn Central* analysis, weighing the economic impact, interference with reasonable investment-backed expectations, and the nature of the government action (*Penn Central* 1978: 124). The results of such inquiries are varied, and at least one state court has found a substantial and total taking caused by SMCRA enforcement (*RTG* 2002). The federal courts, however, have generally ruled against the regulatory takings claims of coal mining operators after such an inquiry. Specifically, the courts have avoided conceptual severance; in other words, when assessing the economic impact of regulations, the profitability of all possessed coal interests, not just those immediately regulated, are considered (*Appolo Fuels* 2002: 723). Additionally, when considering the reasonableness of the operators' investment-backed expectations for property use, the federal courts have ruled that the long-standing presence of a substantial regulatory regime surrounding the coal mining industry must be considered in assessing the reasonableness of expectations (*Appolo Fuels* 2004: 1350), and such consideration generally weakens the plaintiffs' claims that their stated expectations were reasonable.

To summarize, the federal courts have developed a regulatory takings doctrine related to SMCRA implementation that has generally upheld uncompensated regulations. Specifically, the courts have been more apt to place greater weight with the public interest in the avoidance of nuisances caused by the externalities of mining than the claimed property interests of mining operators. Furthermore, the courts have recognized the presence of a pre-existing regulatory regime related to coal mining, and have argued that that presence has established a general expectation that coal mining must occur within regulatory guidelines, and any property claim that requires exceeding those limits is not a legitimate property claim. The next section of this chapter looks at the agencies charged with enforcing SMCRA, and considers the potential for regulatory takings litigation to have a chilling effect on regulatory behavior.

Analyzing the Chilling Effect

To develop a better understanding of the internal workings of SMCRA and how the various past, and possible future regulatory takings challenges, could affect permitting activities, elite interviews were conducted with key personnel in federal OSM and state regulatory authority offices. Subject selection was made based on permitting responsibilities. Interview requests were sent to directors of SMCRA implementing offices, both federal regional OSM offices and state regulatory offices, under varied state regulatory bodies, such as a Department of Natural Resources or a Department of Environmental Protection. Efforts were made to solicit interviews from states with either significant coal production or a history of coal production, and from states that represent the different coal producing regions of the United States. Interviews were conducted in person and by telephone in 2006. While not every office responded to interview requests, interviews were conducted with personnel in state SMCRA implementing agencies in 10 states, representing the Appalachian, Interior, and Western coal producing regions. Interviews were also conducted in five federal OSM offices, including two regional offices and three field offices. Since state agencies have their own unique arrangements, it is difficult to generalize about the titles and ranks of interview respondents. In general, efforts were made to interview personnel with broad managerial oversight over SMCRA implementation. The most common titles of interview respondents in state offices were director, chief, and program manager.

Interviews were conducted with directors of federal OSM offices. Requests were also made to speak with legal counsels from these offices, but such requests were only granted in two state offices and two federal offices.

Research interviews of elites require that extra precautions be taken to insure confidentiality of the respondents (Odendahl and Shaw 2002: 313). I observed quickly during these interviews that, not only was I interviewing a relatively small and determinable population (SMCRA regulators), but also a population who are rather familiar with the identities of other members of the group. For this reason, I decided early on in the research process to exercise extra caution in safeguarding confidentiality by concealing the identity participants, and to forego any direct quotations of the respondents.

Efforts were made to prevent leading the interview subjects, and the interviews were conducted in a manner that focused on general decision-making processes, narrowing down to various perceived threats to those processes, and eventually narrowing further, if needed, to regulatory takings challenges. In general, the interviews revealed a decision-making process in which the likelihood is low that regulatory takings litigation will directly produce a behavioral adjustment characterized as a chilling effect.

One feature of SMCRA regulation that emerged from the interviews is bureaucratization. This feature was found to exist both externally and internally to the regulatory regime. Externally, SMCRA regulation occurs within a larger bureaucratic context, involving other regulatory agencies, enforcing various statutes of federal, state, and municipal origins. Surface mining procedures present a number of risks to an area's hydrology, agriculture, biodiversity, and history, risks which SMCRA requires mining operations to control. Even absent SMCRA, these risk-producing activities would require various permits and related compliance actions. Discharge permits would be required by the Clean Water Act. Considerations may have to be made under the Archeological Resources Protection Act and/or the National Historic Preservation Act. Compliance with US Forest Service regulations may be required. The US Fish and Wildlife Service may require an endangered species consultation. Such steps are mandated before a permit under SMCRA can be issued. In other words, a great deal of decision-making in SMCRA permitting occurs outside of offices authorized to enforce SMCRA. Any chilling effect caused by takings litigation could easily be offset by the requirement of compliance with other regulatory agencies, such as the Army Corps of Engineers or the Forest Service. This external bureaucratization of SMCRA enforcement creates an environment which diminishes the likelihood that regulatory personnel will alter their behavior in anticipation of takings litigation, as those personnel are unlikely to perceive such a threat as directed toward them or their office.

Bureaucratization is also found internally, with knowledge in the regulatory regime being highly compartmentalized. Given the complex, scientific nature of the requirements placed upon surface mining by SMCRA, employment in OSM, or the various state regulatory authorities is based upon some level of scientific expertise. Although the head of the department has the ultimate authority to approve or deny a permit, and respondents relate occasional stories about the politicization of that decision, by and large, they report little to no evidence that their recommendations are consistently ignored. This is particularly true of legal knowledge. Most respondents answered questions about specific legal standards by saying that they would have to consult with their legal counsel. This does not mean that the respondents were ignorant of changes in legal standards. Frequently, respondents indicated that knowledge about changes in legal standards comes to them in the form of a memo from legal counsel, or procedures are changed in writing by directive from above. All in all, the decision-making atmosphere observed was one of compartmentalized ritual. Most respondents indicated that the statute and the regulations are clear as to how things should be done, and if those standards are not met, permits will not be regarded as sufficient, and any legal challenge will be confidently approached with the knowledge that the regulator had followed the rules.

This observation was particularly apt in relation to regulatory takings litigation. Every respondent was aware of regulatory takings litigation. However, the topic of regulatory takings had to be brought up by the interviewer, as most respondents saw it as a possibility, but stated that its occurrence was rare. Only one respondent offered an unsolicited hesitation that such litigation could increase and could result in a chilling effect. By and large, there appears to be a strong culture of obligation within the regulatory agencies. Although the law regarding takings may change to the benefit of property owners, all respondents, without exception, defined their task at hand as one defined by the statute. Most discussions of the threat of litigation involved respondents initially perceiving this threat as being caused by their own deviation from statutory obligation, thus inviting litigation from coal companies or environmental groups, depending on the nature of the deviation.

Furthermore, some of the respondents had, in the past, worked within the coal mining industry, and were sympathetic to the degree of regulation faced by mining operators. However, they stated that they must do their job according to the statutory and regulatory requirements, and, if there is going to be a takings challenge, that is a decision that falls out of their hands. Even respondents in offices that had lost a takings challenge and had to pay compensation (or at least perceived they had to pay) – frequently, such payments come from the general treasure, not the particularly agency – told stories of directives requiring the office to pursue regulation just as before. Interviews made it evident that, for takings litigation to cause a chilling effect, the force of such litigation must overcome this agency culture of statutory obligation, and the countervailing threats of litigation that have, historically, helped forge this culture.

Finally, a set of generalizations can be made about the relationship between the various state and federal regulatory offices and the mining operations. These observations point to the presence of factors outside of the legal terrain of SMCRA implementation that shape the expectations held, and contexts of meaning used by those involved in such implementation. Like the above bureaucratic decision-making rules, these institutions present likely obstacles to a takings litigation chilling effect on regulatory behavior.

All respondents described their general interactions with permit applicants as cooperative today, but contentious in the past. The general story told by personnel in agencies charged with implementing SMCRA is that the initial resistance of the coal mining community to a new set of regulations was high, and it lasted for several years, but that the coal companies have become more readily compliant. A couple of factors are central to this evolution. First, several respondents indicated that it took a while for the mining operations to learn the precise expectations under requirements of the law. SMCRA's history appears to be consistent with the general understanding of the development of all major environmental statutes that developed in the 1970s. Originally, there was a great deal of congressional mistrust directed at agencies, questioning whether they would exercise their newly acquired responsibilities (Melnick 1983). Scheberle's research on federal/state interactions within SMCRA enforcement indicates that oversight of state regulatory authorities by the federal OSM has relaxed, partially due to "the development of performance agreements that evaluate states on the basis of 'on-the-ground results' rather than the number of inspections and citations issued" (Scheberle 2004: 177). The number of oversight visits paid by the federal OSM to state regulatory agencies decreased from more than 5,000 visits per year in the early 1990s to just over 2,000 visits per year in 2003 (Annual Reports). Less pressure on the states to meet a quota of citations can result in more cooperative relationships with the coal mining industry.

Interviews with regulatory personnel indicate that the experiences gained by regulators and those regulated have resulted in more knowledge on the part of surface miners about the legal requirements of SMCRA. Additionally, the development of mining practices has affected that knowledge. As mining has become more corporate, with an increasing number of large companies controlling a bigger chunk of surface coal mining in the US, knowledge about surface mining regulations has become central to corporate decision-making. Furthermore, large corporations have more legal resources at their disposal, which could lead to more litigation, but as the respondents have indicated, this has instead led to more informed decision-making and cost efficient compliance with regulations.

Respondents generally indicated that most takings challenges emerge from poor planning. Agency personnel prefer that potential mining operators consult with the regulatory authority before getting too deeply involved in pursuing mining plans; however, few institutional or informational factors are created by those agencies to inform miners of this preference. Respondents indicated that, when miners do consult with the regulatory authority early in the planning process, the permitting process is completed much more smoothly. The experiences of the respondents demonstrate that larger corporate operations are most likely to have the personnel resources and legal knowledge to seek such information from the beginning. Furthermore, several large operations, particularly those in the West, have more coal estate than they can currently mine. Therefore, current mining practices in those areas are more likely in areas with little reclamation difficulty.

These various temporal factors function as obstacles to a takings-induced chilling effect in a couple of ways. First, the general factor of time, for the reasons explained above, depreciate the likelihood of a regulatory takings lawsuit. As regulatory procedures and expectations become clearer, and as the costs of SMCRA compliance become more internalized, the likelihood of quashed expectations decreases. As takings litigation becomes less likely, the perceived risk to regulatory personnel also decreases, and the power of such litigation to cause a chilling effect is weakened.

Additionally, time shapes the contexts of meaning within which mining, regulation, and litigation occur. A key factor in the judicial determination of regulatory takings is the reasonableness of property use expectations held by the property owner (*Penn Central* 1978: 124). A number of temporal factors have shaped these expectations and, more significantly, the reasonableness of expectations as perceived by regulators. One such factor is the experienced judicial deference in regulatory cases that lessens the agency's collective perception of the risk of takings litigation. However, "one cannot properly understand the nature of the impact of judicial review on administrative procedures without first understanding the nature of administrative procedures" (Sunkin 2004: 45). At a minimum, one should acknowledge the possibility that, when reacting to a judicial stimulus, key regulatory decision-makers must interpret the decision, search for a way to implement the change without fundamentally altering the "*ésprit de corps*" of the agency, and then choose an implementation strategy (Canon 2004: 84). Each of these steps is a point in time in which the regulator has discretion in the manner in which a judicial decision will be implemented, or if it will actually be implemented at all.

In exercising regulatory discretion, the key decision-makers confront the conflicting demands of a potential constitutional requirement of compensation and statutory obligation. Past experience of improved relations between the regulator and the regulated and witnessed improvements in regulatory compliance make takings challenges appear less reasonable. Furthermore, the likelihood of a prolonged backlash is minor compared to the experienced certainty of judicial backlash against statutory noncompliance.

After the passage of social legislation in the 1960s and 1970s by a Congress untrusting of executive commitment, "federal judges have shown themselves to be increasingly suspicious of regulators who stray very far from a narrow interpretation of their statutory authority. … The safer and easier path, both legally and politically, is thus often a narrow and mechanistic application of the authorizing statute" (Nakamura and Church 2003: 7). The end result is an agency culture, defined by obligation to its enabling statute, which must be "overcome" if regulatory takings decisions are to have a chilling effect on regulatory output.

Conclusion

Harrington and Turem argue that the neoliberal reform of regulatory practices "*reconfigures* rather than *replaces* state authority" (2006: 202). In this context, it does appear that the social mobilization of private property rights through regulatory takings litigation is an effort to reconfigure the authority of the courts in relation to administrative agencies. The use by these interest groups of regulatory takings litigation can be seen as an effort, to borrow Harrington and Turem's language, to diminish the courts' role in horizontal accountability, as the applier of congressional standards on regulatory actors, and shift that accountability to a vertical role, in which agencies are held accountable, by the courts, to their principles (the public) (199) through market based administration.

"Pointing to differences in accountability discourses does not mean, however, that there is necessarily a lack of conceptual continuity over time. Indeed, certain continuities are obvious" (Harrington and Turem 2006: 200–201). This chapter has focused on those continuities which, at least in the context of SMCRA implementation, provide a force of regulatory stability in the face of litigious deregulatory pressure.

The preceding observations should not be read to indicate that a chilling effect caused by regulatory takings litigation is impossible. The predictive assumption of a chilling effect caused by regulatory takings litigation rests on assumptions of regulatory behavior rooted in a psychology of economic cost/benefit calculation. Certainly, it is not difficult to imagine that a situation could occur in which budgetary constraints were so high that such assumptions could become manifest. However, my analysis reveals the presence of institutional obstacles to the chilling effect, obstacles which, in the case of SMCRA, must be overcome for regulatory takings litigation to sustain a reduction in SMCRA regulatory outputs.

Some of these factors work by shaping the decision-making rules-of-the-game utilized by regulatory personnel and, as such, can be understood as affecting a key regulator's cost/benefit analysis of the choice between adherence to the statutory requirements of SMCRA, or the possibility of regulatory takings litigation. Key among these factors are a heavily bureaucratized, multi-agency decision-making process, and an agency culture defined by an obligation to statutory requirements. Both of these factors affect the decision-making of regulatory personnel by lessening the perceived risk of a regulatory takings lawsuit, the former by hiding that risk within layers of decision-making, the latter by presenting another risk, historically recognized within the agency as a greater likelihood of getting sued for deviation from the statute.

Other factors shape the contexts of meaning from which regulators understand the values embedded in their regulatory behavior and in the body of laws surrounding their professional career as SMCRA implementing personnel. In other words, regulators find themselves within an evolving hermeneutic environment in which such legal concepts as the reasonability of property use expectations and public responsibility are defined. Respondents to the interviews indicate that certain temporally defined factors affect the way they perceive the threat of regulatory takings litigation. Included in these factors are the historical presence of surface coal mining regulation, changing relationships between regulators and the regulated, and a perception *on the part of regulators* that the courts generally still defer to regulators on the issue of regulatory takings. It is this last set of factors that may be most significant. The time-based factors have changed over time, and with them, the regulators' understandings of risk and right have changed as well. The social mobilization of property rights would have to forge another shift in these factors, but doing so could bring about the changes in regulatory enforcement that they seek, and advocates of strong environmental and land use regulations fear.

Chapter 10
From "Wasteland" to "Wetland": *Palazzolo*, Neoliberalism, and Changing Practices of Coastal Regulation[1]

Laura J. Hatcher

Reframing Property Rights Mobilizations

"Legal mobilization," as an area of study within law and society most often focuses upon the way activists make use of the law to stake out legal claims, to enable social movement mobilization, and to create new understandings of law that will advance the views of activists concerning what is right and just. In these studies the analysis begins, most often, with the moment individuals become aware of an injustice they have suffered (Felstiner et al. 1980–1981). As Michael McCann (2008) points out, legal mobilization tends to focus on the actions of nonofficial legal actors in an analytical move that is also sometimes referred to as "decentering" the courts (see also McCann 1994). Yet the "bottom-up jurisprudence" used in this research often decenters *all* government institutions to such an extent that it is hard to capture the dynamic relationships between the institutions and the actors responding to them. And once decentered, the role of institutional power becomes difficult to analyze.

This becomes especially problematic in analyses of politics where the very nature of the rights are undergoing reconstruction within governmental agencies as well when nonofficial actors do not fit the description McCann has provided so aptly: "the less powerful or marginalized among unofficial ordinary people in civil society" (McCann 2008: 524). Landowners and businessmen do not generally appear to fit this description because they do own property, and as they participate in business, are empowered. Yet they are often involved in property rights mobilizations, particularly along the coasts where economic development and coastal preservation are both priorities. How then can property rights mobilizations

1 Several documents in this study come from the Special Collections Department at the University of Rhode Island. In particular, I wish to thank Associate Professor Sarina Rodrigues Wyant and her staff for the many hours of help in locating documents in the various Governor's and Senator's papers located in their archives. I also wish to thank Wayne McIntosh, Debbie Becher, Dick Brisbin, and Victoria Henderson for their helpful comments on earlier drafts of this chapter.

help us understand legal mobilization more generally? I contend here that careful attention to the historical changes that give rise to property rights mobilizations can highlight the role of changing institutions and institution-building projects. Power shifts with these changes, and as power shifts, property rights activists have developed a rights discourse in response.

The story of *Palazzolo v. Rhode Island* is a case in point. A businessman, Anthony Palazzolo, contested regulations along the south coast of Rhode Island. Eventually, his case was taken up by one of the pre-eminent property rights advocacy groups in the US, the Pacific Legal Foundation. To call either Mr. Palazzolo or his lawyers at the PLF "marginalized" or "disempowered" seems inaccurate when other mobilization analyses begin with individuals who are far more disempowered than either a small business owner or a conservative legal foundation. Moreover, *Palazzolo* is not simply a story of a property rights mobilization that made its way to the US Supreme Court. It is the story of changes to the way the state understood its coastline and the impact those new understandings had on private owners; and, quite importantly, it is the story of how these new understandings eventually created the context in which a property rights mobilization against relatively new legal understandings of the importance of coastal lands could occur. Without those changes, it seems plausible that no such rights claim would have happened.

The enormous power of administrative agencies to change the field in which nonofficial actors work is sometimes missed in legal mobilization studies. Their power is especially important to consider in situations where interactions among various levels of government build new institutions, and create competing areas of law to which activists respond and make use of in their work. In light of the rise of "backlash" movements – a term most often used to describe conservative, neoliberal, and libertarian movements aimed at changing public policy developed during or after the New Deal – taking institutional changes into account in order to understand how and why mobilizations happen has become critical to understanding the political landscape in the late twentieth and early twenty-first centuries in the US. Therefore, the research here advances along a slightly different track than past mobilization studies, though it is clearly inspired by insights produced through legal mobilization theory. In assessing property rights movements, I argue that the tension between administrative rules and constitutional rights are a constitutive dimension of modern governance. Moreover, this chapter represents a shift in my own work, away from analyzing groups such as the Pacific Legal Foundation as "libertarian" (Hatcher 2003 and 2005), toward understanding their activism as *neoliberal* (see also Scheingold and Sarat 2004).

This shift is in part due to the historical lens employed in this project. Libertarian claims would not be possible if the internal logics of the institutions they make claims against had not also changed. While it remains accurate to call property rights activists "libertarian" because their rights claims are consciously aimed at maximizing individual liberty, the term "libertarian" in a social science analysis misconstrues their relationship to neoliberal institutional structures. Finally, because of the *context* in which lawyers and activists for property rights has changed, one can provide an analytically richer understanding of these politics by seeing these activists as constituted through neoliberalism's internal tensions, particularly as neoliberalism has become a feature of administrative agencies.

The basis for my analysis is found by combining a close reading of administrative law as it has developed over the course of the late twentieth century with historical research on the development of institutional structures for coastal regulation. As Harrington and Turem (2006) point out, administrative agencies have received greater deference from judicial actors, particularly in the realm of accountability, especially in the last 25 years. In their view, *Chevron v. Natural Resources Defense Council* (1984) both marked the end of active judicial engagement in structuring the rulemaking process, and the beginning of deference to the administrative agencies. In *Chevron*, the US Supreme Court determined that "the Administrator's interpretation represents a reasonable accommodation of manifestly competing interests, and is entitled to deference" (*Chevron*: 865). This decision overturned a DC Circuit Court of Appeals which, according to the Supreme Court, had read the language of a statute "inflexibly," and announced that in the future "when a challenge to an agency construction of a statutory provision, fairly conceptualized, really centers on the wisdom of the agency's policy, rather than whether it is a reasonable choice within a gap left open by Congress, the challenge must fail." In other words, the courts would, from this point forward, defer to an agency's reading of the statute it is implementing as long as the agency's construction is "fairly conceptualized" (*Chevron*: 866). This deference, Harrington and Turem argue, has had the effect of "wither[ing] somewhat" the internal checks within administrative government that hold the agencies accountable to the public as well as Congress. They describe it as a feature of neoliberal governance (204).

I agree with these scholars, and further suggest that this "withering" has consequences for administrative agencies, not only at the national level, but in states where *Chevron*-like standards have been adopted. It has also created a tension within neoliberal governance that is constitutive of the rights claims made by property rights activists. Thus in cases of property rights mobilizations countering coastal regulations, activists, in part because of the effects that greater deference given administrative agencies have produced, mobilize in opposition to neoliberal governance in order to reinstate older understandings of rights and sovereignty. Not only do they seek to have the internal checks put back into the administrative process, they also seek to strengthen the claims of the individual in the face of new forms of law and thereby undermine regulation.

In short, deferential courts create a vacuum by no longer ensuring the administrative agencies are held accountable for their processes; this provides an opportunity for property rights activists to "push back," asking the courts to recognize the importance of the individual in the process. This activism responds to a lack of and attempts to (re)create an old opposition between individual rights holders and a sovereign who grants them a right that can be used to oppose that sovereign's actions. As with all legal mobilization analyses, the context matters, but it matters in an analysis that takes neoliberalism seriously, not simply because of what it teaches us about when, how and why the law is mobilized; instead, it matters because of what these mobilizations tell us about where power resides within the institutions of government, and what the individual's relationship to it is.

I suggest, here, that neoliberalism appears to have created a contradiction within itself that motivates grassroots activists to make challenges to it. Neoliberal governance, as I discuss in the final section of this chapter, uses scientific knowledge in ways that changes dramatically the way it understands land. Making claims against this governance is the same as making a claim against state authority, but it is also a claim against the scientific understandings underlying the regulations. Property rights activists base their claims upon an older notion of sovereignty that has an *anti-disciplinary claim* about the law embedded in it. When taken together, the tension created in these politics reveals for the analyst the inconsistent, open-textured, and internally conflicted nature of neoliberal governance and its response to rights. This is a point I will come back to in the final section of the chapter, after describing the circumstances that resulted in *Palazzolo v. Rhode Island.*

Development and Use of Coastal Lands

Change in the way property was understood and defined at both the local and national level was hardly a new phenomenon when Anthony Palazzolo bought his land. However, what makes *Palazzolo* significant is that it occurred in Rhode Island, the smallest state in the country with a very large coastline (approximately 420 miles in all), which is one of the state's chief economic resources. Because the state is so dependent on the coast for economic development, the use of what we call today the "coastal zone" was always very important to the government. But Rhode Island's perspective on the coast has also been structured through interactions with national institutions. Research in the state's various archival materials makes clear that its congressional delegation actively participated in the lawmaking process for legislation such as the Coastal Zone Management Act, the National Sea Grant Program, and various other environmental initiatives that occurred in the middle part of the twentieth century. Some of these initiatives included integrating disaster planning with local level planning in the form of flood insurance and disaster relief plans. Others involved the way the coastal zone would be managed in light of changing scientific knowledge about the health of the oceans and pressure from environmental movement activists. Ultimately, these various forces are very similar to the long-term process of changing property practices in the US more generally. And with these changes came restructured property rights.

National Changes

The processes of permitting contesting land use regulation, and the construction of administrative practices around land use planning all underwent changes in the last half of the nineteenth century. These changes laid the groundwork for further changes in the middle of the twentieth century. However, they created tensions within the law that continue to plague judicial decisionmaking around property rights today. It is important to understand that tension and its basis.

Morton Horwitz (1992) points out that "[t]he basic problem of legal thinkers after the Civil War was how to articulate a conception of property that could accommodate the tremendous expansion in the variety of forms of ownership spawned by a dynamic industrial society" (145). Horwitz reminds us that "as the most significant forms of new property were incorporeal [in the nineteenth century], judges were pressed to redefine the nature of interference with property rights more abstractly, not as an invasion of some physical boundary, but as an action that reduced the market value of property" (147). In short, notions of property were no longer simply tied to land. Instead, as John Lewis, in 1888, explained, for some legal thinkers legal doctrine concerning property was to be formed by "look[ing] beyond the thing itself, beyond the mere corporal object, for the true idea of property" (cited in Horwitz 1992: 147). Thus, "property" became a "bundle of rights" rather than a physical piece of land, and the use of the land became part of this bundle. The "'bundle of rights' include[d] every valuable interest which can be enjoyed as property and recognized as such" (Horwitz 1992: 147).

This abstraction, however, created a contradiction in the logic underlying the law. As Horwitz points out, it led to tensions around the notion of "market value," which was understood to be the most objective and practical measure of value. What expectations would owners have concerning the market value of their property? And how should this be tied to the concept of a "bundle of rights"? What uses of their land could owners expect to be acceptable under the law? The *expectations* of owners in the *uses* of their property became an issue in a way that, when a "taking" only involved a physical piece of property, it had not been.

The question arose whether uses of property could actually be *forms* of property. In which case, if the government limits a particular use, does this mean they have taken property and must compensate for it? Horwitz tells us this ultimately raised this question: "how does one avoid the conclusion that any governmental activity that changes expectations and hence lowers the value of property constitutes a taking?" (Horwitz 1992: 149). After all, if property exists at its most basic level as a set of stable expectations, *any* governmental action that changes – or even destabilizes – those expectations becomes constitutionally problematic in the context of the takings clause, and available as the basis for a rights claim.

Among these changes was a shift in the rationale and practices of granting permits for filling land to be developed for economic purposes. One might think these changes would bring about a shift in the expectations of property owners concerning what could be done with the land. After all, as the science of environmental policy took shape in the mid-twentieth century, governments developed new organizational structures as well as administrative practices for determining allowable use of the land. The historical record shows that these changes occurred slowly over a very long period of time, as state and national lawmakers explored different ideas concerning how to both protect and develop the coastline of the individual states as well as the nation as a whole. This slow process meant private property owners did not necessarily understand the meaning of acceptable use, particularly as new administrative agencies developed with new mandates and different ideas concerning the use of coastal land. Ultimately, in the case of Anthony Palazzolo, this meant that the expectations of private owners was particularly unsettled during periods when states were creating new policies around their coastal land and setting up new agencies to implement these regulations. Later, these factors would make coastal states particularly good stomping grounds for property rights activists at the end of the twentieth century.

Rhode Island's Coastal Law

Restructuring the law around its coastal lands was complicated for Rhode Island by the fact that the King's Charter of 1663, among other things, provided that what were then understood as "wastelands" be devoted to publicly beneficial yet water-dependent uses, including building wharves and other activities related to fishing (Conley and Flanders 2007: 104–105). These could be carried out with little interference by the state, except if building somehow interfered with navigation.[2] The practice of "wharfing out," i.e., filling tidelands, was historically controlled by the towns in Rhode Island (Conley and Flanders 2007: 106).

During the nineteenth century, however, the state General Assembly began to take the power to control wharfing away from the towns, and to exert more authority over state waters and tidelands. Among other regulatory mechanisms, in 1815, they established the idea of a "harborline" to mark the boundary between public and private use. Wharfing out could be done up to the harborline but not beyond it, because it could interfere with navigation. In cases such as *Engs v. Peckham* (11 R.I. 210, 1875), the state went so far as to see "the establishment of a harborline operated as a license or invitation to the riparian proprietor to fill or wharf out to that line" (*Engs*, 224). As Dennis Nixon (1990) points out, the breadth of this interpretation meant that there was no parcel by parcel assessment of the appropriate public use of the land, as there would be in the late twentieth century.

This also meant that prior to the parcel-by-parcel assessment being introduced into the law, the assumption by the courts in Rhode Island as well as private owners was that the owner would be allowed to fill the land as long as it did not interfere with the navigability of the water. This principle and its dominant interpretation kept administration of land use fairly simple: if a property owner

2 "Navigational servitude" could not be interfered with because it is a right held by the US federal government according to the Commerce Clause of the US Constitution.

could demonstrate that economic development would follow, filling was acceptable. Motivations for moving away from this standard included a new understanding about the role coast lands play in preservation of property in light of natural disasters, the realization that tourism depended in part on the beauty of the land, and of course, the development of an environmental ethic that involved preservation of ecosystems. What is important for our purposes is to note that this historically grounded simplicity concerning land use regulation meant private property owners could reasonably expect to fill land for economic development, provided they could demonstrate that doing so promoted the public good.

Even though there was a simple standard for determining when tidelands could be filled, it did not mean that owners could expect to do anything they wanted with their land. Rereading the King's Charter, we discover that the shorelines were clearly understood as "wastelands" that required "improvement." The Charter asserted that it "shall not, in any manner, hinder any of our loving subjects, whatsoever … to build and set upon the waste lands belonging to the said Colony and Plantations, such wharves, stages, and workhouses as shall be necessary for the salting, drying, and keeping of their fish to be taken or gotten upon that coast" (King's Charter of 1663). However, the "wastelands" belonged to the Colony, not the users of the coast. After the colony became a state, its coast remained a very important area of economic development. It was to be held by the state, and used freely by the people, provided that the people "improved" it by using it for trade and economic development.[3]

In keeping with this history, in 1843, when the state framed its constitution, the "waste lands" were not simply handed over to individuals to do whatever they wanted with them (Conley and Flanders 2007). The constitution included explicit language that, as Conley and Flanders (2007) have observed, was "[a]ttuned to the significance of the public shore privileges." While the state did actively encourage filling these areas in order to enable their development, and understood this to be a means of improving the coast, it also set rules for how this could be done. Those rules took into consideration the privileges of use that were accorded to the public more generally, not just the fishing industries or others involved in trade. But for the most part, if an owner could demonstrate that filling tidelands would result in economic development and not interfere with navigability, the permits would be granted. The law at this stage empowered those businessmen involved in economic development to a great degree. This would change as the state began to see its coastal lands as playing other significant roles in the "public good."

3 In the late eighteenth and early nineteenth century, this included the slave trade. Indeed, Rhode Island's history with the slave trade is quite notorious. See Conforti 2006 for further discussion.

Changing Understandings of "The Coast"

What sorts of factors would cause a state to change its coastal policy in such a dramatic way? Rhode Island's change took many decades to develop, as has been discussed elsewhere (Nixon 1990; Conley and Flanders 2007; Hatcher 2009). From the state's perspective, coastal and land management took on new urgency after a series of hurricanes resulted in extensive flood damage, property damage, and loss of life. The first of these hurricanes occurred in 1938. Horrific in its speed and force, it has never received an official name as most hurricanes receive, beyond the designation of "the Great Hurricane of 1938." It struck New York's Long Island, Connecticut, Rhode Island, and Massachusetts with full force. In Rhode Island alone, it resulted in 262 deaths, and property damage of approximately $100 million 1938 dollars (approximately $1 billion 2008 dollars). In 1944, another hurricane hit the eastern coast and also caused enormous damage, though not as great as the 1938 hurricane. Then, again, in 1954, Hurricane Carol wreaked devastation similar to the 1938 hurricane. Unlike the 1938 hurricane, Hurricane Carol caused only 19 deaths, while destroying twice as many structures and causing $100 million 1954 dollars in damage (University of Rhode Island, CRC). Cumulatively, the damage caused by these three hurricanes – one a decade for three decades – forced state governments, including Rhode Island, to develop policies to manage damage caused by high winds and flooding. This inevitably meant that individual property owners would have fewer choices concerning what use they put their land to. The power of these choices shifted away from the individual owner, and became a matter of administrative governance.

In direct response to Hurricane Carol (in 1954), the Rhode Island Development Council published a study of the Rhode Island Coastal Region.[4] The report's aim was to consider ways to minimize damage not only along the coast, but also in the state as a whole. In 1956, the state legislature passed the Shore Development Act of 1956 in the hopes of assisting municipalities in protecting the beach areas from further erosion and damage. Implementation of this act was assigned to the Department of Natural Resources, Division of Harbors and Rivers. It was from this agency that Palazzolo and his business partners would, initially, need to apply for permits to build on their land.

In 1959, Anthony Palazzolo became a partner in a business venture involving the development of property along the southern coast of Rhode Island, on a thin bar

---

4 Information concerning this report and early regulatory efforts is drawn heavily from Whitaker 1981. Whitaker's master's thesis, which I discovered while doing field work, is both widely known and frequently cited in reports about the Rhode Island Coastal Resource Management Council and statewide planning. Whitaker discusses the Development Council's 1956 report on pp. 23–24. The Development Council was, according to Whitaker, a precursor to the Department of Economic Development. The report, entitled *The Rhode Island Shore, a Regional Guide Plan Study, 1955–1970* was published in 1955. It attempted to establish a 15 year plan for regulation along the coast.

of land between Winnepaug Pond (a tidal salt pond) and the Atlantic Ocean. It is noteworthy that they were taking ownership just as the state began to change the way it understood the role of the coastal areas in light of these storms. It appears from all the court records as well as the newspaper interviews during the federal court case, that Mr. Palazzolo and his partners knew that the particular section of land would need to be filled in order for it to be developed, and they appear to have believed that if they applied for a permit to dredge and fill, their permit would be granted.

The early transactions that enabled Mr. Palazzolo to participate in the purchase and development of the land are complicated, but have been well documented by David Cole (2002–2003). Cole's analysis is the most detailed chronology of the case to date. Of particular interest is that Mr. Palazzolo became a shareholder and President of Shore Gardens, Inc. (SGI) in 1959 (Cole 2002–2003: 172), and then a year later he bought out his partners. In 1962 SGI, the sole shareholder of which was Anthony Palazzolo, submitted an application requesting a permit to dredge Winnapaug Pond and place the dredged material behind a bulkhead wall to fill the marsh to make it "adaptable for useful development" (described in Cole 2002–2003: 174).

Nearly 10 years later, Henry Ise, the Chief of the Divisions of Harbors and Rivers (DHR) would revisit this early proposal in his review of Mr. Palazzolo's various permitting applications. A careful reading of Ise's analysis is instructive when one considers that it was written in 1971, in the same period that the Coastal Zone Management Act, which established the Coastal Resource Management Council (CRMC) was enacted. The CRMC became the agency that Mr. Palazzolo took to court in the 1980s, but Ise's analysis of Mr. Palazzolo's various proposals is indicative of the way the state's view of its coastline was shifting at the time. This is particularly true when we compare this document to the CRMC's understanding of the coast as it began its court battles with Mr. Palazzolo 10 years later.

According to Ise, the DHR had held a public hearing in the Westerly Town Hall on July 28, 1962 and on the March 1962 application mentioned above. At this meeting, some opposition was voiced by the public based upon the idea that dredging "would be damaging to shellfish growth and contrary to conservation of that natural resource" (Ise 1971: 1). While he mentions this perspective, Ise had other statements that he felt were more compelling in his decision-making process. For example, the Chief of the State Division of Fish and Game had conveyed a statement to the DHR on July 24, 1962 (just before the town meeting) in which the Chief said:

> We have examined the location of the proposed dredging. There is, no doubt, some recreational digging of quahaugs existing in the area, and there would be a temporary loss of this recreation should material be dredged to the depth of four feet. *However, should the area be dredged, the resulting depth would be much more favorable to quahaugs. It would also be a better scallop habitat since there would be less danger of ground frost or winter freezing* (Quoted in Ise 1971: 1, emphasis added).[5]

5 "Quahaugs" are hard shell clams.

Similarly, the Chief of the Division of Fish and Game also submitted a statement a few months before, dated April 13, 1962, which Ise quotes as follows:

> We have examined the south shore of Winnapaug Pond in the area we believe includes the proposed dredging site of Shore Gardens, Inc., from which 60,000 cubic yards of material will be taken and deposited on an adjacent 30 acres of land. Our investigations show that the pond *has a very low potential of shellfish production in the area to be dredged, and that the marsh on which it will be deposited has a low waterfowl or other wildlife value. For these reasons, we have no objection to the proposed project* (Ise 1971: 1, emphasis added).

In addition, Ise quotes a statement submitted by four members of the University of Rhode Island Graduate School of Oceanography (URI). Later, URI would become the primary source of scientific information on the coast for the CRMC. That relationship was, at the time Ise wrote, already forming though not yet made official. The names of the four faculty members are not provided in the Ise document, but Ise says that the following was included in the final paragraph of a "lengthy statement":

> Dredging is ordinarily detrimental to marine bottom life in the immediate vicinity and in varying degrees by silting along the course of the drift. However, in the present instance the rate of circulation is not great, and the proposed location of removal of 60,000 cubic yards of material is from the submerged former clam flats. It can be assumed that the damage by one more operation of this magnitude to local marine life would be *no greater than that caused by the state's operations in the same general area*. However, *if continued in more productive parts of the pond, or if additional breachways were permitted*, leading to this small body of water sufficient to alter present salinity level, it *could seriously affect what appears a very desirable natural resource readily accessible to the public* (Ise 1971: 2, emphasis added).

Looking carefully at these quotes, the idea that dredging and filling would, in one case, actually be good for the wildlife of the pond is quite striking. The scientists at the University of Rhode Island, on the other hand, could see potential damage occurring, but felt that the damage done to the pond would be "*no greater than that caused by the state's operations in the same general area*." We see here evidence that the State of Rhode Island was dredging and filling in the area. Moreover, taken together, there certainly was not complete agreement on the impacts of dredging and filling to the ecology of the area. After all, the Chief of Fish and Game for the state said that such activities could actually be good for the ecosystem of the pond. Keep in mind, however, that Ise begins his discussion of this with the stronger statement of opposition to the dredging and filling voiced in the meeting in Westerly Town Hall. The statements by the experts seem to be used by Ise to mitigate and perhaps even refute the concerns voiced at that Town Hall meeting by what appears to have been a more environmentally-oriented public.

Ise states that on October 5, 1962, the application was returned to Mr. Palazzolo "[o]wing to inaccuracies and the absence of essential basic information." But Ise then turns his attention to another application, submitted in May of 1963. Ise's description is hard to visualize, but essentially Palazzolo wanted to build two entrance channels into the pond, one 600 feet and the other 680 feet long, and both approximately 60 feet wide. Ise does not go into great detail concerning this plan, but Cole tells us that these channels would be "bordered by marina-style residential lots ... to be built by the purchasers of the lots" (Cole 2002–2003: 171). Ise says that there was opposition to this plan from conservationists similar to those raised in the Westerly Hall Town meeting in July of 1962. Thus, Ise says, a decision on the application was deferred until further analysis could be performed. One can infer by the decision to wait on the application and do more analysis that the conservationists were vocal enough that the public officials wanted to ensure careful consideration of their views.

In the meantime, in April of 1966, Palazzolo submitted yet another proposal, this time to build a beach by dredging and grading the land in front of his property. This, according to his application, would require depositing 12,000 cubic yards of dredged material on the land up to about 800 feet inland and averaging a depth of about 12 inches to 16 inches. Unfortunately for Mr. Palazzolo, the state legislature had passed legislation in 1965 that placed the decision for this permit in the hands of the director of the Natural Resources Division. The 1965 law provided the Division of Harbors and Rivers, which was a division within the Department of Natural Resources, with the authority to regulate the filling of coastal wetlands (R.I. Gen. Laws § 46-6-1). The statute actually criminalized behavior that disturbed "the ecology of intertidal salt marshes, or any part thereof," without first gaining a permit from the state. It defines an "intertidal salt marsh" to include areas in which at least some (not all) of the following can be found: salt marsh grace, black grass, seaside lavender, saltwort, salt meadow grass, spike grass, salt marsh bulrush, sand spurrey, and where salt marsh peat exists. The director of Natural Resources, the statute states, "shall refuse to issue such permit if in his judgment the dumping or depositing of mud, dirt, or rubbish, or excavation would disturb the ecology of intertidal salt marshes" (R.I. Gen. Laws § 46-1-1). The state denied Palazzolo's third permit on July 20, 1966, citing the 1965 law. At this point, Mr. Palazzolo filed his first lawsuit in this matter. In August of 1966, he asked the Superior Court to review the decision. The Superior Court remanded the decision back to the Department of Natural Resources on December 30, 1966, citing the insufficiency of the record in its court order. In part, the Ise document in 1971 is a response to this court case.

The 1965 Act (and its amendments in 1967) is evidence of the very important changes concerning the way those salt marshes and the coast line more generally was understood by state regulators. Yet, it was only the beginning of the changes to come. In March of 1969, just a few months after taking office, Governor Frank

Licht set up a committee to look into and consider how best to regulate the coastal area. The Technical Committee on the Coastal Zone released its preliminary findings and recommendations a year later, in March of 1970. Governor Licht charged the Technical Committee to consider what "effective management" of the Narragansett Bay would require (Governor's Report on the Coastal Zone, 1970). This committee eventually produced an extensive report outlining both the challenges and opportunities of coastal management. After a great deal of heated debate, many of the Technical Committee's recommendations were incorporated into legislation passed by the state legislature as the Rhode Island Coastal Resources Management Act of 1971 (CRMA). This statute established the Coastal Resource Management Council (CRMC).

The CRMC is a complex organization, in part, because like many environmental agencies it was given the power to regulate with a two fold, somewhat contradictory, mandate: to both preserve the coast and promote its economic development.[6] Moreover, the CRMC was granted authority, "over land areas (those areas above the mean high water mark)" and limited "to that necessary to carry out effective resources management program."[7] Quite importantly, the CRMC's jurisdiction, like many coastal management agencies in the US, is defined by the mean high water mark (i.e., think of the scum line that forms after high tide in tidal zones – this is roughly the line that is used to determine the CRMC's jurisdiction). This area includes the tidal waters of the salt ponds along the southern coast, where Palazzolo's land was, as well as all land adjacent to tidal rivers. Since there are 420 miles of coastline in Rhode Island (a state that is approximately 48 miles long and 37 miles wide), and tidal waters include parts of the rivers running through towns and cities into the bays, (including its capitol city, Providence), the CRMC is responsible for permitting and regulating a very large portion of the land in a very small state. Its creation marks a major shift in Rhode Island's perspective on its coast, because it was created with much broader powers to manage land than its predecessor ever had.

While the Governor and state legislators were busy passing the enabling legislation for the CRMC in 1971, the Department of Natural Resources finally responded to Mr. Palazzolo's applications. Remember that he originally filed in

6 See Rhode Island Laws, Chapter 23, Title 46. The goals of the program are to carry out the "policy of this state to preserve, protect, develop, and where possible, restore the coastal resources of the state for this and succeeding generations through comprehensive and coordinated long-range planning and management, designed to produce the maximum benefit for society from such coastal resources; and that preservation and restoration of ecological systems shall be the primary guiding principle upon which environmental alteration of coastal resources will be measured, judged, and regulated" (§42-23-1).

7 Rhode Island Laws, §42-23-6(B). The statute continues, "This shall be limited to the authority to approve, modify, set conditions for, or reject the design, location, construction, alteration, and operation of specified activities or land uses when these are related to a water area under the agency's jurisdiction, regardless of their actual location …".

1962, filed twice in 1963, and then again in 1966. He went to court, and the court had sent the case back to the administrative agency for further review. Thus, when Henry Ise determined on April 1, 1971, that Mr. Palazzolo's permit applications were in order, Palazzolo had already been waiting nine years for an answer to his applications. Ise determined that Mr. Palazzolo could decide between the two applications submitted in May of 1963 or April of 1966. He gave Palazzolo 60 days to make up his mind. However, before Palazzolo could make his decision, the newly created Coastal Resources Management Council, which came into being through the 1971 legislation, asserted its authority, and rescinded the permits until further review could be done under their new mandate.

As one reviews this history, it becomes clear that it is at this point we can conclude Rhode Island owners could no longer expect to fill and dredge by simply showing that economic development would occur through their efforts. Instead, their applications would be considered, not only in consideration of economic development, but also in the context of preserving the coastline.

Mr. Palazzolo, at times with long periods between applications, applied for permits with the CRMC. In 1983, he applied for a permit to do the same thing he had proposed to do in the 1966 permit that the Division of Harbors and Rivers had found acceptable: build a bulkhead along Winnapaug Pond and fill the 18 acres behind it. The CRMC turned him down. He refiled the application, and the CRMC turned him down a second time. Finally, in 1988, Palazzolo filed a complaint alleging inverse condemnation, and demanded that the state pay him $3.1 million for the property. He came to this number by calculating what the land would be worth had he been able to develop it according to his 1966 permit plan. But he was no longer willing to file one permit after the other. He now alleged a constitutional violation of his right to private property, whereas previously he had requested the courts to order the agencies to reconsider their decisions.

At this time, he had not met his future lawyers, the Pacific Legal Foundation. Instead, for several years, Mr. Palazzolo struggled in the state courts using local attorneys. As the case made its way through the Rhode Island courts, Mr. Palazzolo's arguments were rejected again and again, and more than once for lack of ripeness. The judges contended that he had not yet made use of all his administrative remedies. They pointed to doctrines of public nuisance and the public trust to point out that even if all remedies had been exhausted, there was nothing in the record to show that they would order that the agencies grant the permits. Judge Frank J. Williams, in a 1992 case, pointed out that there was still some economic viability left in the land if Mr. Palazzolo was to develop the two acres of dry land that was part of his acreage. From the state court's perspective, Mr. Palazzolo needed to continue to work within the permitting process. The CRMC had denied his permit, arguing that the 18 acres of land that Mr. Palazzolo wanted to fill amounted to 12 percent of the marshes surrounding the pond – filling this area would jeopardize the future of Winnapaug Pond. The Superior Court upheld the CRMC, and later the Rhode Island Supreme Court rejected his appeal, arguing that the case was not ripe as Mr. Palazzolo had not yet "explored development options less grandiose than filling 18 acres of salt marsh" (quoted in Levitz 2000). This was the decision that ultimately made its way to federal Supreme Court review.

Once the Pacific Legal Foundation stepped in and the US Supreme Court agreed to hear the case, it garnered a great deal of press attention. While his lawyers may be part of the conservative movement, one reporter wrote, Mr. Palazzolo self-identified as a "New Deal Democrat" (Flint 2002). The government, Mr. Palazzolo felt, had a role to play in the lives of citizens. However, in the case of his property, he felt that the government had overstepped the bounds of appropriate action, and were denying him uses that he felt the law itself allowed him. He explained in an interview, "I never got one penny off this land. All I got is tax bills … You think those guys fighting the Revolutionary War wanted us to have to ask the next person, 'Can I do this with my land?' [Expletive]." Later he explained to the same reporter that the Rhode Island Attorney General (Sheldon Whitehouse) and state administrators "are not people you can sit down and talk with. They just keep rubbing my nose in it." Finally, Mr. Palazzolo explained, "I wanted to build a nice project … The kids had to go to school. We had to eat. It wasn't like this, the way it is now – I wouldn't have bought the frigging land."

His sense that the regulations had been unfair seemed deeply rooted in the changing nature of land use policy over the course of the 40 years in which he had battled with state regulations. The use he thought he would be able to make of the land was not available to him – and Palazzolo felt strongly, according to every interview he did in the press, that he should have been allowed to dredge and fill the land, because the law itself allowed him to do so. The CRMC and other state officials who were denying him uses he thought were acceptable were, in his mind, breaking the law. He made the startling claim, in the weeks before the Supreme Court case, "This land had rights … After the sweep of a pen, it had no rights. Where did they go to? The state got them. How much did it pay for them? Zero." If we were to replace the word "rights" in this quote with the word "uses," Mr. Palazzolo's point appears to be that the state has the use of the land. The owner's uses disappeared "with a stroke of the pen."

Palazzolo told Nina Totenberg of NPR in an interview in February of 2001, "I have met with Coastal [i.e., CRMC] on site and asked them what I could do with this, and they said, 'Nothing.' They keep looking at me straight in the eye and say, 'Nothing.' And that kind of doesn't sit right. I mean, I always felt that here in Rhode Island, well, in this country, you have the right to own property and to use it, providing you do not harm anybody, and I was not harming anybody." Mr. Palazzolo clearly asserts the view that to own property is to control its uses, even as he made reference to the notion of "not harming" any individual.

The Pacific Legal Foundation entered the picture after finding the conflict during Internet searches aimed at locating precedent setting cases. This organization has the historically important distinction of being the first conservative public interest law firm in the United States (Hatcher 2005, Teles 2008). Since its beginning in the early 1970s, it has developed from an organization mostly interested in disputing the findings of Environmental Impact Statements in California and filing briefs of *amicus curiae* in Supreme Court cases, to an organization that deals in many different areas of law and actively searches for cases to sponsor in federal litigation.

Eric Grant, one of their staff attorneys, was assigned to the case, though it was James Burling who eventually argued it before the Supreme Court. The actual mobilization once these nationally known lawyers became involved moved quickly, and the case jumped from being an issue in a small state to a potentially important precedent-setting case. As this occurred, the complicated permitting process that Mr. Palazzolo had been involved in receded in the background, as the constitutional issue of whether the state could "take" land through regulation dominated the discourse. However, the form of "taking" that had occurred involved the decision of what use the land could be put to, not whether the land itself had been physically taken by the state.

The final twist in the story of *Palazzolo* came when the precedent set in the Supreme Court case was not really what either side had argued before the Court. The Supreme Court sent the case back to the Rhode Island courts to be reviewed again under tough standards concerning the economic impact on a property owner of land use regulations. This fact meant the State Attorney General, Sheldon Whitehouse, could declare a victory in the case, because it showed that the Court rejected Palazzolo's theory of property, and he felt certain Rhode Island would prevail in state court (Lord 2001).

Yet, the Supreme Court managed to set a precedent concerning ripeness that was understood by many property rights advocates to be a "win" for their cause. In essence, the Court decided the issue of whether an owner can claim a regulatory taking of property subject to wetlands regulation *after* the acquisition of the property. The 5-4 decision, authored by Justice Anthony M. Kennedy found that the Rhode Island Supreme Court had erred in determining that the case was not ripe for judicial review, though the Rhode Island court had been correct in asserting that Palazzolo had not yet established a deprivation of all economic value in his claims. The US Supreme Court remanded the case back to the state courts to provide Mr. Palazzolo with the opportunity to establish deprivation of all economic value. It is noteworthy that at this point the case, once again, became an administrative law matter. The state courts eventually found that Mr. Palazzolo had not yet exhausted his permit applications, thus deferring to the claims made by the CRMC as early as the 1990s concerning the possible uses of the dry land within Mr. Palazzolo's acreage.

The local press reports that Mr. Palazzolo, after losing yet again in court, is selling his land. He says he cannot afford to build the home that would be allowable on the upland where he could be permitted to build. Without a building on it, the property itself has been valued at over half a million dollars (Santiago 2008).

Reconfigured State Authority and Property Rights

In many ways, the story of *Palazzolo v. Rhode Island* is the story of reconfigured state authority that changed property rights in substantial ways. State authority to regulate land has been, according to many scholars, reconfigured along with the rest of state authority over the course of the twentieth century (Turem and Harrington 2006, Soja 1989). Increasingly, urban and land use planning has been used, as Edward Soja pointed out in 1980, as a tool of the state for organizing space for the benefit of capital accumulation and crisis management (see also Brisbin, et al. in this volume for a discussion of land use planning more generally). We saw both of these in the story of *Palazzolo v. Rhode Island.*

Property rights activists draw upon the liberal political tradition and its notions of sovereignty and individual rights to protect legal subjects from overzealous government. Contemporary movements do this while also adapting to new institutional designs that employ administration through scientific understandings of land and natural disasters. Assessments made by regulators of "use" balance scientific analyses and economic calculations about the land. We see in the case of Mr. Palazzolo's permits that the issues of how his activities would impact the ecosystem were always a part of the agencies' responses to him – however, the regulators' understanding of these impacts changed depending on the point in time as well as which agency considered the permits. The agencies were, in part, responding to the changing laws being created by the state legislature.

Rights claims by neoliberal property rights groups such as the Pacific Legal Foundation strategically counter logics of administrative agencies by pointing to the merits of individual decision-making (i.e., the belief that Mr. Palazzolo should be able to determine the use of land he owns) in contrast to the legitimacy of agency choices. While doing so, property rights activists continue to rely upon the authority of a sovereign to grant rights and enforce the law for its basis. But they are contesting the laws that the sovereign has made. For example, Mr. Palazzolo and his attorneys argued that the CRMC had overstepped its bounds by determining that he could not use the land in ways he thought were appropriate. As quoted above, Mr. Palazzolo felt the uses had changed with "one stroke of the pen."

Neoliberal rights claims, grounded in the notion of a legal subject that is a rational individual who needs protection against the state's actions, uses the very state power it contests to make rights claims. A decision to go to court is, after all, a form of request to the government to consider the legitimacy of its own actions. Our example, here, is the claim that property has been taken without due process and just compensation. I argue that we can analyze this as a claim that the government's understanding of how the land can be used has changed in a way that shifts the power away from the individual property owner to bureaucrats. The property rights claim is made to resist government decisions that changed the structure of land use itself.

As Foucault (1980) pointed out in his "Two Lectures," calling upon the rights of sovereignty does not truly resist the law, but instead reinforces law's legitimacy by asking law to recognize the freedom it grants. In his lecture of *5 April 1978*, Foucault develops this idea in a direction that is helpful to us. He explains that the insertion of freedom is an essential ingredient in governing:

> Henceforth, a condition of governing well is that freedom, or certain forms of freedom, are really respected. Failing to respect freedom is not only an abuse of rights with regard to the law, it is above all ignorance of how to govern properly. The integration of freedom, and the specific limits to this freedom within the field of governmental practice has now become an imperative (Senellart 2004: 353).

Kirstie McClure (1995) argues that Foucault sought a "new form of right, one which must indeed be anti-disciplinary, but at the same time liberated from the principle of sovereignty" (cited in McClure 1995: 150). In the case of property rights mobilizations, the claims are often made against land use regulations grounded in scientific understandings about hurricanes and environmental protection of ecosystems. These regulations are very much indebted to forms of disciplinary knowledge – i.e., the science of ecosystems, wildlife biology, and the like. As I have argued elsewhere, there is something distinctively anti-disciplinary about property rights claims, especially when activists make a claim about the right of citizens to use their property as they see fit in order to oppose the decisions of administrators. These decisions are generally framed in terms of scientifically grounded law and regulation (Hatcher 2003: 452). The form of right used by property activists is not liberated from the laws they oppose, even as it contests contemporary governance, but instead calls upon an older form of sovereignty still embedded in constitutional government to counter the regulation developed through administrative practice.

The Pacific Legal Foundation (PLF) became involved only after the case had already been filed and spent years in litigation in the Rhode Island courts. They provided a means of gaining national attention for this issue, but their involvement was not the main impetus for the rights claim. Mr. Palazzolo's position relative to power in the state had changed dramatically in the time between entering into a partnership to develop land, and his Supreme Court case. As the state adopted regulations based in environmental science to regulate its coast, it increased the power of the agencies regulating land in substantial ways. While the PLF's participation substantially changed the attention the case received, the mobilization itself started when Mr. Palazzolo, without this larger national movement actor, decided that the state was not making fair decisions concerning his permits. The fact that he was not going to be allowed to build on the land was, to him, an injustice because of his belief that he was asking to use the land in a way that the state had already found acceptable. In his mind, Rhode Island governance had stripped him of his rights – rights that came with ownership of the land – and had done so in a way that made it unaccountable to its own administrative process. Palazzolo turned to the courts for redress, but quickly found that the courts would turn back to the administrative agencies involved.

The claim that a regulation has violated the takings clause of the Constitution is, in part, a means of delegitimizing the science of environmental administration and land use planning in ways that are "anti-disciplinary," in the sense that Michel Foucault suggested in his work. What is intriguing about neoliberal claims against these changes to the administrative state is that they push back at the deference courts pay to administrative agencies by pressing the courts to consider the supremacy of the individual's decision making process over those of the neoliberal state's.

By looking at *Palazzolo* within the context of historically changing institutions, we can see how the institution-building project embarked upon by the state created the dispute. Had Mr. Palazzolo's permit applications been reviewed a little earlier, he may well have developed his land as he wanted to. The move to make an individual rights claim in this context is also indicative of the change in the institutions over the course of time, and this particular claim – that a use of land amounts to a taking – could not have happened before the institutions themselves changed their understanding of private property. The overlapping of older rights claims and new institutions of governance structured a form of rights claim that was not purely anti-disciplinary in Foucault's sense, but counters contemporary notions of governance through an older notion of individual rights. This makes the analysis of *Palazzolo v. Rhode Island* especially apt for understanding how institutional power matters in legal mobilization studies.

Bibliography

Ackelsberg, I. 2007. Interview. All for the Taking: 21st-Century Urban Renewal (dir. George McCollough).

Ackerman, B. 1977. *Private Property and the Constitution*. New Haven: Yale University Press.

Action Group on Erosion, Technology and Concentration (ETC). 1996. "*US Government Dumps the Hagahai Patent*" Available at: http://www.etcgroup.org/en/materials/publications.html?pub_id=461 [accessed: May 1, 2009].

Acuerdos de Paz. 2003. *Acuerdos de Paz de Guatemala*. MINUGA, Misión de Verificación de las Naciones Unidas en Guatemala: pp. 242.

Alexander, G.S. 1997. *Commodity and Propriety: Competing Visions of Property in American Legal Thought, 1776–1970*. Chicago: University of Chicago Press.

ALMG 1990. Documentos del seminario: Situación actual y futuro de la ALMG. Guatemala City, Patrocinio del Ministerio de Cultura y Deportes.

Alvarez, J.E. 2008. "The Factors Driving and Constraining the WTO's Incorporation of International Law" in J. Merit, V. Donaldson, and A. Yanovich, (eds) *The WTO at Ten: Governance, Dispute and Developing Countries*. Huntington, NY: Juris Publishing.

AMARC. 2005. *Democratizando la palabra: Informe regional sobre los marcos regulatorios de la Radiodifusión en Centroamérica*. El Salvador, Asociación Latinoamericana de Educación Radiofónica, Asociación Mundial de Radios Comunitarias.

AMARC. 2007. *Informe anual 2007 de la radiodifusión comunitaria en Guatemala: Once años en espera del cumplimiento de los Acuerdos de Paz*. Guatemala City, AMARC.

Amherst Seminar. 1988. "Introduction to the Special Issue on Law and Ideology." *Law and Society Review* 22, 629–39.

Andrews, L.B. 2001. *Future Perfect: Confronting Decisions About Genetics*. New York: Columbia University Press.

Annual Reports of the Office of Surface Mining. 1978–2003. *United States Department of the Interior.*

Associated Press. 2001. "Westerly Man, State to Argue Today Before U.S. High Court." *The Providence Journal-Bulletin*, February 26, 8B.

Babcock, R.F. 1966. *The Zoning Game: Municipal Practices and Policies*. Madison: University of Wisconsin Press.

Babcock, R.F. and Siemon, C.L. 1985. *The Zoning Game Revisited*. Boston: Oelgeschlager, Gunn and Hain.

Baker, C.E. 1975. "The Ideology of the Economic Analysis of Law." *Philosophy and Public Affairs* 5: 3–48.

Barros, D.B. 2005. "The Home as a Legal Concept," *Santa Clara Law Review* 46: 256.

Barry, J.M. 2005. *The Great Influenza: The Epic Story of the Deadliest Plague in History*. New York: Penguin Books.

Baum, L. 2006. *Judges and Their Audiences: A Perspective on Judicial Behavior*. Princeton: Princeton University Press.

Becher, D. 2009. *Valuing Property: Eminent Domain for Urban Redevelopment, Philadelphia* 1992–2007. PhD Thesis for the Department of Sociology, Princeton University, Princeton, NJ, 344.

Becher, D. Forthcoming. "The Participant's Dilemma: Bringing Representation and Conflict Back In," *International Journal of Urban and Regional Research*.

Beckert, J. 1996. "What Is Sociological About Economic Sociology? Uncertainty and the Embeddedness of Economic Action." *Theory and Society* 25(6): 803–840.

Been, V. and Beauvais, J. 2003. "The Global Fifth Amendment? NAFTA's Investment Protections and the Misguided Quest for an International 'Regulatory Takings' Doctrine." *New York University Law Review* 78, 30–143.

Benedict, J. 2009. *Little Pink House: A True Story of Defiance and Courage*. New York: Grand Central Publishing.

Benson, P., Fischer, E., and Thomas, K. 2008. "Resocializing Suffering: Neoliberalism, Accusation, and the Sociopolitical Context of Guatemala's New Violence." *Latin American Perspectives* 35(5): 38–58.

Berliner, D. 2003. *Public Power, Private Gain: A Five Year, State-By-State Report Examining the Abuse of Eminent Domain*. Arlington, VA: Castle Coalition.

Berman, P.S. 2007. "A Pluralist Approach to International Law". *Yale Journal of International Law* 32, 301–29.

Blomley, N. 2003. "Law, Property, and the Geography of Violence: The Frontier, the Survey, and the Grid." *Annals of the Association of American Geographers* 93(1): 121–141.

Blomley, N.K. 2005. "The Borrowed View: Privacy, Propriety, and the Entanglements of Property," *Law and Social Inquiry* 30 (4), 617–61.

Bluestone, B. and Harrison, B. 1990. *The Great U-Turn: Corporate Restucturing and the Polarizing of America*. New York: Basic Books.

Botello-Samson, D. 2008. "The Benchmark of Expectations: Regulatory Takings and Surface Coal Mining." *Journal of Natural Resources and Environmental Law* 22(1), 1–37.

Boudreaux, K. and Yandle, B. 2002. "Public Bads and Public Nuisance: Common Law Remedies for Environmental Decline." *Fordham Environmental Law Journal* 14, 55–88.

Brisbin, R.A., Jr. 1997. *Justice Antonin Scalia and the Conservative Revival*. Baltimore: Johns Hopkins University Press.

Brisbin, R.A., Jr. and Hunter, S. 2006. "The transformation of Canadian property rights?" *Canadian Journal of Law and Society* 21 (1), 135–59.

Buchanan, A. 2003. *Justice, Legitimacy and Self-Determination. Moral Foundations for International Law.* Oxford and New York: Oxford University Press.

Bull, B. 2005. *Aid, Power and Privatization: The Politics of Telecommunications Reform in Central America.* Northampton, Mass.: Elgar Publishing Inc.

Bullock, S. 2006. Interview.

Bureau of Economic Analysis. 2009. *Foreign Direct Investment*: 1980–2006. Available at: http://www.bea.gov/international/di1fdibal.htm.

Burgos, S. 2001. "Status Report of First Year of the Asez – Nti Pilot Early Action Planning Project." December 2001. *Philadelphia Empowerment Zone*, Philadelphia.

Butler, H.N. and Macey, J.R. 1996. "Externalities and the Matching Principle: The Case for Reallocating Environmental Regulatory Authority." *Yale Journal On Regulation* 14, 23–66.

Caldeira, G. and Wright, J. 1988. "Organized Interests and Agenda-Setting in the U.S. Supreme Court." *American Political Science Review* 82, 1109–1128.

Canon, B.C. 2004. Studying Bureaucratic Implementation of Judicial Policies in the United States: Conceptual and Methodological Approaches, in M. Hertogh and S. Halliday (eds) *Judicial Review and Bureaucratic Impact: International and Interdisciplinary Approaches*. New York: Cambridge University Press.

Castañeda y Castañeda, M.S. 2008. Interview. Guatemala City, Guatemala.

Castle Coalition. 2007a. 50 State Report Card: *Tracking Eminent Domain Reform Legislation Since Kelo. Institute for Justice*, Washington, DC, 56.

Castle Coalition. 2007b. Untitled Photograph. Institute for Justice, Washington, DC.

CEH. 1999. *Memory of Silence* [Tz'inil Na'tab'al]. Guatemala City, Comisión para el Esclarecimiento Histórico (Commission for Historical Clarification).

CERIGUA. 2006. "Radios comunitarias en la mira del Ministerio Público." *Centre for Investigative Reports on Guatemala*. Guatemala.

Chan, S. 2008. "U.S. Supreme Court Refuses to Hear Atlantic Yards Case." *The New York Times*. June 24.

CIDH. 2003. "Justicia e inclusión: Los desafíos de la democracia en Guatemala", Comisión Interamericana de Derechos Humanos (Inter-American Commission on Human Rights), Organization of American States.

City of New London. 2001. New London Development Council. 2001. Comprehensive Economic Development Strategy.

Claeys, E.R. 2008. "*Kelo*, the castle, and natural property rights", in *Private Property, Community Development, and Eminent Domain*, in R.P. Malloy (ed.). Burlington, VT: Ashgate, 15–33.

Coase, R.H. 1998. "Comment on Thomas W. Hazlett: Assigning Property Rights to Radio Spectrum Users: Why Did FCC License Auctions Take 67 Years?" *The Journal of Economics and Law* 41 (October): 577–580.

Coastal Resources Management Act. Title 46, Chapter 23, Section 46-23-1. Providence: Rhode Island General Laws.

Cohen, J.R. 2002. "Maryland's 'Smart Growth': Using Incentives to Combat Sprawl," in *Urban Sprawl: Causes, Consequences, and Policy Responses* (ed.) G. Squires. Washington, DC: Urban Institute Press, 293–324.

Cojtí Cuxil, D. 1996. "The Politics of Maya Revindication." In *Maya Cultural Activism in Guatemala*. E. F. Fischer and R. M. Brown. Austin, University of Texas Press: 19–50.

Cole, D.E. 2002. "Analytical Chronology of Palazzolo v. Rhode Island." *Environmental Affairs* 30: 177.

Collins, P. 2008. *Friends of the Supreme Court: Interest Groups and Judicial Decision Making*. New York: Oxford University Press.

Commission on Marine Science, Engineering and Resources. *Our Nation and the Sea* 1969. US Government Printing Office. Available at http://www.lib.noaa.gov/ [accessed: October 10, 2008].

Community Leadership Institute, Philadelphia Folklore Project, et al. 2004. I Choose to Stay Here. Philadelphia Folklore Project: 21 min.

Community Leadership Institute. 2008. *The Taking of Bodine: Never Forget. Precious Places*. S.V. Center, Scribe Video Center: 10 min.

Conforti, J.A. 2006. *Saints and Strangers: New England in British North America.* The Johns Hopkins University Press.

Conley, P., and Flanders, R. 2007. *The Rhode Island Constitution: A Reference Guide*. Praeger Publishing.

Contreras, G. 2008. "Reclutan a Kaibiles Por Emisoras Piratas." *Siglo Veintiuno*. Guatemala City, Guatemala.

Cooper, P.J. 1988. *Hard Judicial Choices: Federal District Court Judges and State and Local Officials*. New York: Oxford University Press.

Corkery, M. and Chittum, R. 2005. "Eminent Domain Uproar Imperils Projects." *Wall Street Journal*, August 3, A1.

Corntassel, J.J. 2007. "Partnership in Action? Indigenous Political Mobilization and Co-optation During the First UN Indigenous Decade (1995–2004)." *Human Rights Quarterly* 29: 137–166.

Council of the City of Philadelphia. 2002 Public Hearing, Committee on Rules, December 9, 2002.

Coyle, D.J. 1993. *Property Rights and the Constitution – Shaping Society through Land Use Regulation*. Albany, NY: State University of New York Press.

Cullingworth, J.B. 1993. *The Political Culture of Planning: American Land Use Planning in Comparative Perspective*. New York, NY: Routledge Inc.

Cullingworth, J.B. 1997. *Planning in the USA: Policies, Issues, and Processes.* New York: Routledge.

Cultural Survival. 2008. "*Guatemala Radio Project*." Available at: http://www.culturalsurvival.org/programs/grp/program2 [accessed at: August 30, 2009].

Cutler, C. 2003. "Critical Reflections on the Westphalian Assumptions of International Law and Organization: A Crisis of Legitimacy." *Review of International Studies* 27, 133–50.

Dahl, R.A. 1963. *A Preface to Democratic Theory*. Chicago: University of Chicago Press.

De Soto, H. 1989. *The Other Path*. New York, Basic Books.

De Soto, H. 2000. *The Mystery of Capital: Why Capitalism Triumphs in the West and Fails Everywhere Else*. New York, NY: Basic Books.

Decker, R.O. 1976. *The Whaling Center: A History of New London.* Chester, Conn.: Pequot Press.

DeGrove, J.M. 2005. *Planning Policy and Politics: Smart Growth and the States* Cambridge, MA: Lincoln Institute of Land Policy.

Delaney, D., Ford, R.T., and Blomley, N. 2001. Preface: "Where is Law?", in *The Legal Geographies Reader: Law, Power, and Space* (eds) N. Blomley, D. Delaney, and R.T. Ford. Malden, MA: Blackwell Publishers, 13–32.

Department of Foreign Affairs and International Trade of Canada. 1999. Submission of the Government of Canada in Metalclad v. United Mexican States.http://www.economia-snci.gob.mx/sphp_pages/importa/sol_contro/consultoria/Casos_Mexico/Metalclad/1128/1128_990728_Canada.pdf.

Department of Foreign Affairs and International Trade of Canada. 2004. Submission of the Government of Canada in Methanex v. Government of the United States. http://www.state.gov/documents/organization/28854.pdf.

Department of International Negotiations of Mexico. 2004. *Submission of the Government of Mexico in Methanex v. Government of the United States*. http://www.state.gov/documents/organization/28829.pdf.

Dickenson, D. 2007. *Property in the Body: Feminist Perspectives*. Cambridge, UK: Cambridge University Press.

Dietz, T. 2002. "The Drama of the Commons", in *The Drama of the Commons*, edited by E. Ostrom, et al. Washington, DC: National Academy Press.

Dougherty, V. 2007. Interview.

Downs, A. 2001. "What Does 'Smart Growth' Really Mean?" *Planning*, 67 (4), 20–26.

Dryzek, J. 1999. "Critical Theory as a Research Program." *In The Cambridge Companion to Habermas. S. White*. Cambridge, Cambridge University Press: 97–119.

Ducot, C.R. and Dudley, R.L. 1986–7. "Dimensions Underlying Economic Policymaking in the Early and Later Burger Courts," *The Journal of Politics* 49: 521–539.

Duneier, M. and Carter, O. 1999. *Sidewalk*. New York: Farrar, Straus and Giroux.

Dworkin, R. 1984. "Rights as Trumps," in *Theories of Rights*, edited by J. Waldron. Oxford: Oxford University Press, 153–167.

Egan, T. 2005. "Ruling Sets Off Tug Of War Over Private Property," *The New York Times*, July 30, A1.

Epp, C.R. 2008. "Implementing the Rights Revolution: Repeat Players and the Interpretation of Diffuse Legal Messages." *Law and Contemporary Problems* 71 (1): 41–52.

Epp, C.R. 2009. *Making Rights Real: Activists, Bureaucrats, and the Creation of the Legalistic State*. Chicago: University of Chicago Press.

Epstein, L. 1985. *Conservatives in Court*. Knoxville, University of Tennessee Press.

Epstein, L. and Knight, J. 1997. "Mapping Out the Strategic Terrain: The Informational Role of *Amici Curiae*." In Clayton, Cornell and Howard Gillman (eds), *Supreme Court Decision-Making: New Institutionalist Approaches*. Chicago, IL: University of Chicago Press.

Epstein, R. 1985. *Takings: Private Property and the Power of Eminent Domain*. Chicago: University of Chicago Press.

Escalante, M.A. 2005. "El Rol del Gobierno en La Protección de Derechos y La Supervisión de Conflictos." Presentation at the conference Convergence or Competition: Radio Spectrum Management in Guatemala and Latin America. Universidad Francisco Marroquín, Guatemala City, Guatemala.

Eskridge Jr., W.N. 1991. "Reneging on History? Playing the Court/Congress/President Civil Rights Game." *California Law Review* 79(3): 613.

Ethical Framework. Available at: https://genographic.nationalgeographic.com/staticfiles/genographic/StaticFiles/AboutGenographic/Introduction/Genographic-Project-Ethics-Overview.pdf [accessed August 30, 2009].

Ewick, P. and Silbey, S. 1998. *The Common Place of the Law: Stories from Everyday Life*. Chicago: University of Chicago Press.

Executive Order 13406. 2006. "Protecting the Property Rights of American People" (June 23).

Fasken Martineau DuMoulin LLP. 2001. Investor's Memorial and Post-Hearing Submission of Claimant, ADF Group v. Government of the United States. http://www.state.gov/documents/organization/5964.pdf.

Fee, J. 2005–2006. "Eminent Domain and the Sanctity of Home." *Notre Dame Law Review* 81: 783–820.

Felstiner, W.L.F., Abel, R.L., and Sarat, A. (1980–1981). "The Emergence and Transformation of Disputes: Naming, Blaming, Claiming …" *Law and Society Review* 15(3/4): 631–654.

Fischel, W.A. 1995. *Regulatory Takings: Law, Economics, and Politics*. Cambridge: Harvard University Press.

Fishman, R. (ed.) 2000. *The American Planning Tradition: Culture and Tradition*. Washington, DC: Woodrow Wilson Center Press.

Flynn, S. 2006. "Across the Country, Americans Fight to Protect Their Property. Will the Government Take Your Home?" August 6, 2006. *Parade*. New York, New York, Parade Publishers: 6-8.

Ford, R.T. 1999. "Law's Territory (A History of Jurisdiction)," *Michigan Law Review* 97 (4), 843–930.

Foucault, M. 1980. "Two Lectures." In *Power/Knowledge: Selected Interviews and Other Writings, 1972–1977*. Colin Gordon (ed.) Pantheon Books.

Fox, L. 2007. *Conceptualising Home: Theories, Laws and Policies*. Oxford and Portland, Oregon: Hart Publishing.

French, M.A. 1992. "After 10-Year Tangle, Cornrows Still Divide District Hairdressers." *Washington Post*, January 26.

Friends of Fort Trumbull. n.d. Friends of Fort Trumbull. Available at: http://www.fortfriends.org/FORT_TRUMBULL/history.htm [accessed on March 15, 2009].

Fukuyama, F. 2002. *Our Posthuman Future: Consequences of the Biotechnology Revolution.* New York: Farrar, Straus and Giroux.

Fulton, W. 1996. *The New Urbanism: Hope or Hype for American Communities?* Cambridge, MA: Lincoln Institute of Land Policy.

Galanter, M. 1974. "Why the Haves Come Out Ahead: Speculations on the Limits of Legal Change." *Law and Society Review* 9: 95–160.

Galbi, D.A. 2003. "Revolutionary Ideas for Radio Regulation." *Law and Economics WPA* 0304001: 150.

Gale, D.E. 1992. "Eight State-Sponsored Growth Management Programs." *Journal of the American Planning Association* 58 (4), 425–40.

Gantz, D. 2006. The United States and NAFTA Dispute Settlement: Ambivalence, Frustration and Occasional Defiance. http://ssrn.com/abstract=918542.

Gerring, J. 1999. "Culture versus Economics: An American Dilemma," *Social Science History* 23: 2, 129–172.

Gill, S.R. and Law, D. 1989. "Global Hegemony and the Structural Power of Capital." *International Studies Quarterly* 33: 475–499.

Gillman, H. 1999. "The Court as an Idea, Not a Building (or a Game): Interpretive Institutionalism and the Analysis of Supreme Court Decision-Making," in *Supreme Court Decision-Making* (eds) C.W. Clayton and H. Gillman. Chicago: University of Chicago Press.

Gillett, G. and McKergow, F. 2007. "Genes, Ownership, and Indigenous Reality." *Social Science and Medicine* 65: 2093–2104.

Ginsburg, F. 1991. "Indigenous Media: Faustian Contract or Global Village?" *Cultural Anthropology* 6(1): 92–112.

Godsil, R.D. and Simunovich, D.V. 2008. "Protecting Status: The Mortgage Crisis, Eminent Domain, and the Ethic of Homeownership." *Fordham Law Review* 77: 949.

Goffman, E. 1961. *Asylums; Essays on the Social Situation of Mental Patients and Other Inmates*. Garden City, N Y.: Doubleday.

González Arrecis, F. 2007. Regularán radios comunitarias. AMARC. Retrieved June 2, 2008, from http://legislaciones.item.org.uy/index?q=node/132, February 14.

Goodwin, J., Jasper, J.M. and Polletta, F. 2001. *Passionate Politics: Emotions and Social Movements.* Chicago: University of Chicago Press.

González, A.F. 2007 (February 14). "Regularán Radios Comunitarias." AMARC. Retrieved June 2, 2008, from http://legislaciones.item.org.uy/index?q=node/134.

Government of Guatemala 1985 [1993]. *Constitución Política reformada por Acuerdo Legislativo* No. 18–93 del 17 de Noviembre de 1993.

Government of Guatemala 2007. "Política para Resolver la Problemática de las 'Radios Ilegales.'" Government of Guatemala. Guatemala City, *Diario de Centroamérica*: 10–13.

Gramsci, A. 1971. *Selections from the Prison Notebooks*. New York: International Publishers.

Greenhouse, L. 2000. "Supreme Court Roundup: Justices Press for Clarity in a Property Rights Dispute." *The New York Times*, February 27, 18A.

Greenhouse, L. 2002. "Win the Debate, Not Just the Case." *New York Times*. July 14.

Guttmacher, A. E. and Collins, F. S. 2005. "Realizing the Promise of Genomics in Biomedical Research." *JAMA* 294(11): 1399–402.

Hackney, J.R. 1997. "Law and Neoclassical Economics Theory: Science, Politics, and the Reconfiguration of American Tort Law Theory." *Law and History Review* 15(2) 275: 322.

Hackney, J.R. 2003. "Law and Neoclassical Economics Theory: A Critical History of the Distribution/Efficiency Debate." *Journal of Socio-Economics* 32: 361–390.

Hagle, T.M. and Spaeth, H.J. 1992. "The Emergence of a New Ideology: The Business Decisions of the Burger Court," *The Journal of Politics,* 54: 1, 120–134.

Hall, T.D. and Fenelon, J.V. 2009. *Indigenous Peoples and Globalization: Resistance and Revitalization*. Boulder, CO: Paradigm Publishers.

Hamilton, R.A. 2001. "Counting on Pfizer?" *New York Times*. April 29.

Harrington, C. 1984. "The Politics of Participation and Nonparticipation in Dispute Processes." *Law and Policy* 6, 203–30.

Harrington, C.B. and Turem, Z.U. 2006. "Accounting for Accountability in Neoliberal Regimes, in Public Accountability": *Designs, Dilemmas and Experiences*, edited by M.W. Dowdle. New York: Cambridge.

Harry, D. 1994. "The Human Genome Diversity Project: Implications for Indigenous Peoples." *Abya Yala News* 8.

Hartford Courant. 1998. Editorial: A Pick-Me-Up at Pfizer.February 5.

Harvey, D. 2007. *A Brief History of Neoliberalism.* New York, Oxford University Press.

Hatcher, L. 2003. "Green Metaphors: Language, Land, and Law in Takings Debates." In *Current Legal Issues* (5): 445–464.

Hatcher, L. 2005. "Economic Libertarians, Property, And Institutions: Linking Activism, Ideas And Identities Among Property Rights Activists." In Austin Sarat And Stuart A. Scheingold (eds). *The Worlds Cause Lawyers Make: Structure And Agency In Legal Practice*. Palo Alto: Stanford University Press.

Hatcher, L. 2009. The Odyssey of *Palazzolo*: Public Rights Litigation and Coastal Change. *Fordham Urban Law Journal* 36(4): 849–862.

Hathaway, W. 1998. Pfizer Expansion May Bring More Than 1,000 Jobs – New Facility Part Of $185 Million New London Plan. *Hartford Courant.* February 4.

Hayek, F. A. 1945. "The Use of Knowledge in Society." *American Economic Review* 35(4): 519–530.

Hazlett, T.W. 2001. "The Unlimited Bandwidth Myth, The Spectrum Auction Faux Pas, and the Punchline to Ronald Coase's 'Big Joke': An Essay on Airwave Allocation Policy." *Harvard Journal of Law and Technology* 14(2): 335–469.

Hazlett, T.W., Ibárgüen, G., and Leighton,.W. A. 2006. "Property Rights to Radio Spectrum in Guatemala and El Salvador: An Experiment in Liberalization." *Law and Economics Research Paper* 06-07.

Hazlett, T.W., Ibárgüen, G., and W.A. Leighton, W.A. 2007. "Property Rights to Radio Spectrum in Guatemala and El Salvador: An Experiment in Liberalization." *Review of Law and Economics* (December): 437–484.

Henderson, V. 2008. "Sound As a Dollar? The Propertization of Spectrum Resources and Implications for Non-Profit Community Radio in Guatemala". Unpublished Master's Thesis, Queen's University.

Herrera, Ó.F. 2006. "Simpatizantes de Radio Pirata Queman Subestación." *El Periódico*. Guatemala City, Guatemala.

Herrera, V.H. 2007. "En Guatemala Funcionan Más de 800 Radios Clandestinas." Available at: http://legislaciones.item.org.uy/index?q=node/357. [accessed June 10, 2008].

Hoover, D. and den Dulk, K.R. 2003. "Christians Go To Court: Legal Mobilization in the United States and Canada." *International Journal of Political Science* 25(1): 9–34.

Horowitz, D.L. 1977. *The Courts and Social Policy*. Washington, DC: The Brookings Institution.

Horwitz, M. 1992. *The Transformation of American Law: 1870–1960*. Oxford University Press.

Howse, R. 1999. "From Politics to Technocracy – And Back Again: The Fate of the Multilateral Trading Regime." *The American Journal of International Law* 96, 94–117.

Huber, P. 1998. "A People's Constitution." In *Regulator's Revenge: The Future of Telecommunications Regulation.* T. W. Bell and S. Singleton. Washington, DC: Cato Institute: 29–38.

Hunter, S. and Leyden, K. 1995. "Beyond NIMBY: Explaining Opposition to Hazardous Waste Facilities.*" Policy Studies Journal* 23 (4), 601–19.

"I Choose to Stay Here." (dir. Community Leadership Institute, Philadelphia Folklore Project and B. Dornfel, 2004).

IACHR. 2001. Fifth Report on the Situation of Human Rights in Guatemala, Inter-American Commission on Human Rights, Organization of American States.

IACHR. 2003. "Justicia e Inclusión: Los Desafíos de la Democracia en Guatemala", Comisión Interamericana de Derechos Humanos (Inter-American Commission on Human Rights), Organization of American States.

Ibárgüen, G. 1992. "Privatizar las Ondas de Radio." Guatemala City, Centro de Estudios Economico-Sociales.

Ibárgüen, G. 2002. "What Guatemala Can Teach the FCC." *Wall Street Journal* (The), A11.

Ibárgüen, G. 2003. "Liberating the Radio Spectrum in Guatemala." *Telecommunications Policy* 27: 543–554.

Ibárgüen, G. 2004. "Case Study on Guatemala." Paper submitted to the Workshop on Radio Spectrum Management for a Converging World. Geneva, International Telecommunications Union.

Ibárgüen, G. 2008. Interview. Guatemala City, Guatemala.

Indigenous Peoples Council on Biocolonialism. 1997, "Ukupseni Declaration, Kuna Yala on the Human Genome Diversity Project", available at: http://www.ipcb.org/resolutions/htmls/dec_ukupseni.html.

Institute for Justice. 2000. Case filing: CV-01-0557299-S.

Institute for Justice. 2007. "50 State Report Card: Tracking Eminent Domain Reform Legislation Since *Kelo*." www.ij.org [accessed: March 24, 2009].

Institute for Justice. 2008. Financial Statements With Independent Auditors' Report Years Ended June 30, 2008 And 2007.

Institute for Justice. 2009. Available at: http://www.ij.org [accessed: March 24, 2009].

Ise, H. 1971. Decision of the Chief of the Division of Harbors and Rivers in the Matter of: Applications of Anthony Palazzolo. Frank Licht Papers, Box 75, File 1078. Courtesy of the University of Rhode Island, Special Collections (Governor Licht Papers).

Jones, Day, Reavis and Pogue 2002. Second Amended Claim of Investor, Methanex v. Government of the United States.http://www.state.gov/documents/organization/15035.pdf.

Kagan, R.A. 2000. "How Much Do National Styles of Law Matter?" In *Regulatory Encounters: Multinational Corporations and American Adversarial Legalism*, edited by R.A. Kagan and L. Axelrad. Berkeley: University of California Press, 1–30.

Kagan, R.A. 2001. *Adversarial Legalism: The American Way of Law. New Haven*: Yale University Press.

Karlin, A. 2006. "Property Seizure Backlash." *Christian Science Monitor*, July 6, A1.

Keck, M.E. and Sikkink, K. 1998. *Activists Beyond Borders: Advocacy Networks in International Politics*. Ithaca: Cornell University Press.

Kingsley, C. 2005. "'Hands Off My Home' Campaign Addresses Eminent Domain Case," *St. Louis Daily Record*, July 15.

Knaap, G. and Nelson, A.C. 1992. *The Regulated Landscape: Lessons on State Land Use Planning from Oregon.* Cambridge, MA: Lincoln Institute of Land Policy.

Kronman, A.T. 1993. *The Lost Lawyer: Failing Ideals of the Legal Profession.* Cambridge: The Belknap Press.

Kuttner, R. 1999. *Everything for Sale: The Virtues and Limits of Markets.* Chicago: University of Chicago Press.

Lacy, M.G. 1992. "The United States and American Indians: Political Relations." In *American Indian Policy in the Twentieth Century*, edited by V. Deloria. Oklahoma City: University of Oklahoma Press.

Lagnado, L. 2002. "Disconnecticut: Needy New London Saw Cure For Its Ills In Pfizer's Arrival." *Wall Street Journal.* September 10.

Landis, J.D. 2006. "Growth Management Revisited." *Journal of the American Planning Association*, 72 (4), 411–30.

Lawson-Remer, T. 2006. "Values under siege: NAFTA, GATS, and the propertization of resources." *NYU Environmental Law Journal* 14(2): 481–520.

Lee, H.C. and Tirnady, F. 2003. *Blood Evidence: How DNA Is Revolutionizing the Way We Solve Crimes.* Cambridge, MA: Perseus Publications.

Leighton, W.A. 2008. Interview. [Telephone].

Ley General de Telecomunicaciones 1996. *Ley General de Telecomunicaciones. Decreto 94–96 y sus reformas Decretos 115-97 y 47-2002 del Congreso de la República de Guatemala.* Government of Guatemala, Ediciones Arriola.

Lithwick, D. 2009. "Driven Out." *New York Times*. March 15.

Liu, E. 2005. "Radiodifusión de Conflictos Dentro del Mercado." Presentation at the Conference *Convergence or Competition: Radio Spectrum Management in Guatemala and Latin America*. Universidad Francisco Marroquín, Guatemala City, Guatemala.

Loeppky, R.D. 1998. "Control from within? Power, identity, and the human genome project." *Alternatives: Global, Local, Political* 23(2): 245–266.

López, E. 2006. "Investigan a Dos Diputados Por Radios Pirata." *Siglo XXI.* Guatemala City: Online.

Lord, P. 2001. "Turf Battle Supreme – Property Rights Affirmed; Payment Denied." *Providence Journal-Bulletin*, June 29, 2001, Page. 1A.

Loretti, D. 2007. Estudio sobre la incompatibilidad con los principios de derechos humanos sobre libertad de expresion del castigo penal de la radiodifusion no autorizada. Guatemala City, Guatemala, AMARC.

Lueck, D. 1995. "The Rule of First Possession and the Design of the Law." *Journal of Law and Economics* 38(2): 393–436.

Lynd, S. 1988. "The Genesis of the Idea of a Community Right to Industrial Property in Youngstown and Pittsburgh" in *The Constitution and American Life* (ed.) D.P. Thelen. Ithaca: Cornell University Press: 266–295.

Mahoney, J.D. 2005. "Kelo's Legacy: Eminent Domain and the Future of Property Rights." *Supreme Court Review* 103–133.

Mahoney, P.G. 2001. "The Common Law and Economic Growth: Hayek Might Be Right." *The Journal of Legal Studies* 30(2): 503–525.

Maltzman, F. and Wahlbeck, P.J. 1996. "May it Please the Chief? Opinion Assignments in the Rehnquist Court." *American Journal of Political Science,* 40: 421–443.

Maltzman, F., Spriggs, J, and Wahlbeck, P.J. 2000. *Crafting Law on the Supreme Court: The Collegial Game.* Cambridge: Cambridge University Press.

Mather, L. and Yngvesson, B. 1980–1. "Language, Audience, and the Transformation of Disputes." *Law and Society Review* 15, 775–822.

McBride, S. 2006. "Reconfiguring Sovereignty: NAFTA Chapter 11 Dispute Settlement Procedures and the Issue of Public-Private Authority." *Canadian Journal of Political Science* 39, 1–21.

McCann, M. 1994. *Rights at Work: Pay Equity Reform and the Politics of Legal Mobilization.* University of Chicago Press.

McCann, M. 2008. "Litigation and Legal Mobilization." in *The Oxford Handbook of Law and Politics*, edited by K. Whittington, R.D. Kelemen and G.A. Caldeira. Oxford: Oxford University Press, 522–40.

McCann, M., and Dudas J. 2006. "Retrenchment and Resurgence? Mapping the Changing Context of Movement Lawyering in the US," in *Cause Lawyers and Social Movements,* edited by A. Sarat and S. Scheingold, Palo Alto, California: Stanford University Press, 37–59.

McCay, B.J. 2002. "Emergence of Institutions for the Commons: Contexts, Situations, and Events." In *The Drama of the Commons*, edited by E. Ostrom. Washington, DC: National Academy Press.

McClure, K. 1995. "Taking Liberties in Foucault's Triangle: Sovereignty, Discipline, Governmentality and the Subject of Rights." In: *Identities, Politics and Rights* (eds) A. Sarat and T.R. Kearns. University of Michigan Press.

McCollough, G. 2005 All for the Taking: 21st-Century Urban Renewal, Berkeley Media LLC.

McGuire, K.T. 1994. "*Amici Curiae* and Strategies for Gaining Access to the Supreme Court," *Political Research Quarterly* 47(4), 821–837.

Mead, A. 1997. "Genealogy, Sacredness and the Commodities Market." *Cultural Survival Quarterly* 20: 46–53.

Melnick, R.S. 1983. *Regulation and the Courts: The Case of the Clean Air Act.* Washington, DC: The Brookings Institution.

Meltz, R, Merriam, D., and Frank, R. 1999. *The Takings Issue: Constitutional Limits on Land Use Control and Environmental Regulation.* Washington DC: Island Press.

Mendelson, W. 1964. "The Untroubled World of Jurimetrics." *The Journal of Politics* 26(4): 914–922.

Mérida, H. 2007. "AMARC denuncia ante la CIDH al Gobierno de Berger." *El Periodico*. Guatemala City, April 16.

Merrill, T. 1986. "The Economics of Public Use." *Cornell Law Review* 61–116.

Mitchell, T. 1991. "The Limits of the State." *American Political Science Review* 85, 77–96.

MNN. (2008). "Christian Radio Forced Off the Air in Guatemala. Mission Network News", Online. Available at: http://www.mnnonline.org/article/11465. Last accessed August 20, 2009.

Molnar. H. 1989. "Aboriginal Broadcasting in Australia: Challenges and Promises". Paper presented at the International Communication Association Conference, March.

Moran, K. 2004a. "City To Assess State Of Fort Trumbull Development – Eminent – Domain Lawsuit Not the Only Source of Frustration." *New London Day.* September 30.

Moran, K. 2004b. "Groups Seek Legal Remedy for Eminent Domain – Fort Trumbull Case Spawns Briefs Filed with Supreme Court." *New London Day.* December 16.

Moser, C. and McIlwaine, C. 2001. "Violence in a Post-Conflict Context: Urban Poor Perceptions from Guatemala." Washington, DC: World Bank.

Muir, W.K. 1973. *Law and Attitude Change.* Chicago: University of Chicago Press.

Murphy, W. 1964. *Elements of Judicial Strategy* Chicago: University of Chicago Press.

Nadler, J. and Diamond, S. et al. 2008. "Government Takings of Private Property: Kelo and the Perfect Storm" in *Public Opinion and Constitutional Controversy* (eds) N. Persily, J. Citrin, and P. Egan. Oxford: Oxford University Press: 287–310.

Nakamura, R.T. and Church T.W. 2003. *Taming Regulation: Superfund and the Challenges of Regulatory Reform.* Washington, DC: Brookings Institution Press.

National Conference for State Legislatures (NCSL). 2007a. "Property Rights Issues on the 2006 Ballot." Available: http://www.ncsl.org/statevote/prop_rights_06.htm [accessed: March 15, 2009].

National Conference for State Legislatures (NCSL). 2007b. Eminent Domain: 2005 State Legislation. Available: http://www.ncsl.org/programs/natres/post-keloleg.htmPoletown [accessed March 15, 2009].

National Conference for State Legislatures (NCSL). 2007a. Eminent Domain: 2006 State Legislation. http://www.ncsl.org/default.aspx?tabid=17593 [accessed: May 8, 2010].

National Constitution Center. 2008. "Associated Press – National Constitution Center Poll." Available at: http://surveys.ap.org/data/SRBI/APNational%20Constitution%20Center%20Poll.pdf.

National Human Genome Research Institute. "Background on Ethical and Sampling Issues Raised by the International HapMap Project", (http://www.genomica.net/RICERCA/HAPMAP/HAPMAP_etica.htm) [accessed April 26, 2009].

Natural Resources Group. 1969. *Report on the Administration of Narragansett Bay*. Providence: State of Rhode Island.

Nelson, D. 1996. "Maya Hackers and the Cyberspatialized Nation-State: Modernity, Ethnostalgia, and a Lizard Queen in Guatemala." *Cultural Anthropology* 11(3): 287–308.

New London Day. 2004. *Eminent Domain Chronology*. September 29.

New London Development Council. 2001. *Comprehensive Economic Development Strategy*.

Nielsen, L.B. and Albiston, C.R. 2006. "The Organization of Public Interest Practice: 1975–2004." *North Carolina Law Review* 84: 1591–1621.

Nilsen, A.G. and Cox, L. 2006. "The Bourgeoisie, Historically, Has Played a Most Revolutionary Part": Understanding Social Movements from Above. In C. Barker and M. Tyldesley (eds), *Eleventh International Conference on Alternative Futures and Popular Protest 2006 – Conference Papers,* Volume 3, Faculty of Humanities and Social Science, Manchester Metropolitan University. Available at http//eprints.nuim.ie/458 [accessed: August 29, 2009].

Nixon, D.W. 1990. "Evolution of Public and Private Rights to Rhode Island's Shore," *Suffolk University Law Review* 24(2): 313–330.

NotiCen 2006. "Community Radio Struggles for Legitimacy in Guatemala." *Latin American and Iberian Institute*. Albuquerque.

Novak, W.J. 1996. *The People's Welfare: Law and Regulation in Nineteenth-Century America.* Chapel Hill: University of North Carolina Press.

O'Conner, K. and Epstein, L. 1982. "*Amicus Curiae* Participation in the U.S. Supreme Court: An Appraisal of Hakman's Folklore." *Law and Society Review* 16: 311–320.

O'Connor. J. 2001. *The Fiscal Crisis of the State.* New Burnswick, NJ: Transaction.

Odendahl, T. and Shaw, A.M. 2002. "Interviewing Elites", in *Handbook of Interview Research: Context and Method*, edited by J.F. Gubrium and J.A. Holstein. Thousand Oaks: Sage Publications.

Office of International Claims and Investment Disputes, Office of the Legal Advisor, US Department of State. 1999. Submission of the Government of the United States of America in *Metalclad v. United Mexican States*. http://www.state.gov/documents/organization/4178.pdf.

Office of International Claims and Investment Disputes, Office of the Legal Advisor, US Department of State. 2000. Fourth Submission of the United States of America, *Pope & Talbot, Inc. v. Government of Canada*. http://www.state.gov/documents/organization/4098.pdf.

O'Leary, R. 2006. "Environmental Policy in the Courts", in *Environmental Policy: New Directions for the Twenty-First Century*, sixth edn., edited by N.J. Vig and M.E. Kraft. Washington, DC: CQ Press.

Palazzolo v. Rhode Island. Oral Transcript. Available at http://www.supremecourtus.gov/oral_arguments/argument_transcripts.html.

Palencia, G. 2008. "Édgar Archila: 'Se debe cumplir ley de radiocomunicaciones.'" *Prensa Libre*. Guatemala City, Guatemala.

Paul, E.F. 1988. *Property Rights and Eminent Domain*, New Brunswick, NJ: Transaction Publishers.

Pearce, C.C. 1997. Investor's Memorial for Metalclad Corporation. http://www.economia-nci.gob.mx/sphp_pages/importa/sol_contro/consultoria/.Casos_Mexico/Metalclad/escritos/Memorial_Metalclad.pdf.

Peet, R. 2002. "Ideology, Discourse, and the Geography of Hegemony: From Socialist to Neoliberal Development in Postapartheid South Africa." *Antipode* 34(1), 54–84.

Pérez, L. 2006. "Radios comunitarias, sin respaldo." *Prensa Libre*. Guatemala City, May 21.

Perin, C. 1977. *Everything in Its Place: Social Order and Land Use in America.* Princeton, NJ: Princeton University Press.

Perry, H.W. 1991. *Deciding to Decide: Agenda Setting in the United State Supreme Court*. Cambridge: Harvard University Press.

Peterson, A. 1989. "The Takings Clause: In Search of Underlying Principles Part I – A Critique of Current Takings Clause Doctrine." *California Law Review* 77: 1304.

Pettigrew, P.S., Bautista, L.E.D., and Zoellick, R.B. 2001. Letter from Principal Counsel, Trade Law Division to Chapter 11 Tribunals.http://www.dfait-maeci.gc.ca/tna-nac/phases-en.asp#comm.

Philpott, D. 2001. *Revolutions in Sovereignty: How Ideas Shaped Modern International Relations*. Princeton, NJ: Princeton University Press.

Platt, R.H. 1996. *Land Use and Society: Geography, Law, and Public Policy.* Washington, DC: Island Press.

Posner, R.A. 1973. *Economic Analysis of Law*. Boston, Little Brown.

Posner, R.A. 1979. "Utilitarianism, economics, and legal theory." *Journal of Legal Studies* 8: 103–140.

Preciphs, J. 2005. "Eminent domain ruling knits rivals." *Wall Street Journal*, 8 July, A1.

Prensa Libre. 2008. "Se están desvaneciendo." *Prensa Libre*. Guatemala City: 4–5, July 27.

Price, J.H. 2005. "Florida Town Considers Eminent Domain," *Washington Times,* October 10.

Pritchett, C.H. 1948. *The Roosevelt Court: A Study in Judicial Politics and Values*. New York: Macmillan.

Private Property Rights Protection Act of 2005. US House of Representatives, 109 H.R. 4128 (enacted November 3, 2005).

Puro, S. 1981. "The United States as *Amicus Curiae*." In S.S. Ulmer (ed.), *Courts, Law and Judicial Processes.* New York: Free Press.

Rabkin, J. 1989. *Judicial Compulsions: How Public Law Distorts Public Policy*. New York: Basic Books.

Radin, M.J. 1982. "Property and Personhood." *Stanford Law Review* 34: 957–1013.
Ramírez, G. 2007. "Pautarán propaganda 29 emisoras pirata." Siglo Veintiuno. Guatemala City, Guatemala.
Raustiala, K. 2003. "Rethinking the Sovereignty Debate in International Economic Law." *Journal of International Economic Law* 6, 841–878.
REMHI. 1998. *Guatemala: Nunca Más*. Informe del Proyecto Interdiocesano de Recuperación de la Memoria Histórica. Guatemala City, Oficina de Derechos Humanos del Arzobispado de Guatemala.
Resnik, D.B. 1999. "The Human Genome Diversity Project: Ethical problems and solutions." *Politics and the Life Sciences* 18: 15.
Rhode, D.W. and Spaeth, H. 1976. *Supreme Court Decision Making*. San Francisco: W.H. Freeman.
Rigden, P. 1997. "Companies Covet Genes; Ethics and Profits Compete in the Patenting of Human Genetic Materials." *Alternatives Journal*. FindArticles.com. Available at: http://findarticles.com/p/articles/mi_hb6685/is_n3_v23/ai_n28691106/ [accessed August 28, 2009].
Robinson, W.I. 2004. *A Theory of Global Capitalism: Production, Class, and State in a Transnational World,* Baltimore: Johns Hopkins University Press, 2004.
Rodríguez Guaján, C.R. 2007. Interview. Santa Cruz Balanyá, Chimaltenango, Guatemala.
Rose, N. 1996. "Governing 'Advanced' Liberal Democracies", in *Foucault and Political Reason: Liberalism, Neoliberalism and Rationalities of Government* (eds) A. Barry, T. Osborne, and N. Rose. Chicago: University of Chicago Press, 37–64.
Rosenberg, G.N. 1991. *The Hollow Hope: Can Courts Bring About Social Change?* Chicago: University of Chicago Press.
Rouse, R. 2001. "Tonga joins list of laboratory communities." *Nat Med* 7: 8-8.
Ruddy, J.J. 2000. *Revisiting New London.* Charleston, SC: Arcadia Press.
Ruiters, G. 2005. "The Political Economy of Public Private Contracts: Urban Water in Two Eastern Cape Towns." In The *Age of Commodity: Water Privatization in Southern Africa* (eds) D.A. McDonald and G. Ruiters. London; Sterling, VA: Earthscan.
Russell, P. H. 2005. *Recognizing Aboriginal Title: The Mabo Case and Indigenous Resistance to English-Settler Colonialism. Toronto*; Buffalo: University of Toronto Press.
RWB. 2006, March 21. "Authorities Close Nine Community Radios for Having No License." Reporters Without Borders.
Ryan, P. 2005. "Treating Wireless Spectrum as a Natural Resource." *Environmental Law Institute* 35: 10620–10629.
Sabino, C. 2007. Guatemala, la historia silenciada. Vols. I and II. Guatemala City, Fondo de Cultura Económica.

Sagalyn, L.B. 2008. "Positioning Politics: *Kelo*, Eminent Domain, and the Press" in *Land and Power: The Impact of Eminent Domain in Urban Communities.* (ed.) T.N. Castano. Princeton, N.J. Princeton University: 39–48.

Sandefur, T. 2005. "The 'Backlash' So Far: Will Citizens Get Meaningful Eminent Domain Reform?" 2006 *Michigan State Law Review*, 709–777.

Santiago, E.M. 2008. "Decades Later, Palazzolo Selling Pond Site," *The Westerly Sun*, July 8, 2008.

Sarat, A. and Scheingold, S. 2004. *Something to Believe In: Politics, Professionalism, and Cause Lawyering*. Stanford University Press.

Scheberle, D. 2004. *Federalism and Environmental Policy: Trust and the Politics of Implementation*, second edn. Washington, DC: Georgetown University Press.

Scheingold, S.A. 1974. *The Politics of Rights; Lawyers, Public Policy, and Political Change.* New Haven: Yale University Press.

Scheingold, S.A. 1978. *The Politics of Rights: Lawyers, Public Policy, and Political Change.* New Haven: Yale University Press.

Schneiderman, D. 2008. "Investment Rules and the New Constitutionalism." *Law and Social Inquiry* 25, 757–787.

Schorr, D.B. 2005. "Appropriation as Agrarianism: Distributive Justice in the Creation of Property Rights." *Ecology Law Quarterly*. 32. 3–71.

Schubert, G. 1959. *Quantitative Analysis of Judicial Behavior.* Glenoe, IL: Free Press.

Schubert, G. 1962. "The 1960 Term of the Supreme Court: A Psychological Analysis," *American Political Science Review,* 56: 90–107.

Schubert, G. 1965. *The Judicial Mind: The Attitudes and Ideologies of Supreme Court Justices, 1946–1963*. Evanston, IL: Northwestern University Press.

Schubert, G. 1974. *The Judicial Mind Revisited: Psychometric Analysis of Supreme Court Ideology*. New York: Oxford University Press.

Schultz, D. 2002. "The Phenomenology of Democracy," in *Social Capital: Critical Perspectives on Community and Bowling Alone* (eds) S.L. McLean, D.A. Schultz, and M.B. Steger. New York University Press, 74–99.

Schultz, D. 2006. "The Property Rights Revolution that Failed: Eminent Domain in the 2004 Supreme Court Term," *Touro Law Review* 21: 929–988.

Schultz, D. 2007. "Comprehensive Plans, Corporate Thuggery, and the Problem of Private Takings," New York State Bar Association, *Government, Law and Policy Journal* 9(6) (Spring, 2007).

Schultz, D. 2009. *Evicted! Property Rights and Eminent Domain in America*. Westport, CT: Praeger Press.

Schultz, D. and Gottlieb, S.E. 1998. "Legal Functionalism and Social Change: A Reassessment of Rosenberg's *The Hollow Hope*," in *Leveraging the Law: Using the Courts to Achieve Social Change* (ed.) D. Schultz. New York: Peter Lang Publishing, 169–214.

Segal, J.A. 1988. "*Amicus Curiae* Briefs by the Solicitor General During the Warren and Burger Courts: A Research Note." *The Western Political Quarterly* 41(1): 135–144.

Segal, J.A. and Spaeth, H. 1993. *The Supreme Court and the Attitudinal Model*. New York: Cambridge University Press.

Segal, J.A. and Spaeth, H. 2002. *The Supreme Court and the Attitudinal Model Revisited*. Cambridge: Cambridge University Press.

Senellart, M. (ed.) 2007. "Lecture of 5 April 1978." In *Michel Foucault – Security, Territory, Population: Lectures at the Collège de France, 1977–1978*. Translated by Graham Burchell. Palgrave MacMillan.

Shore Development Act of 1956. Rhode Island Laws, Chapter 23, Title 46.

Sinha, A. 2006. "Global Linkages and Domestic Politics: Trade Reform and Institution Building in India in Comparative Perspective." Paper Presented to Law and Society Meeting, Baltimore, MD.

Smart, T. 1992. "These Radicals Have the Right Wing Cheering." *Business Week* 24 (February).

Snow, D.A. and Anderson, L. 1987. "Identity Work Among The Homeless – The Verbal Construction And Avowal Of Personal Identities." *American Journal of Sociology* 92, 1336–71.

Snow, D.A. and Benford, R 1988. "Ideology, Frame Resonance, and Participant Mobilization." *International Social Movement Research* 1: 197–217.

Soja, E.W. 1989. *Postmodern Geographies: The Reassertion of Space in Critical Social Theory*. London: Versa.

Somin, I. 2004. "Overcoming Poletown: County Of *Wayne v. Hathcock*, Economic Development Takings, and the Future of Public Use." *Michigan State Law Review* 2004: 1005–1038.

Somin, I. 2007. "The Limits of Backlash: Assessing the Political Response to Kelo." *George Mason University Law and Economics Research Paper Series*: 07–14.

Southworth, A. 2008. *Lawyers of the Right: Professionalizing the Conservative Coalition*. University Of Chicago Press.

Spaeth, H. 1963. "Warren Court Attitudes Toward Business: The B Scale." In *Judicial Decision-Making*, (ed.) G. Schubert. New York: Free Press.

Sparrow, M.K. 2000. *The Regulatory Craft: Controlling Risks, Solving Problems, and Managing Compliance*. Washington, DC: Brookings Institution Press.

Spiller, P. and Spitzer, M. 1992. "Judicial Choice of Legal Doctrines," *Journal of Law, Economics and Organization* 8: 8–48.

Spiller, P.T. 2006. "Efficiency, Quantification, and Valuation of Spectrum." Presentation to the conference *Improving Spectrum Management through Economic or Other Incentives*. Washington, DC, National Telecommunications and Information Administration: pp. 262 (transcript).

Spiller, P.T. and Cardilli, C.G 1999. "Towards a Property Rights Approach to Communications Spectrum." *Yale Journal on Regulation* 16(1): 53–83.

Stack, C.B. 1974. *All Our Kin: Strategies for Survival in a Black Community*. New York: Harper and Row.

Steger, M. 2002. *Globalism: The New Market Ideology*. Lanham, MD: Rowman and Littlefield.

Steinberg, M.K., Height, C., and Mosher, R. et al. 2006. "Mapping Massacres: GIS and State Terror in Guatemala." *Geoforum* 37(1): 62–68.

Stern, S. 2009. "Residential Protectionism and the Legal Mythology of Home." *Michigan Law Review* 107: 1093–1144.

Summers, R. 2000. *Essays in Legal Theory*. Boston: Kluwer Academic Publishers.

Sunkin, M. 2004. "Conceptual Issues in Researching the Impact of Judicial Review on Government Bureaucracies," in *Judicial Review and Bureaucratic Impact: International and Interdisciplinary Perspectives*, edited by M. Hertogh and S. Halliday. New York: Cambridge University Press.

Talen, E. 2005. *New Urbanism and American Planning: The Conflict of Cultures*. Routledge Press.

Teles, S. 2008. *The Rise of the Conservative Legal Movement: The Battle for Control of the Law.* Princeton University Press.

Thallam, S. 2008. *2008 Report – International Property Rights Index*. Washington, DC: Property Rights Alliance, available at http://www.internationalpropertyrightsindex.org/UserFiles/File/022508ot-report%20(2).pdf.

The International HapMap Consortium 2005. "A Haplotype Map of the Human Genome." *Nature* 437: 1299–1320.

The Mataatua Declaration on Cultural and Intellectual Property Rights of Indigenous Peoples, 1993. Retrieved August 30, 2009, http://www.wipo.int/export/sites/www/tk/en/folklore/creative_heritage/docs/mataatua.pdf.

The National Geographic Society. "A Landmark Study of the Human Journey", Available at: https://genographic.nationalgeographic.com/genographic/index.html [accessed: April 26, 2009].

The Rhode Island Shore, A Regional Guide Plan Study: 1955–1970. 1955. Providence: State of Rhode Island.

The Taking of Bodine: Never Forget (dir. Community Leadership Institute).

Thompson, B.H. 2000. "Tragically Difficult: The Obstacles to Governing the Commons." *Environmental Law*. 30: 241–278.

Tishkoff, S.A., et al. 2009. "The Genetic Structure and History of Africans and African Americans." *Science* 324: 1035–1044.

Tocqueville, A. 1840/1969. *Democracy in America*, (ed.) J.P. Mayer and translated by G. Lawrence. New York: Harper Perennial.

Totenberg, N. 2001. *Morning Edition*. National Public Radio. Aired February 26, 2001.

Townsend, R. and Wilson, J.A. 1987. "An Economic View of the Commons," in *The Question of the Commons* (eds) B.J. McCay and J.M. Acheson. University of Arizona Press.

Tribe, L. 2000. *American Constitutional Law* 3rd. West Press.
Ulmer, S. 1960. "Supreme Court Behavior and Civil Liberties," *The Western Political Quarterly* 13: 288–311.
UN Declaration on the Rights of Indigenous Peoples, Adopted by General Assembly Resolution 61/295 on 13 September, 2007. Retrieved August 30, 2009 (http://www.un.org/esa/socdev/unpfii/en/drip.html).
University of Rhode Island, Coastal Resource Center. *Fact Sheet: Hurricanes in Rhode Island*. Available at http://nsgl.gso.uri.edu/riu/riug97006.pdf [accessed: February 11, 2009].
US Census. 2008.
US Coast Guard Academy. 2009. *United States Coast Guard Academy – USCGA Timeline*. http://www.cga.edu/display.aspx?id=331 [accessed March 15, 2009].
US Patent and Trademark Office. "U.S. Patent Statistics Chart. Calendar Years 1963–2008" Available at: http://www.uspto.gov/go/taf/us_stat.htm [accessed: May 1, 2009].
Vasciannie, S. 1999. "The Fair and Equitable Standard in International Investment Law and Practice." *British Yearbook of International Law* 70: 99–166.
Venkatesh, S.A. 2006. *Off the Books: The Underground Economy of the Urban Poor*. Cambridge, Mass: Harvard University Press.
Voices of American Law: Kelo v. New London. 2006. Video. Durham, NC: Duke University School of Law. DVD.
Wald, P. 2006. "Blood and stories: how genomics is rewriting race, medicine and human history" *Patterns of Prejudice* 40: 303–333.
Waldron, J. 1990 "Homelessness and the Issue of Freedom", *UCLA Law Review* 39: 95–324.
Warner, K. and Moltoch, H. 2000. *Building Rules: How Local Controls Shape Community Environments and Economies*. Boulder: Westview Press.
Webb, A.L. 2003. *Neighborhood Transformation Investigated: Exclusive Report, shoddy record-keeping and missing expense reports could cost the city millions*. Philadelphia City Paper, Philadelphia, PA.
Weber, W. 2000. "Tonga sells genetic heritage to Australian firm." *The Lancet* 356: 1910.
Wheeler, S.M. 2008. "State and municipal climate change plans: the first generation," *Journal of the American Planning Association* 74 (4), 481–96.
Wheeler, S.M. and Beatley, T. (ed.) 2009. *The Sustainable Urban Development Reader*. New York: Routledge.
Will, G. 2004. "Despotism in New London." *Washington Post*. September 19.
Williams, D.V. 2007. "Customary Rights and Crown Claims: Calder and Aboriginal Title in Aotearoa New Zealand", in H. Foster, J.H.A. Webber, and H. Raven, *Let Right Be Done: Aboriginal Title, the Calder Case, and the Future of Indigenous Rights*, Vancouver: UBC Press.
Williams, E. 1991. "Hairdresser Regulations Cramp its Styling, Cornrow Salon Says." *Washington Times*. November 7.

Winer, L. 2003. "The Constitutional Case Against 'Free' Airtime". *Policy Analysis* 481, 6 August. Cato Institute.

Wolf, M.A. 2008. "Hysteria versus History: Public Use in the Public Eye." In *Private Property, Community Development and Eminent Domain* (ed.) Robin Paul Malloy. Burlington, VT: Ashgate.

Wong, S. 2001. "Strong Medicine Pfizer's New Complex Is Clear Evidence Of Drug Sector's Emerging Vitality In State." *Hartford Courant*. 3 June.

World Bank. 2008. "Broadcasting, Voice, and Accountability: A Public Interest Approach to Policy, Law, and Regulation." S. Buckley, K. Duer, T. Mendel and S.Ó Siochrú. Washington, DC, The World Bank Group.

Xunic, A. C. 2008. Interview. Sumpango, Sacatepéquez, Guatemala.

Yergin, D. and Stanislaw, J. 2002. *The Commanding Heights: The Battle for the World Economy*. New York: The Free Press.

Cases

ADF Group v. Government of the United States, [2003], http://www.state.gov/s/l/c3741.htm.

Annicelli v. South Kingston, [1983] 463 A.2d 133.

Appollo Fuels, Inc. v. United States, [2002] 54 Fed.Cl. 717.

Appollo Fuels, Inc. v. United States, [2004] 381 F.3d 1338.

Berman v. Parker, [1956] 348 U.S. 26.

Board of County Commissioners v. Lowery, [2006] OK 31.

Carole Media LLC v. N.J. Transit Co., [2008] 550 F.3d 302.

Chancellor Manor v. United States, [2003] 331 F.3d 891.

Chevron v. Natural Resources Defense Council, [1984] 467 U.S. 837.

City of Norwood v. Horney, [2006] 110 Ohio St.3d 353.

County of Wayne v. Hathcock, [2004] 471 Mich. 445, 684 N.W.2d 765.

Dartmouth College v. Woodward, (1819) 4 Wheat 518.

Dolan v. City of Tigard, (1994) 512 U.S. 374.

Eastern Minerals International, Inc. v. United States, [1996] 36 Fed. Cl. 541.

Engs v. Peckham, [1875] 11 R.I. 210.

First English Evangelical Lutheran Church of Glendale v. County of Los Angeles, (1987) 482 U.S. 304.

Fletcher v. Peck, (1810) 9 Cranch 87.

Fort Trumbull Conservancy LLC v. Alves, [2008] 286 Conn. 264.

Goldstein v. Pataki, [2008] 516 F.3d 50.

Hawaii Housing Authority v. Midkiff, [1984] 467 U.S. 229.

Kelo v. City of New London, [2001] Case response: CV-01-0557299-S.

Kelo v. City of New London, [2004] 268 Conn. 1.

Kelo v. City of New London, [2005] 545 U.S. 469, 2005.

Kelo v. New London, Connecticut, [2002] 2002 Conn. Super. LEXIS 789.

Keystone Coal Association v. DeBendictis, (1987) 480 U.S. 470.

Lingle v. Chevron, U.S.A. Inc., (2005) 544 U.S. 528.
Lochner v. New York, (1905) 198 U.S. 45.
Lucas v. South Carolina Coastal Council, [1992] 505 U.S. 1003.
Metalclad Corporation v. United Mexican States, [2000] http://www.economia-snci.gob.mx/sphp_pages/importa/sol_contro/consultoria/Casos_Mexico/Metalclad/Metalclad.htm.
Methanex v. Government of the United States, [2006] http://www.state.gov/s/l/c3741.htm.
M&J Coal Company v. United States, [1995] 47 F.3d 1148.
Nollan v. California Coastal Commission, (1987) 483 U.S. 825.
Palazzolo v. Rhode Island, [2001] 533 U.S. 606.
Penn Central Transportation Co. v. New York City, [1978] 438 U.S. 104.
Pennsylvania v. Mahon, (1922) 260 U.S. 393.
Poletown Neighborhood Council v. Deitroit, (1981) 304 N.W. 2d 455.
Pope & Talbot, Inc. v. Government of Canada, [2000] http://www.international.gc.ca/trade-agreements-accords-commerciaux/disp-diff/ethyl.aspx?lang=en.
Presley v. City of Charlottesville, VA, [2006] 464 F.3d 480.
Regents of the University of California v. Bakke, (1978) 438 U.S. 265.
Rith Energy, Inc. v. United States, [1999] 44 Fed. Cl. 108.
R.T.G. v. Ohio, [2002] 98 Ohio St. 3d 1.
San Remo Hotel v. San Francisco, (2005) 545 U.S. 323.
S.D. Myers Inc. v. Government of Canada, [2001] http://www.international.gc.ca/trade-agreements-accords-commerciaux/disp-diff/ethyl.aspx?lang=en.
Swedenburg v. Kelly, [2005] 544 U.S. 460.
Tahoe-Sierra Preservation Council v. Tahoe Regional Planning Agency, [2002] 535 U.S. 302.
UPS v. Government of Canada, [2007] http://www.international.gc.ca/trade-agreements-accords-commerciaux/disp-diff/ethyl.aspx?lang=en. United States v. 14.02 Acres, [2008] 530 F.3d 883.
U.S. v. Carolene Products Co., (1938) 304 U.S. 144.
Waste Management II v. United Mexican States, [2004] http://www.economia-snci.gob.mx/sphp_pages/importa/sol_contro/consultoria/Casos_Mexico/Waste_2_management/Waste_2_management.htm.
Western Seafood Co. v. United States, [2006] 202 Fed. Appx. 670.
Zelman v. Simmons-Harris, [2002] 526 U.S. 639.

Index